"*New Ideas About New Ideas* offers a new lens through which to interpret, appreciate, and participate in the world around you. If you are searching for that elusive creative 'edge' where the best ideas can be generated, you can't afford to miss this book."

—Michael Wolff, author, *Burn Rate*

"Innovation is the biggest challenge facing Corporate America. Shira White's new book is loaded with helpful concepts that will get your company moving in the right direction."

—Al Ries, co-author,
The 22 Immutable Laws of Branding and Positioning:
The Battle for Your Mind

"There is no doubt that creativity and innovation are required to propel business forward. Shira White's extremely insightful and very readable book describes the best of creative thinking and innovative pursuits in the world of business today. The need to understand these approaches and learn from successful practitioners is universal in any business climate."

—Dr. Carol A. Cooper, Director,
Value Management, Bayer Corporation

"The 'spark' that ignites the innovation process is not readily understood by many looking to compete in the new millennium. Shira White's book presents diverse perspectives on the driving forces behind the most creative companies today. It provides a benchmark for those who want to look beyond their horizons for growth."

—Michael L. Williams,
Manager of Quality and Business Excellence,
The Dow Chemical Company

NEW IDEAS

ABOUT

NEW IDEAS

NEW IDEAS

ABOUT

NEW IDEAS

Insights on Creativity

from the

World's Leading Innovators

SHIRA P. WHITE

with G. Patton Wright

FT Prentice Hall
FINANCIAL TIMES

An imprint of **Pearson Education**

London · New York · Toronto · Sydney · Tokyo · Singapore · Hong Kong
Cape Town · Madrid · New Delhi · Madrid · Paris ·
Amsterdam · Munich · Milan · Stockholm

PEARSON EDUCATION LIMITED

Head Office:
Edinburgh Gate
Harlow CM20 2JE
Tel: +44 (0)1279 623623
Fax: +44 (0)1279 431059

London Office:
128 Long Acre
London WC2E 9AN
Tel: +44 (0)20 7447 2000
Fax: +44 (0)20 7447 2170
Website: www.business-minds.com

———————————————

First published in the United States in 2002 by Perseus Publishing
First published in Great Britain in 2002

© Shira P. White 2002

The right of Shira P. White to be identified as Author
of this Work has been asserted by her in accordance
with the Copyright, Designs and Patents Act 1988.

ISBN 0 273 66168 X

British Library Cataloguing in Publication data
A CIP catalogue record for this book can be obtained from the British Library

10 9 8 7 6 5 4 3 2 1

Printed and bound in Great Britain by Henry Ling Ltd, Dorchester

The Publishers' policy is to use paper manufactured from sustainable forests.

To Max

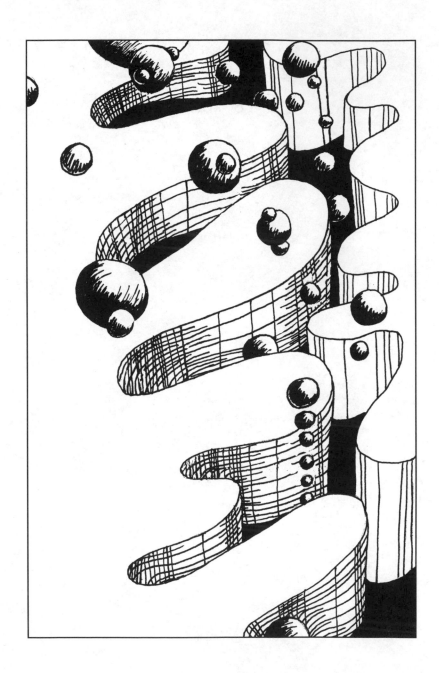

Contents

Preface   x

Introduction
Sizzling Spaces: Making Innovation Happen   1

1 **Spark Soup**: Where Innovation Begins   23

2 **Bubbling**:
New Approaches to Idea Development   51

3 **Bargaining with the Future**:
The Valuation Struggle   93

4 **Going Live**:
Bringing New Ideas to Life   131

5 **Integrated Circuitry**:
Mechanisms of Innovation Action   173

6 **Rocket Design**: Innovating the Organization   215

7 **Making an Apple Pie**:
Beyond the Organization   267

Featured Organizations and Individual Profiles   297

Notes   311

Credits   317

Index   319

About the Author   334

Preface

When I sit down to paint or write, sometimes I see something that inspires me. Other times, I want to create something, but the blank canvas stares back at me, waiting and waiting and waiting for insights to come.

Where does innovation begin? Where does a new idea come from? If you want to innovate on purpose, where and how do you start? And how can you do it over and over again? How do you support new development when everything is crashing around you?

This book was still in process when the New Economy took the dive when the happy economic bubble burst and, later, when the World Trade Center got bombed. In an instant, we went from an era when new ideas about the way we work and live were sparking all over the place—with new companies, new products, and new ways of looking at the world—to a time of falling prices, cutting costs, slashing jobs, scaling back, and retreating with a back-to-basics attitude. People were beginning to get gun-shy, or downright scared. The bright new ideas that floated around during the Bubble now seemed leaden. For many, pioneering activities came to a major slowdown or sometimes a complete halt. New development began to give way to a fight for survival. Many felt less pressure to innovate—maybe they should have felt more.

In 2000-2001, stock market valuations declined considerably in large part because they had reached "irrational" altitudes—their inflated prices were not supported by the fundamentals and were bound to fall. But the underlying level of business creation and dynamism, which reached unparalleled heights in the prior five years, had created tremendous value.

There are important reasons why, in economic slowdowns, downtimes, distress, and crises, people should be even more interested in innovation in developing new ideas, new products, and new solutions:

1. The old ideas either aren't working or aren't enough.
2. New ideas are what will lift us back to prosperity.
3. Competition is usually quieter.
4. Development costs are often lower.
5. Cost of entry is lower.
6. Acquisitions are often cheaper.
7. Mistakes are often cheaper.

Innovative companies can build strength during slowdowns and downtimes and come out of them with broader product lines, stronger channels, greater share, and a bigger jump-start on recovery. New ideas not only raise people above mediocrity and crowds, but are also the only thing that will solve the current problems they face and lift them out of the ditches they are in. That's why, while everyone else tightly compresses, companies committed to creativity and innovation often expand their development efforts.

In good times or bad, it may or may not be the best time to launch a new product or start a new business, depending on the circumstances, but it is always a good time for a new idea that can flourish even within tight constraints. It is always a good time for a new solution that doesn't require resources you don't have or can't get. It is always a good time to develop another perspective of the world around you and another glimpse of the future. The point is that whatever economic conditions happen to be as you read this book, new approaches to innovation can make all the difference in your world.

This book is all about ideas even more than it is about the companies and people that are profiled. No one should read this book and come away with the notion that success is automatically guaranteed if he or she adopts a particular company's new idea. Instead, the reader can pick and choose, modify and adapt, adopt and reject, crafting a customized approach to innovation to suit the circumstance.

The concept for this book came about as I began to observe big differences between innovation leaders and everyone else. Even those people and organizations who were committed to investing in new product development, creativity training, and other innovation goals seemed to need more than what they had to work with. I began to see it first when I worked as a creative director at several Madison Avenue advertising agencies, as they mistakenly approached new product development assignments exactly the way they approached creating new ad campaigns. When I left to start my own innovation development consulting firm, my mission was to seek out and develop new ways to advance innovation.

I began to explore new areas and new possibilities with clients to develop some different ways and means. I began to write articles and deliver speeches on "New Ideas about New Ideas" and "New Ideas about Old Ideas," which met with great enthusiasm from colleagues, clients, friends, and critics. It became clearer and clearer, the more I talked with people who were charged with creating innovation success, that the older, classic approaches to new product and business development were no longer enough. As this realization spread, I was asked to write a book that presented new insights and concepts. The material for this book draws from my own consulting practice and from diverse sources at the leading edges of the world.

I looked around for the "hot, hip, and happening." And I gathered a fascinating collection of cutting-edge corporate leaders, artists, architects, scientists, writers, composers, choreographers, and filmmakers, to name a few. Due to their demanding schedules, typically I was originally offered only thirty-minute interviews with each. But once we got started, our talks opened up floodgates. We often ended up talking for many more hours than that and often meeting again for more. This kind of exchange can happen only when people are really jazzed about the conversation. It happened frequently during my interviews with these corporate, cultural, and educational innovation leaders. We got to questions that no one else had really asked them before, about subjects that are core to their existence: creativity and innovation. And that inspired them. They rewarded me with fascinating insights and enthusiastic support.

Interviewing over one hundred talented leaders was an exhilarating experience. Developing friendships with several has been even more wonderful. Gathering their insights and weaving them together with my own thoughts have brought an extraordinary opportunity. What started as a big idea has continued to grow as more possibilities began to unfold along the way. As with many big ideas, this book project was a big undertaking, demanding an enormous effort. I have many people to thank.

First, I am beholden to Pat Wright, who guided me through the process of writing this book, as a mentor and a friend, keeping me, as a first-time author, grounded—being a counterpoint, devil's advocate and, on occasion, a writing coach. Pat devoted a tremendous amount of time and effort in helping to bring *New Ideas About New Ideas* to life. Next, I am thankful for my editor, Nick Philipson, who saw potential in this book before anyone else did. Nick has championed this book from the beginning, slaying an occasional dragon or two along the way. Nick challenged me to stretch in new directions with my writing. I am extremely grateful for the wisdom and strength of my agent, Jim Levine, who went far beyond the call, fighting for my creative vision, helping to guide me, and fortifying the book with his own helpful insights.

I also thank: Dale and Doug Anderson; Nancy Slonim Aronie;

Eliot Bailen; Shelby Barnes, Intellectual Ventures; Jeff Blumenthal, Salomon Smith Barney; Christina Braun; Kathleen Lusk Brooke, Purrington House; Elizabeth Carduff; Lisa Cherno, KPMG; Carol Z. Cooper, Bayer Corporation; Jon Cooper, Big Pie Media; Jane Covner; Stan M. Davis; Leonard Dobbs; Larry Dresdale; Susie Eisner Eley; Randy Englund, Hewlett-Packard; Betsy Ennis, Guggenheim; Steve Eppinger, MIT; Michael Flier; Jason Fox, Annie Ohayon Media; Pepi Marchetti Franchi, Guggenheim Museum; Jennifer Frutchy; Peter Fuhrman; Milton Glaser; Kimberly Glyder; Seth Godin; Claude Goetz; Dalit Goldberg; Richard Hamermesh, Harvard University; Erik Hansen, Tom Peters Company; Janice Heiler, Xerox; Rick Levine; Teri Luke; Mary Marsters, The Rennselaerville Institute; Shelly Mansfield, Enron; Jennifer McKeane, Palm; Trina McKeever, Serra Studios; Keith Mendenhall, Frank O. Gehry; Rob Mitchell, BMW; Michael Neuwirth, Acirca; Lauri Novick, ALS Foundation; Dulce Paredes, Nabisco; Mark Palmer, Enron; Dulce Paredes, Kraft; Marco Pavia, Martin Pazzani, Foote Cone & Belding; Jacqueline Peluso; Nanette Porcelli; Tom Purves, BMW; Jane Raese; Al Reis; Elissa Rogovin; Audrey Rohan; Negeen Roshan; Kim Sabo, Progressive; Andrea Sanders; Chris Snow Schackne; Michael Schrage; Judy Serrin; Arlinda Shtuni, Andrew Shotland, NBC; Geoff Smart; Jerry Szilagyi, Orbitex; Tatiana Stead, Capital One; Lissa Warren; Alan Webber, Fast Company; Michael Weinstein, Ark Restaurants; Jane Wesman, Wesman Associates; Bill Westerman, IDe; Geoffrey Wexler, Jo Fineman White; Sander White; Shirley White; Mike Williams, Dow Chemical Company; Max Wiseltier; Peter Wirth, Genzyme; Michael Wolff; and Judith Zissman.

Finally, I thank the people I interviewed for this book for their interest, creative insights, time, effort, and support—Roger Ackerman (Corning); Laurie Anderson (performance artist); Joshua Bell (violin virtuoso); John Seely Brown (Xerox); Rudy Burger (MIT Media Lab Europe); Satjiv Chahil (Palm); Dale Chihuly (artist);

David Cole (Acirca); Marge Connelly (Capital One); Jill Ker Conway (Lend Lease); Dan Dillon (Welch's); David Ditzel (Transmeta); Frank Gehry (architect); Philip Glass (composer); Brian Greene (Columbia University); Timothy Greenfield-Sanders (photographer); Caroline Kovac (IBM); Tom Krens (Guggenheim Museum); Ken Lay (Enron); Annette Lemieux (artist); Jeff Levy (eHatchery); Peter Lewis (Progressive); Dennis Liberson (Capital One); John Loose (Corning); Tod Machover (MIT Media Lab); Gail Maderis (Genzyme); Steve Massarsky; Michael McGrath (PRTM); Nathan Myhrvold (Intellectual Ventures); Betsey Nelson (Macromedia); Philip Noguchi (US Food & Drug Administration); Joe Paradiso (MIT Media Lab); Glenn Renwick (Progressive); Mark Rodriguez (Acirca); Timothy Rowe, (Cambridge Incubator); Mike Ruettgers (EMC^2); Richard Serra (artist); John Sherriff and Jeff Skilling (Enron); Geoff Smart; Henri Termeer (Genzyme); Sam Waksal (ImClone); and Robert Wilson (artist).

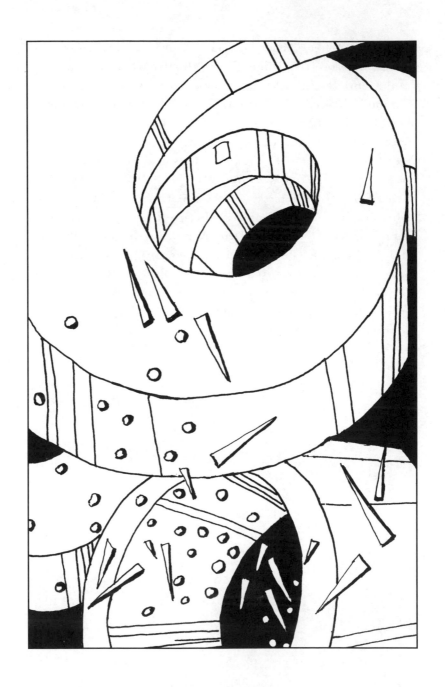

INTRODUCTION: SIZZLING SPACES

Making Innovation Happen

I knew art before anything else. My earliest memories are of doodling and drawing, creating shapes and patterns, playing with colors and designs. In every circle, I was the "artistic" one, the one who always evoked the admission from onlookers, "Wow, look at that, and I can't even draw a straight line!" I thought about art, even when doing other things—the art of walking down the street, the art of cooking a meal, the art of playing with dolls, the art of negotiation. I was propelled toward being an artist, and I went to art school.

As I began to realize that few artists survive on what they earn from their creations, I began studying for my MBA. I could never quite convince myself that business success had to come at the expense of art or creativity. I took on the challenge of finding some way that would link creativity to business—for example, by developing new products for other companies or by helping to unleash creative talents in their employees and managers.

One of my first tests came soon after I started grad school. Management of Information Systems (MIS) was a mandatory course, but it was too structured and full of rules for my way of thinking. One MIS assignment, which asked me to review a business case and develop a solution for it, required weeks of work. I studied parallel cases and presented my solution, feeling proud of my accomplishment. But when my paper was returned, it had a big, fat, red *D* slashed across its cover.

I had never received a *D* before—big, fat, or otherwise. I was an artist, I was smart, and I was used to getting *A*s in everything. I was the only one there not in a pinstripe suit.

I began poring over the comments on the paper. I couldn't figure out the error of my ways, so I approached the professor after class to ask for an explanation. She ticked off her thoughts on the problem.

I listened. "OK, I think I see what you are saying, but why did I get a *D*?"

She reiterated her explanation. Again, I said, "Yes, that makes sense, but why did you give me a *D*?" She went at it again.

So did I. "Look," I said, "I understand *your* answer to the problem. What I don't understand is why *my* answer is wrong."

"It wasn't the answer I was looking for," she replied simply, feeling a bit annoyed.

"Wait a second," I said, feeling both shocked and exasperated. "You mean you gave me a *D*, not because my answer was 'wrong,' but because it wasn't the one *you* were looking for?"

"Yes, that's right," she beamed.

I was penalized for coming up with a viable, creative solution, which just happened not to be the solution that *she* devised for the problem. Under those precepts, new solutions since the beginning of time—the wheel, vaccines, credit and ATM cards, rock and roll, software, anesthesia, airplanes, ice cream, and glass—would never have come to be. Different ideas are inherent in innovation, yet they are screened out by most people and institutions.

This professor knew nothing about my background, education, experiences, interests, or character. I was one among hundreds of young grad students churning through her cookie-cutter classes. She looked up from her papers, put her hand on her more than ample hip, looked me in the eye, and said, "Honey, if you want to be creative, go to art school. You're in business school now."

Honey! I froze in horror—cold, white light, the sound of my own heartbeat thumping in my ears, my muscles tensing, my breathing shallow—looking down at myself from the ceiling—outraged. What the hell was I doing in business school? What was I thinking?

Clutching my briefcase, I ran from the classroom out onto Trinity Place. In the area around Wall Street, throngs of brokers and analysts were heading home for the day.

I felt like quitting business school. I stopped at a restaurant bar for a drink to regroup and reassess. It turned out that one of my marketing professors walked in and, seeing me, asked why I looked so freaked. After listening to my account of the run-in with his colleague, he showed me an opening. It didn't have to be the way it seemed in the MIS class, he said. He shared my belief that the business world could use all the art, all the out-of-the-box thinking, all the innovative problem solving that it could find. His encouragement helped turn me around and convince me that I should give business another chance. If it hadn't been for his encouragement that afternoon, my MBA quest would have been over, right then and there.

Creativity can be integrated into every aspect of business—strategy, management, products and services, operations, culture, organizational design, and the lives we lead beyond the workplace. We can learn more from the world's most creative and successful people by seeing the art in how they work—and how they live their lives outside of work. There are CEOs, managers, entrepreneurs, students, young artists, potential geniuses inhabiting garages and tinkering with the world's next shatteringly new invention—avoiding the traps that my MIS instructor set in prescribing one problem/one solution and by generally presenting "work" as an artless pursuit.

CONTINUOUS LEAPS

Innovation has become a lot more important to corporate leaders, in the last decade in particular, because of changes in the business environment brought on by increased technological capabilities, speed, hypercompetition, and faster rates of diffusion enabled by greater connectivity. But while many companies say they are "making innovation happen," for most of them, innovation is based on old ideas, principles, and processes. At best, their innovations are incremental—miniscule improvements in products and services. While there is nothing wrong in achieving small gains, this view of innovation shuts out the truly startling cases of *leap innovations*.

Leap innovations occur when someone discovers an entirely new approach to a problem, an approach that changes life in some significant way. Although a leap innovation often results in new products, services, or processes, it differs somewhat from what Clayton Christensen and Geoffrey Moore call a "discontinuous innovation." That is, the leap innovation emphasizes the act of moving into the unknown or unexplored, rather than just breaking with predictable patterns of innovation.[1] Furthermore, it is not merely product-centric. A leap innovation can occur in any pursuit and can happen anywhere within the universe of an organization, in any function—research, new product development, recruiting, managing information, financing creative projects, or improving the life of work, and the work of life, in every aspect. The biggest leaps are the innovations that transform our whole world, the way the light bulb, personal computer, Internet, and the Human Genome Project have changed how we live and work. Leaps come from creative action.

Continuous leaps and continuous transformation can go hand in hand, as they have at Corning, Inc. for more than 150 years. Originally a light bulb manufacturer, Corning has literally changed the world as it changed itself with over a dozen leap innovations, described in greater detail in Chapter 1, "Spark Soup." To convey the magnitude of Corning's leaps, consider its latest adventures in the biotech world. How, you may ask, could a glass company, known for its blue-flowered cookware, become a leader in biotech? It is simple. Corning did what it always has done—keeping its eye on the future, it pushed pioneering research, leveraged its technologies and manufacturing capabilities, and took a daring plunge (see the sidebar "Corning's Life Sciences Division").

Making innovation happen is cited as the biggest challenge today for organizations.[2] Even as the challenges of economic recession and encroaching terrorism move to the forefront of our consciousness, as times get tough for whatever reason, innovation is the only way to a better time. We begin this book by introducing new concepts about how to spark a leap innovation, as well as new economic, cultural, and technological challenges that innovators will face. Incremental or leap, innovation is ultimately critical to survival. That goes for the simplest paramecium making its way through the swamp as much as it does for the largest organizations in the worlds of business, government, education, and philanthropy.

HOT, HIP, AND HAPPENING

Beyond Corning, a number of cutting-edge organizations and individuals are continually innovating. Many thrive on paradox and uncertainty. Some act fast and loose, seemingly unconscious or unconcerned with personal failure or critical opinion. Not that these things are insignificant, but the truly innovative are so absorbed in the act of creating that they shoot past patterns that the rest of the world is locked into. In short, creative leaders create sizzling "spaces," both actual and virtual, where ideas spark and inspired geniuses are free to roam unexplored territory.

In conducting the research for this book, I talked with some of today's most innovative thinkers and leaders, including top creative artists, scientists, educators, and executives who are doing some-

CORNING'S LIFE SCIENCES DIVISION

One of Corning's businesses produces glass-based products such as test tubes and slides for scientific laboratories. Leveraging its proprietary technologies used in producing coated slides and test chambers, Corning bet on the future of genomics and developed a line of DNA microarrays, a kind of biochip, which it launched in 2000. It entered an industry dominated by Affymetrix, which had had virtually no competition for its first four years. Only a few other players, such as Motorola and Agilent, jumped in after Corning did.

Microarrays have become indispensable in the pharmaceutical industry for collecting and analyzing the enormous amount of information long locked inside human and other species' genes. Corning, the market leader in fiber optics, leveraged that leap technology, which it invented over twenty years before to make strands of optical fiber thinner than a human hair. The company also called up a micro-printing process that had been used years ago to put those blue cornflower patterns on its one-time ubiquitous cookware. John Loose, Corning's CEO, points out that millions of people had prototypes for microarrays in their kitchens in the late 1950s.[3]

One of Corning's clear advantages is that its technology can produce biochips ten to twenty times faster than its competitors can. Each glass slide, which measures one inch by three inches, is micro-imprinted with about 10,000 unique gene sequences. Using a process of matching RNA and DNA patterns, scientists are able to identify the makeup of cells, both in healthy and diseased states, and they are finding the keys to new preventions and cures.

Corning's microarrays dramatically shortened drug discovery and regulatory processes by a factor of more than 1,000. The technology expanded into medical diagnostics, and its applications should continue to expand exponentially beyond that. Some predict that the market, including non-human species analyses, could reach tens of billions of dollars by 2010.[4] As Corning helped to connect the world through leaps in fiber optic telecommunications, it is helping to revolutionize the way we view and cure devastating disease.

thing different and doing it differently. Although their success may not last forever, or may dip and rise again, for significant periods of time they are hot, hip, and happening—we call them H^3 for short. While this terminology may make some chuckle or roll their eyes, most people we talked to especially liked the term and found that it serves as a useful nomenclature in identifying this extraordinary group. Brief profiles of the interviewees and organizations appear at the end of this book. The important thing is that these traits distinguish these people and organizations from everybody else. These H^3s reveal the most creative approaches and principles in making innovation happen successfully. They are passionate. They love to create, discover, and invent over and over again.

This book goes beyond well-known examples of innovation to reveal powerful insights from some of the world's most creative companies and individuals. It features their unique approaches to coming up with new ideas, bringing them to life, funding new projects and businesses, designing and managing organizations, and living a creative life beyond the traditional workplace.

The stories behind these H^3 organizations and individuals are told in greater detail in the chapters to follow, but for the moment, it is important to hear the common themes that run through all of their stories.

> Popular opinion never produces innovation.
> —Satjiv Chahil,
> chief marketing officer,
> Palm, Inc.

THE CREATIVE PRIORITY

> I believe you can choose to approach the world creatively or not creatively. There's always the possibility of turning over any task in an unusual, creative way.
> —*Tod Machover, composer, director,* Opera of the Future,
> *MIT's Media Lab*

When innovation is a key goal, creative talent is the most precious resource. It carries more weight in every endeavor. Many H³s have found ways to organize around talent—recruiting, supporting, and rewarding people who operate with creative passion and aptitude. The artist is more valued than the manager. The artist can see past others and can express what others cannot even begin to put into words.

Such was the case with people who designed websites and needed both better visual tools and better hand-coding tools, but had never been able to articulate that need. The hyper-talented, creative engineers at Macromedia, the cutting-edge software company and market leader in products for web designers, figured how to put these two kinds of tools together into one ingenious software program called Dreamweaver. The new program dramatically changed how web designers work and think. As executive vice president and CFO Betsey Nelson puts it, "You know, I am sure there are other smart minds out there, but *we* brought it to life and got it out there. I give great credit to our engineering team—our talent."

Nelson believes that talent is at the top of the valuation scale. She can see how creative talent drives her company. "Look at any project team. Their vision is usually so large that they cannot get all the things they want to do into one version. And they keep going past expectations with each step they take. They just go to it. It's very impressive."

In many traditional organizations, however, people who have investments in the "old model" are not always happy to see new talent coming along with a bright and shiny new design. These traditionalists tend to have a knee-jerk reaction to anything new—a new way of thinking, a new idea, a new way of doing things. Typically, the need to change is in conflict with the need to stay the same. The tension is played out in every exploration of a new idea. H³s, however, believe that in order to survive they have to keep an innovation edge on competitors and stay ahead of environmental threats—they have to make leaps. "It's highly unlikely you're going to get leap innovation from most of the people that you already have," warns Nathan Myhrvold, former CTO of Microsoft and current CEO of Intellectual Ventures, an entrepreneurial partnership and investment company. "If you have this problem—and it's a long-standing problem— it's almost a self-fulfilling prophecy."

Innovation is a core part of H^3 strategy, driving every decision at every level, from hiring and firing to operations to manufacturing to R&D to funding to structuring the entire organization. It has, for example, led ImClone, a New York–based innovator in cancer therapies, through difficult decision paths in commercializing its breakthrough cancer drug, C225. One option was to license the drug to a big pharmaceutical company that, in turn, would reap all the profits. "Licensing was a chicken's way out of making sure that Wall Street said, 'Oh it's great, Eli Lilly's licensed it. Or Bristol's licensed it,'" explains Sam Waksal, ImClone's CEO. Under such an agreement, ImClone would have received a royalty, and the big pharmaceutical company would have taken over all the work, claimed all the gold and reaped all the glory. "If we licensed our new drug, we would have to just sit around and report to Wall Street every quarter on what somebody *else* was doing, not on what *we* were doing. Licensing would have taken all of the control out of our hands and put it into someone else's. It made no sense to me. It just made no sense whatever," says Waksal, who is more interested in leveraging ImClone's own exceptional talent and keeping more of the company's innovation rewards in-house.

Creative priority impacts every design and every process. As you read, you will see the contrast between traditional leaders and creative leaders in how they allocate and share resources, for example, or how they form and manage relationships. For instance, it is easy to cut innovation resources when things get tough. While it's true that you can't continue to support exploration if you can't maintain support of current operations, some H^3s choose to uphold their investment in exploration and development even during rocky times.

But it does not always follow that the more you spend on R&D,

the better chance you have at innovation success. So much depends on the nature of the industries involved and the competitive landscape. "I don't see a huge level of correlation in many cases between the amount of money that a company spends on research and how they're going to thrive in the industry," reports Rudy Burger, CEO of MIT's Media Lab Europe. "Kodak is a fabulous example of that. It's not clear to me, going all the way back to [former CEO] George Fisher, he had to understand the nature of the juggernaut bearing down on Kodak. Kodak sank countless hundreds of million of dollars into digital imaging research technologies, yet that money in most cases has been completely wasted."

> It is important that your vision actually gets you excited when you imagine it—and that you are able to spend time with it. I don't believe that somebody could be creative without spending some time with themselves, pushing ideas through, and imagining on their own.
>
> —Tod Machover

There would have been far cheaper ways of acquiring the technology. Kodak had a creative priority but went about it the wrong way by trying to outspend the competition. Digital imaging wasn't the threat. The real threats could be detected in the quandaries: How do you turn a paper and chemical company into a new-age digital company? How do you make the leap from technology to product? Kodak was asking the wrong question (or chasing the wrong problem) and therefore pouring resources down the drain.

If creativity resides only in marketing or in R&D or in engineering, for example, but not in the rest of the organization, innovation is next to impossible. If it is possible, it is not sustainable. We're conditioned, over time, to become very specialized in fields of study and practice. For most, creativity has become an activity reserved for certain functions, designated for certain people such as creative directors, or relegated to certain times and situations. For example, most organizations and teams are still locked into relying upon the hackneyed brainstorming session. If creative initiatives are limited to brainstorming, it's tough for the few sparks that you do get to catch fire. Usually they sputter and fizzle out. Innovation flow is often interrupted or stopped by the boundaries of specialization. "In a way, I think we're all like the autistic child that's been locked up," says composer and artist Robert Wilson. "When we get out, it's very threatening to us. It's like another world."

For H³s, however, innovation is not a discrete activity. It is not compartmentalized. There are no creative boundaries. And artistic concerns—aesthetics—are *not* beside the point. The entire H³ culture breathes creativity. Innovation is at the core of every process, cutting across every domain and bringing new innovation forces together.

Creative priority directs everything from personal development to organizational development and strategy development. It sets up patterns of behavior and style in both individuals and groups. It dictates inflow and outflow of data and ideas.

H³s believe that you can gain more knowledge and creative insight if you surrender to uncertainty. This principle may seem counter-intuitive, even threatening, to those of us who demand empirical proofs. Columbia University physicist Brian Greene, for example, had a great math teacher who challenged the class by giving the students unsolved problems. "We would spend the term trying to solve them," Greene remembers. "Along the way, we would get a new insight, then another new insight, then another, until someone finally cracked the problem. He allowed the *unknown* to dictate the curriculum, as opposed to the traditional way of letting the known dictate the curriculum." For Greene, science is about relishing deep immersion in the unknown, in the dark. "It can be frightening but energizing," he says. "I enjoy being at sea. Finding the light is rare. We find light on little islands of understanding."

Building or redesigning an organization around a core innovation strategy—in order to maximize innovation—requires making new kinds of decisions, thinking of things you normally don't pay much attention to. For example, how do you put talent at the top of the list? How do you decide about organizational structure? Not everyone has the talent that is needed to reach innovation goals. You can't have an organization where you say, "OK, your job is coming up with three new ideas within the next thirty days." It doesn't work that way. You get lucky with some people and not with others. There tends to be a fairly small collection of people who have most of the best ideas. "What works for me is to be able to spot that 10 percent more quickly," says Dave Ditzel, founder and CTO of Transmeta, underscoring one of a variety of insights on creative organization. Transmeta was started and staffed with people Ditzel found in that top 10 percent, and they developed a new microprocessor called the Crusoe Chip, which gave Intel an unprecedented level of competition.

Creative priority is not limited to small companies or technology industries. Progressive is an insurance company that has maintained a creative priority throughout its forty-five year history. It is the fourth largest auto insurance company in the world. "Creativity is the soul of Progressive," says CEO Glenn Renwick. "Our mission is to look for customer experience discontinuities until we eliminate them—to rethink systems. Our culture attracts people that embrace change and get satisfaction and business return from thinking about problems differently." Progressive's entire culture centers on creativity.

Many H3s have creative guidance systems that keep them in an active innovation space, for example, in gathering data. They listen to many diverse voices. And, it's very important for them to listen to their own.

Many people assume it is easier to make leap innovations in a computer chip company than in a company that primarily makes juice and jelly products. Part of the issue is our conditioning: We don't believe in the possibility of truly new ideas in many industries, organizations, or even our personal lives. "The problem that the food industry runs into is that everyone thinks they've done everything already," explains Dan Dillon, CEO and president of Welch Foods, Inc. "They don't want to make the investment because they don't see the return on investment. Companies are selling the same food products they sold twenty years ago, with maybe slight variation. New products in our industry might be going from a glass package to a plastic package." Still, Dillon believes that his is an innovative organization.

Welch's is the marketing and food-processing arm of the National Grape Cooperative Association—similar to Ocean Spray for cranberry growers—with 1,461 member growers. It harvests over 300,000 tons of grapes annually. Though Welch's was founded in 1869 and is intentionally as steeped in tradition as can be, and conservative in many ways, Dillon still tries, where he believes he can, to lead the company down new paths. "The technologies drive a lot of these things," he explains. "You might think, when you see our new technologies, that there is not a major change, but it could be a very major change. It is not the kind of giant leap forward that you might find in other industries, but it could still be very important. For example, taking grape jelly and putting it into a squeezable package, or taking single-serve juice and going from glass to plastic cans—that would be considered a big change."

Not that Welch's hasn't tried for more. The company spent tens of millions of dollars trying to develop a frozen smoothie product that required partial thawing in a home microwave. It was a total bust. After a few of those big innovation missteps, Welch's pulled back.

"Real successes for us," Dillon says, "are closer-in successes. For example, we took concentrate, normally sold as frozen concentrate, and put it into a shelf-stable container. That was a major shake-up for our industry." Taking the concept even further, Welch's merchandised this concentrate in a clever way, which immediately got consumers' attention, understanding, and acceptance: Welch's displayed the cans horizontally, just as frozen concentrate is displayed, and stocked it in the dry foods section. "We asked the question, 'Would consumers make the leap with us?' and BANG, it became a $65 million business," says Dillon. Á la Chiquita with its dominance in the banana market, Welch's has leveraged its name by entering the supermarket fresh fruit aisle with its own brand of fresh grapes and strawberries.

Twenty-six percent of the products Welch's currently markets are less than five years old, an impressive record for a food products company, although most of their new products are incrementally new. While the company is to be commended for the strides it has taken, its innovations raise important questions: Are leaps possible? Are leaps desirable? I believe the answer is "yes" to both. There may be new uses for grape products in other industries such as pharmaceuticals. There may be significant process and distribution innovations that can be leveraged. Welch's may have processing technologies that can be applied to completely different businesses. There may be ways to innovate the organization's structure. There may be management innovations that could move mountains.

Then the question becomes "How can leaps be developed in any company within any industry?" Beginning with identifying opportunities, finding both old problems and new, generating new ideas, then developing and executing those concepts, this book presents new food for thought that any industry, organization, or individual can use.

Old problems are being solved in new ways outside the spheres of work as well, in the community and the home. We also explore the way many H[3] leaders have begun to leverage their innovation capabilities to help advance solutions and opportunities within charitable institutions, philanthropic organizations, volunteer programs, and personal relationships.

Creative priority guides leadership at innovative organizations. It sets a variety of limits and levels for all management decisions. For example, the best orchestra conductors know when not to conduct but instead to relinquish control to the orchestra and allow the players' creative talent to take center stage. The worst conductors try to dictate everything. As violin virtuoso Joshua Bell recalls, "One conductor that I didn't like very much used to say to the orchestra, 'I don't want you listening to each other, I want you following my stick.' Everyone's creativity was taken away. I often like to play without a conductor."

Creative leaders are needed to make innovation happen. They create operational spaces for themselves and their organizations that spark, feed, and nurture innovation success. The trick is to recognize a whole suite of different ways that are possible to solve problems—and to make exciting things come alive. "Make the various ways to do these things not only available, but make them familiar," says Tod Machover of MIT's Media Lab.

> Creativity is laced through what all of us scientists do in our day-to-day work because we're confronted with unsolved problems. And the goal is to get sharp, powerful, elegant explanations and solutions to those problems. Typically, that requires insight and a leap of understanding to be able to find pattern.
>
> —Brian Greene, professor of physics at Columbia University

ASSORTED SPACES

David Ditzel was at Sun Microsystems when JAVA started. Led by Sun Vice President Wayne Rosing, the JAVA programming language was originally intended to do something very different. "Wayne was a very creative guy, " Ditzel recalls. "He hired about 300 very brilliant people, but they didn't have a clearly focused mission. They couldn't figure out where they were going with the business. Eventually the whole program was canceled, and only twelve people were left. Those people looked at the core technology, and they changed the vision of what they were supposed to accomplish. They were able to combine the technical talent—James Goslin, on one side, and business talent Kim Polese on the other side—and figure out how to articulate a new vision and create a successful message. They completely redefined what JAVA was at that point. And they were able to soar when they finally got it off into a different space and another culture."

Some H^3s do well with large structures; some do better with small. Some count their employees on one hand; others have tens of thousands on the payroll. H^3s range from solo artists such as Laurie Anderson, Timothy Greenfield-Sanders, and Annette Lemieux to small organizations such as biotech generator Im-Clone, with 270 employees, to giants such as Corning with 40,000. Some alter their size and configuration to fit the innovation opportunity and to maintain maximum sizzle. Many link or intersect with outsiders to gain new insights on the market, competitors, and themselves.

> If someone says to you, "Try to see your own eyes," what do you do? You can look forward really intently, and no matter how hard you try to do it directly, you can't. But then, if you come up with a clever thing—called the mirror—then you can do it. Sometimes, you need a mirror to refocus your attention in a way that you couldn't simply do by exerting more effort, more energy! Because no matter how hard you try to see your eyes, you can't do it.
>
> —Brian Greene

Age is not a dominant factor: Transmeta had its IPO in 2000; Corning, Inc. is over 150 years old. Nor is location a main issue: Great innovators are not all clustered in the high-tech areas such as Silicon Valley or Research Triangle Park. Although some do have their headquarters in those hot spots, others can be found anywhere around the world.

H^3s are not predominantly associated with any one industry, such as high-tech, biotech, or pharmaceutical—the industries that first come to mind when someone mentions innovation. They can be in any line of endeavor, from farming to insurance to banking to textile manufacturing to construction. There is no limit. Some are fast-movers who quickly take the lead in their respective industries or arts. The market is their petri dish; they and their products are experiments.

CONTINUOUS SIZZLE

The cry for a retreat to conservatism came in 2001 as a lot of the dot-coms, telcoms, and other maverick industries took a nasty beating.

Betsey Nelson of Macromedia testifies to these challenges. "Overall, we have been pretty conservative financially," she explains. "I think that's to our benefit, certainly in terms of the market. Conservatism was out of favor the first couple of years I was here, but obviously, it's come back into favor as the market has adjusted and started paying more attention to things like long-term profitability caps. This downtrend for us has actually been excellent. It's really shaken out some of the other stuff that was kind of fluffy in the market and it gives us opportunities to look for acquisitions or partnerships. Prices have really come down a lot. We continue to climb, as people understand our business and see the path we're on."

The conservatives' cry became louder—even to the point of reversing the casual dress codes most people had adopted: We seemed to be headed back to suits. There was a giant sucking sound, as companies reeled in their outposts. They slashed experimental programs, scaled back R&D, closed off on outside consultants and other external relationships, reabsorbed spin-offs, and added opacity to communications. While not a surprise—in fact, it was a typical reaction—we might expect the opposite to happen, that creativity would be more encouraged and supported during tough times because it takes acts of creativity to survive and rise above difficulties.

I heard a colleague say that people weren't into hearing about innovation and new ideas anymore, not after everyone got burned by the fires of the New Economy. "It's back to basics," he said. "Everybody either wants a sure thing or something really basic and really safe." I wondered how people would be able to climb out of the hole if they didn't resort to creative problem solving and innovation development.

Maybe some of the ideas that crashed were bad ideas in the first place, or maybe they were flawed in some key way that could be fixed. Or maybe those ideas could trigger better ideas. Just because a company's business model was baseless doesn't mean that company had no useful management methodology or philosophy. Just because the economy soured doesn't mean that every creative company in it screwed up. Not *all* of the models were garbage.

If anything, one thing the leaders got right in the New Economy was that they cherished creativity, built creative cultures, and developed resources to promote and support innovation. But an "innovation" that cannot demonstrate success or added value is not an innovation. It is merely a potentially interesting concept waiting for the right conditions or the right insight. Many of the New Economy companies never reached or could not sustain success with their new ideas.

We always need new ideas—and we need new ideas about how to get, grow, and better manage them.

This book is filled with examples and insights from a luminous group of exceptionally creative organizations and individuals who triumph through innovation. Whether you are with a large company, small team, or on your own, whether you are old or young, whether you are rich or poor, whether times are good, bad, happy, or sad, new ideas can move you to a better place and keep you standing while others fall around you.

H^{3}s can always slide backwards or calcify, and stodgy companies can learn a new dance. Mavericks can become complacent or misguided. Traditional companies can, with courage, become cutting-edge in their practices and in their points of view. They may even, mirabile dictu, experience a vast change in how they are perceived by others in the marketplace, by investors, and by the public.

Creativity and innovation have always been important, but because of technological advances, speed of communications, growth of information, and rapid change during the past decade or so, the need for creativity has never been greater. Fast times loosen our reins and inspire our bravado. Slow times strongly challenge us to solve problems, find alternative solutions, and break out ahead of the pack. It is true at any time: Creativity is the ultimate competitive advantage.

As the stories in the following chapters illustrate, those companies and individuals who work more creatively rise above the rest, discover new problems, and find new solutions that escape the notice of conventional, less innovative companies. And they have a far better time doing it.

CAVEATS

> You can get so tied up in what's right that you lose the music.
>
> —*Joshua Bell*

Some of the organizations and leaders featured in this book may or may not be on top or even around tomorrow. A company's success and longevity are based on many things—its ability to innovate is but one. Its "failure" may be for other reasons, beyond its innovation practices. In many cases, the innovators and the executers are not the same people. Sometimes, corporate systems foul good ideas. An industry may founder. A key decision may be poor. During the writing of this book, a number of innovative companies I profiled began to experience heavy troubles. Enron, in particular, has experienced dramatic volatility, with a stock price as high as nearly $85 per share, diving to depths of bankruptcy in late fall 2001. Enron is a case of extraordinary creative thinking that developed new business models, new markets, and new products. Some of the company's creative practices have been periodically questioned by investors and regulators.

It is not unusual for eyebrows to be raised about new ideas but questions and skepticism should not be deterrents. It is sometimes difficult to discern the line between which norms and rules are OK to break and which are not OK. Enron came under tremendously heavy fire and eventually collapsed after it took a more than $1 billion charge in the third quarter of 2001, which triggered an investigation by the SEC,[5] which raised serious questions about Enron's financial reporting and its limited partnerships. Whether or not Enron operated within legal bounds and will be able to justify its creativity in these areas remains to be seen. Regardless, its innovation attributes can still be relevant and important, and we can learn a lot from its creative strategies and advantages. Even if Enron gets shut down or acquired, its brilliant legacy remains: The company developed a new, thriving forward market for commodities and hedging—a market within which others will continue to compete.

We can also learn from a company's missteps and evolutions. We can respect the innovators for trying new things, and we can try to figure out how we can benefit from their experiments. Thomas Edison did not have a stellar record as a businessman, yet he set up a company that became one of the largest and most successful in the world—General Electric. In the long run, we may witness distressed and fallen H3s rise again, perhaps to even greater heights.

The path from an emerging idea to marketplace success is loaded with land mines. Yet it foolish to be deterred. Innovation success is critical to general success. As those who "get" it say, "Innovate or die!"

This is not a "how to" book about *how to innovate.* Nor is it merely descriptive of *what constitutes the creative process.* It is not a series of case studies or academic analyses. We showcase new ideas from an eclectic collection of leading-edge organizations and individuals, with flashes of insight and compelling stories that will inspire you.

You won't like every idea. Some ideas work better for one group than another or for one situation but not another. You may consider some ideas flawed, but they still may contain some value to you if you modify them to suit your needs.

Don't expect hard evidence that these ideas "work." Can you say for sure that a new idea about creative cultural development, for example, yielded a specific return on investment? Probably not. In many cases, the proof is hard to find, but there is anecdotal evidence, and there are many things pointing to causal relationships.

Look carefully at present solutions. Experience them, if you can, or link up with someone who can. And understand that these are the answers of today, but not of tomorrow. However solid the answers are, they are not the ultimate, all-encompassing answers. No answer is an absolutely perfect solution. The imperfections, bumps, cracks, gaps, and holes you see in today's answers are the emerging portals to tomorrow. These are the sizzling spaces of future sparks.

. 1 .

SPARK SOUP

Where Innovation Begins

Once in a while you get shown the light
In the strangest of places
If you look at it right.
—*The Grateful Dead*

Chips were getting really fast, big, and hot. Some ran on as much as one hundred watts in power, generating enough heat to boil water. Software was becoming far more important than the hardware. There was a growing battle between complexity and compatibility. "I didn't like what I saw," Dave Ditzel explains. "I was a chief scientist for Sun Microsystems at the time. My job, in part, was to look out into the future to see where things were going. Where did we want to go in ten years?"

Ditzel saw that design teams were getting huge. Projects were a lot more expensive and taking much, much longer than they should. Years ago, you could design a chip in a year or two. Now it was taking from five to eight years. "The more you get huge teams, the more you dilute the overall ability to have a few key people take charge and lead," says Ditzel. He calls it "the Chinese army approach." He ticks off the formula: "You just hire an army of people, get organized, and work the daily, weekly, and monthly schedules. You have lots of managers and management meetings. You can crank out products that way." As Ditzel sees it, this is the "classic Intel approach"— highly successful for Intel but not the model that he feels personally comfortable with. "It's not the one where a lot of innovation happens," he exclaims. Those were the issues Ditzel was struggling with at Sun before he finally bolted, struck a spark with his Crusoe Chip innovation, and founded his own, more streamlined chip company, Transmeta, where he now serves as vice chairman and chief technology officer.

The Crusoe Chip is a manifestation of Ditzel's development of a new hybrid computer technology, the first to combine hardware and software solutions to address the problems with high temperature, complexity, and compatibility. Recruiting geniuses such as Linus Torvalds, who created the Linux operating system, Ditzel and his new company set to work on the Crusoe family of processors. The Crusoe is so cool it's hot. While Intel's Pentium III, for instance, reaches temperatures of over 220 degrees Fahrenheit during the playing of a DVD, the Crusoe processor plays the same DVD at only 118 degrees.[1] Because it runs so much cooler, the Crusoe extends the battery life of a typical laptop such as Sony's VAIO from only a few hours, at best, up to a full workday. The Crusoe can also lower the cost of laptops and PCs since they no longer have to depend on noisy fans to cool off internal parts.

Why couldn't Ditzel develop the Crusoe while he was still at Sun? He had been thinking about different technology ideas for several years. But it's very difficult to get a project started and finished in an established company because established companies like to do things that are small, evolutionary changes. "If you want to do something that's radically different from what they have, then that means going

against the system," explains Ditzel, "so you have the doubly difficult task of trying to invent something new—having to constantly
fight and try to explain why it's better, why it's different, why you
shouldn't be doing the same old thing over and over again."

In short, Ditzel was going for a *leap innovation,* not just another incremental improvement. To do that, often smart, creative people
realize they themselves have to leap into a new world, a new company, a new environment—a new mix—where an idea spark has a better chance of catching fire. In a brand new company, there is a
single-minded focus to make that one new idea succeed.

Some people operate as if their whole world is a spark soup—a
fluid amalgam of data, in a creative broth, with swirling impres-
sions, spoonfuls of sensation, and bursts of electricity. Some companies operate that way too. They immerse and can interact with all
of the ingredients. They constantly try to change the recipe. They
are H^3s—they are hot, hip, and happening. They bring together different elements in an attempt to create new sparks. The new sparks
that survive become new elements in the soup. And so it goes. Conditions change. Tastes change. In-
gredients come together in new
ways. New sparks emerge. For H^3s,
it's a way of life.

Contemporary glass artist Dale
Chihuly is immersed in a vibrant
life of sapphire spirals, amethyst
orbs, and molten emerald gyra-
tions. His sculptures can be sub-
lime in their complexity and delightful in their simplicity. He uses
the world as both his palette and
his canvas. With a kaleidoscope of
projects such as the Fiori di Como,
a 2,100-square-foot piece made
up of 2,000 hand-blown, in-

tensely colored glass pieces in floral-inspired shapes, which hangs from the main ceiling of the Bellagio Hotel in Las Vegas; a sixty-five-ton ice wall at the King David Museum in Jerusalem; the four enormous free-blown glass and steel mega-ton sculptures that grace

the Atlantis resort in the Bahamas; installations and exhibitions in over 200 museums around the world; an art-based apprentice program, which rehabilitates a multitude of troubled teens; and dozens of other spectacular projects around the world—he is everywhere. He lives everywhere. He maintains spaces everywhere. For Chihuly, life is all a spark soup.

Laurie Anderson has her own recipe as she springs from composing to painting to writing to performing to designing spaces and musical instruments to filmmaking—from high-technology to paint, from obscurity to fame—in and out and in again. She lives it. She wears it. It is in the way she talks. It is in what delights her. It is in what moves her as well as in what she moves. It is in her friends and collaborators. It is in her sponsors. Lou Reed, Paul Allen, David Bowie, Robert Wilson, Philip Glass, Brian Eno, and Peter Gabriel form a dazzling constellation of her collaborators. Anderson's critically acclaimed *Life on a String* album was released in August 2001. She often works on several big projects simultaneously, such as a film score, an installation (one will be presented by the Musée d'Art Contemporain of Lyon, France, in 2002), and a pavilion (one in Switzerland will open in summer 2002).

Chihuly and Anderson are two examples. But for virtually all the creative artists I spoke to, their lives are a spark soup, bubbling with possibilities, simmering with opportunities, loosely flowing, continually churning challenges and problems, and perpetually popping with new ideas. There is not a lot of regulation. There is no weighty structure. There are openings everywhere to let new ingredients in.

New things don't tend to come out of heavy organization, unless something rebels and mutates. Consider the possible beginning of the universe. Many scientists today believe it began with a spark in a soup of four gases: The stars and planets emerged from a swirling soup of cosmic bits. Many cosmologists believe that the universe was once tightly packed and extremely hot. According to Brian Greene, "At the moment of the big bang the whole of the universe erupted from a microscopic nugget whose size makes a grain of sand look colossal."[2] In the microseconds after this explosion, the universe began cooling rapidly and expanded into a swirling "thermal soup of quarks, electrons, photons, and other elementary particles."[3] Ultimately, the galaxies, stars, and planets emerged from the soup of cosmic particles, and the first living organisms came forth out of ocean cauldrons. As ingredients were added and temperatures changed, evolution occurred, and is still occurring, in an endless genesis.

Science itself evolves as new truths are discovered—as later generations stand, as Sir Isaac Newton claimed he stood, on the shoulders of giants—as new ingredients are added to the spark soup. If you look at the timeline of biotechnology (see sidebar: "Bio Timeline"), for example, you will see the endless genesis of biological solutions to disease and the management of living organisms, dating back thousands of years. Big shifts can take decades. Sometimes new solutions come in bunches as they did at the end of the nineteenth and beginning of the twentieth centuries, a record decade of discovery, when concepts as simple as washing one's hands before eating or performing surgery and taking medicines such as antibiotics and interferon effectively doubled human longevity. The recent genomics

> If I have seen further, it is by standing upon the shoulders of giants.
>
> —Sir Isaac Newton,
> in a letter to Robert Hooke

BIO TIMELINE HIGHLIGHTS[4]

1750 B.C.: The Sumerians brew beer.

500 B.C.: The Chinese use moldy soybean curds to treat infections.

A.D. 1796: Edward Jenner inoculates a child with a viral vaccine, saving him from smallpox.

1590–1879: Scientists discover cells, bacteria, proteins, enzymes, genes, DNA, chromosomes. Microscopes, diagnostic stains, and centrifuges are invented and improved for further research.

1911: A cancer-causing virus is found.

1920: Growth hormones are discovered.

1928: Penicillin is used to treat infections.

1900–1950: Experiments in genetic recombinations, jumping genes, cell culturing, interferons, and synthetic antibiotics are conducted.

1960–1969: Hybrid DNA-RNA molecules are created, human and mouse cells are fused, the genetic code is cracked, and enzymes are synthesized.

1970–1979: The 1970s bring the beginning of gene cloning, synthesis, targeting, and splicing along with embryo transfers, monoclonal antibodies, DNA sequencing, and genetically modified organisms.

1980–1989: DNA fingerprinting is developed. Exxon patents an oil-eating microorganism, which can help in cleanups. Genetic markers for specific inherited diseases are found. Congress funds the Human Genome Project. Genetically modified crops are introduced.

1990–2001: Recombinant DNA technology is introduced into the U.S. food supply. Gene therapy is approved by FDA. Researchers clone sheep, monkeys, and cows. Advances are made in identifying genes associated with breast cancer, colon cancer, and Parkinson's disease. The first complete animal genomes are sequenced.

---

triumphs are set to make the first decade of the twenty-first century another record-setter.

Creativity is not neat and orderly. It is not organized. It is difficult, if not impossible, to measure. Flashes of brilliance can come from anywhere, triggered by anything. It takes a lot of guts to swim in a fluid environment, chock full of new stimuli, riddled with risk and uncertainty. It is hard when something so ephemeral is so important, but without innovation, we are destined to stay where we are or even slip backwards. Innovative ideas are the only things that move us forward, yet paradoxically, creative pursuits are often the first things to be curtailed when times get tough. The typical reaction to adversity, down markets, reversals of fortune, and fear is to cut back and hunker down. R&D and T&E budgets are cut. Outside consultants are banished. Chancy prospects are not supported. Everything is tightened as we get frightened. We saw it in the fall from the heights of irrational exuberance, as Alan Greenspan called the attitude of the seemingly unstoppable bullish investors of the late 1990s, falling further when the war on terrorism began. Yet, it is innovation that will pull us out, not interest rate cuts and conservatism. It is the new idea that lies below our radar, the new spark waiting to be struck, that will lift us to new prosperity and new life.

ENDLESS GENESIS

> Surviving means being born over and over again.
> —*Erica Jong*

There is a restlessness among H³s, a refusal to be satisfied, to believe that they know everything. The new idea pods burst open, and millions of feathery parachutes set sail across the meadow. There is no finality. Companies don't die in the Silicon Valley hotbed. New life springs from their vestiges. Creative organizations—wherever they are, however big or small, old or new—never stop creating themselves. H³ talent is constantly thinking of new possibilities, new potentials. They live to score "the next new new thing."[5] They are forever striking matches.

Corning has been in an endless genesis since 1851 (see sidebar: "The Transformations of Corning, Inc.: A Timeline"). "One of our key inventions was in lighting the world," says Roger Ackerman,

---

THE TRANSFORMATIONS OF CORNING, INC.:
A TIMELINE[6]

1851: Company is founded.

1879: Light bulb is developed with Thomas Edison, making electric light possible.

1915: Pyrex is invented, making heat-resistant glass innovations possible.

1934: Silicone is invented, spawning thousands of new-to-the-world products.

1947: Cathode ray tube is invented, making TV possible.

1960s: LCD screens are invented, eventually making advanced mobile devices such as laptop computers possible.

1970s: Optical fiber is invented, revolutionizing telecommunications and making the Internet possible.

1990s: Advances in photonics for high-speed optical systems enable greater bandwidth and connectivity to improve access and utilization of networks, including the Internet.

2000: Microarrays are developed to exponentially advance biotech research.

---

recently retired chairman and CEO of Corning, referring to the company's work with Thomas Edison in inventing the light bulb. Over and over, the company's innovations have changed the world: from the light bulb to the cathode ray tube (which gave us TV), to Pyrex and silicone, and most recently to fiber optics, which enabled the creation of truly global and practically instantaneous telecommunications and the Internet. Corning's hair-thin strands of glass delivered the Information Age.

In the 1980s, Corning's directors came to the conclusion that they no longer wanted to be in the now-very-mature light bulb business. They sold it and repeated that move in the 1990s with their Pyrex cookware business, among others. Many companies sell off mature product lines, but Corning has transformed its whole identity over and over again, keeping the company on the cutting edge of new technologies and new industries. As Ackerman puts it, "We're constantly reinventing ourselves. We've shed our skin several times. We've always been willing to let go—not hang on and try to retrench."

Instead of focusing only on profitability to satisfy the demands of Wall Street, Corning has focused on the future. "We were looking at what would become an incredibly enormous need to transfer information extremely quickly," explains Ackerman, "and so, we invented fiber optics, optical networks, and much of the technology needed to make optical communications possible." The glass company became a leading high-technology company, specializing in fiber optics, flat glass for LCD screens, ophthalmic lenses, and many other cutting-edge products. Corning's various businesses generated sales of nearly $7.3 billion in 2000.

Genesis after genesis unfolds. Corning is now positioned to lead the next major life-changing wave. The company is at the very center of the convergence of telecommunications, computer, and television technologies. This old company doesn't stay old. It continues to grow at incredible rates like a healthy, precocious upstart, although it suffers periodic declines as many other technology companies do.

Every new idea is a solution to a problem. The light bulb was a new solution to darkness and inconvenience; a new painting is a new solution to the "problems" of empty space and visual dilemma; a new piece of music is a new solution to silence or a respite from cacophony. The arts give us new ways to move the soul. In an endless genesis, every new idea is a solution to a problem, and every new solution begets new problems.

If you look at today's solutions, you can see yesterday's problems on one side and tomorrow's problems on the other.

> ... yesterday's problem → today's solution → tomorrow's problem → near-future solution → future problem → future solution → future problem *ad inf.*

Every problem and every solution plugs into a bigger system. If you think in a continuum, you can look around you today at new answers, whether they are products, methodologies, philosophies, or aesthetic statements, and you can get important clues to what tomorrow's problems will be. Biotech is the ultimate model for endless genesis, for the perpetual pattern of problem-solution-problem-solution (see previous page). Antibiotics solved a problem but created a new one—namely bugs resistant to the drugs. And systems intersect with other systems. The systems are changed by each new development—positive or negative. System pathways are not always clear to see, but they are there. Try to trace the connections, the causes and effects. Try to detect changes in energy flow.

If you focus only on today's problems, as many do, you won't see as far ahead as you would if you focused on today's solutions.

> The next message you need is always right where you are.
>
> —Ram Das

Consider the challenge of effectively managing inventory. It's been problematic ever since we began counting beans. One of the biggest problems has always been thievery. Accurate counts and devices to detect sticky fingers and find stolen goods have been difficult to achieve and maintain. Crooks can be quite adept at thwarting identification marking systems. As the U.S. Treasury demonstrated in its redesign of paper money, a traditional way of dealing with counterfeiting is to create identification marks that are increasingly complex and harder to duplicate or remove. Watermarks, glyphs, and barcodes, for instance, have been offered as "solutions" to the problems of counterfeiting and branded product diversion, but thieves have found ways to outsmart all of these—then it's back to the drawing board.

You may have experienced this dynamic if you've ever owned a radar detector. Every time a new radar detector gains popularity, the police develop a newer radar gun that defies the latest detector technology, and you have to buy yet another, newer radar detector to keep your edge in preventing speeding tickets—that is, until cops get even better technology. Needless to say, the radar gun manufacturers are quite happy to play this game of leapfrog since the next iteration of their products comes with more bells and whistles and higher price tags.

At each iteration, each side hopes it has found a permanent solution, but no one ever does. The best one can hope for is to prolong the solution's lifespan, to stall the opponent while anticipating his next move. The Eastman Chemical Company developed a new way to confound counterfeiters, which should keep them scratching their heads for quite some time. Eastman invented an invisible marker. You can't steal, copy, or remove something you don't know is there. The marker consists of a new molecule that Eastman created, which is visible only when ex posed to a very narrow range of the infrared spectrum. We at the SPWI Group helped Eastman Chemical develop new product and business strategies for this innovative technology. The results, ClirCode invisible inks and marking media, are now used to print invisible barcodes and glyphs.[7] They can be seen only through a special highly sophisticated scanner—one that will take the bad guys some time to reverse-engineer—but of course, eventually they will find a way as the vicious circle continues.

PERFECT PROBLEMS

The battle has been raging, officially, for almost thirty years, endlessly, since Nixon declared the war in 1974.[8] Millions have fallen around the world. Many people were against the Vietnam War, but no one is against this one—the War on Cancer.

We've made some inroads to beat back the enemy. But we're still fighting. As in the steaming jungles of Vietnam, it's hard to see where the killers are coming from. We're still in an unfamiliar world. When you don't know what to look for, it's hard to find it. When you don't understand the codes of cancer, it's hard to break through.

"We can send a man to the moon. Why can't we find the cure for cancer?" is a commonly heard query. What is so hard? What is the big problem?

As we know, problems can be seen in a negative light, or they can be seen as opportunities. Einstein, for instance, equated the word "problem" with a puzzle or a nut to crack rather than a burden or a proposition laden with negative connotations. For him the universe was like a giant math problem, a brainteaser, or even better, a very good mystery.

All problems have more than one interpretation. Most of the time, they remain well hidden or tangled up in issues having to do with human psychology, history, economics, social conditions, environmental change, technology, and culture. When problems present themselves in bundles, as they most often do in life, it's difficult to determine which one is the "perfect" problem to attack— the one that will lead you to the next big leap innovation, whether it is fiber optics, a PDA, Viagra, sunscreen, or a snowboard.

Cancer is a horrible, devastating disease, but within it are opportunities for solutions. We simply haven't found them yet. We are getting closer because we are beginning to redefine the medical condition. Thousands of super-smart cancer researchers hunted and searched for almost a century, envisioning new weapons of destruction, but they didn't know much about what they were trying to kill. They began to realize that cancer is not simply one disease or one problem, but rather is over 400 discrete diseases, each with its own particular formula of growth signals and responses, each with its own macabre conversation. The researchers began to observe that these killers—tumors, mutations, or damaged genetic sequences—were constantly sending out chemical signals to outwit the body's healthy cellular processes, while building up a cruel arsenal of metastases or blockages. One frontliner, Dr. John Mendelsohn, figured out how to interrupt these lethal messages after a long search for clues, in microscopic places, for answers that would stop the devastation.

Mendelsohn began his path to discovery as a student of Dr. James Watson at Harvard University in the 1960s, shortly after Watson, together with his partner Francis Crick, won the Nobel Prize for the discovery of the DNA molecule's double helix structure. Shortly thereafter, Mendelsohn and a number of other researchers began to wage the long and complicated War on Cancer.

No one had yet figured out the right problem to study until, in 1980, Mendelsohn zeroed in on a protein expressed by tumors, called EGF (Epidermal Growth Factor) and a magnet-like site called EGFR (Epidermal Growth Factor Receptor). Normal cells divide over and over, making fresh new copies of themselves while the older cells die off. But sometimes, there is an error in the copy machine, which can result in a genetic mutation called an oncogene—the bad seed that grows into cancer. Oncogenes send deadly signals that cause cells to replicate out of control. With nothing to stop them, they build up into tumors: the more they grow, the more signals they send, and the more signals they send, the more they receive and grow. When the growth factor binds to its receptors, it turns the cell into a cancer factory, unleashing metastases, healthy cell invasion, tumor cell repair, and an ever-increasing number of blood vessels to feed the tumor. The cell stimulates its own exponential multiplication.

But what if the signal could be intercepted? Mendelsohn thought that the factory might be shut down. It was a "perfect" problem— perfect enough, that is, to set off a cascade of industry activity and spawn thousands of new promises.

Mendelsohn set out, together with a team, to develop a new monoclonal antibody to block the signal of destruction and death. Along the way, he became the chairman of the Medicine Department at Sloan-Kettering, the pinnacle of cancer research-based medical centers. After twelve years, struggling to raise funds to develop and test his hunch, Mendelsohn met up with two brothers, Sam and Harlan Waksal, an immunology Ph.D. and a pathologist, who had just started a little biotech company, ImClone, and were looking for a new drug platform on which to build.

When Mendelsohn presented his findings, suddenly the creative sparks began flying. Sam Waksal, CEO of ImClone, recalls the precise moment, rare in business and life, when one gets to think later-ally: "A lot of people wanted to put a label on the discovery, calling it chemotherapeutic or radioactive, then to use it as a guided missile to blast away a targeted tumor," he explains. "Others wanted to vacci-nate. I looked at the data and said, 'What's happening is that the an-tibody is acting as a drug to shut off the signal to the cancer cell. It's blocking the tumor's ability to survive.' With that underlying mecha-nism, the chemotherapy and radiation damage the cancer cells' DNA and block the tumor in certain ways. The antibody comes in and blocks it at a different phase of its life cycle, not allowing the tu-mor cell to re-regulate itself. And that was the first time that any-body had thought of the problem and the solution in that way."

Perfect problems can sometimes take a long time to solve. Despite the breakthrough, it took C225, the name given to Mendelsohn's breakthrough drug, twenty years to get from lab to market, with quite a few roadblocks and setbacks along the way, including Im-Clone's near-bankruptcy. But in 2000–2001, C225 began moving swiftly through the mandated phases of clinical trials—much faster than usual—illustrating its ability to reverse the deadliest of cancers even among some of the most dire cases, where no other treatment had worked and patients, who had run out of options, were deemed "terminal" or "hopeless." Of course, C225 is not a panacea, but it remains one of a handful of truly promising drug therapies for many kinds of cancer.

Most biotech start-ups opt to license out their discoveries to big pharmaceutical companies because they don't have the cash, the in-frastructure, or the clout to commercialize the product on their own. Waksal, however, vehemently believed that ImClone had found the perfect problem and that C225 was a prize-winning solution in its ability to interrupt the cancer "signals." He poured over $100 mil-lion—an enormous sum for a relatively small company—into its de-velopment. In an unprecedented move, Waksal opted to keep all rights to the drug in-house—a move others never dared to make before.

Signal interruption is a perfect kind of problem because it represents a totally new change in the model of cancer treatment and yields unprecedented success. Mendelsohn went on to become president of the M. D. Anderson Center in Houston, another top cancer hospital in the country, while continuing to serve as a board member and scientific advisor to ImClone. ImClone Systems became a cutting-edge biotech dynamo, with a $3 billion market cap. Even more impressive is the company's revenue growth since 1995: 37 percent (sixty months), 13 percent (thirty-six months), and 1,833 percent (twelve months).9 Although it had not shown a profit in its seventeen-year life, Wall Street analysts projected $500 million in sales for C225 for the treatment of colon cancer alone, with $1 billion for all EGF-fueled cancers, including head and neck, gastrointestinal tract, prostate, breast, kidney, and lung tumors.

THE "PERFECT" QUESTIONS

The perfect problem is found by asking the perfect question. Untangling the right question often requires us to adopt a new vantage point or a new set of definitions. *How did the universe begin?* It seems like a reasonable question to ask. "We always put the word 'begin' in quotes because . . . what do you mean by 'begin'?" physicist and Columbia University professor Brian Greene muses. He deliberately "fuzzes out" the question, teasing out the meanings of the word *begin*, and looking to see if there is a better question. The assumptions about the word *begin* can vary greatly, as can the interpretations of the problem that is raised. "Does 'begin' mean that at some moment the universe clicked on?" Greene asks, as if it were a light to be switched on or off. "Or does the question refer to a particular moment in which the notion of time came into existence?" If time is a human construct—we are, after all, the only animals on earth who watch clocks, keep calendars, and count down the seconds to the New Year—then every question has to be weighed in terms of its social, psychological, and cultural implications. Maybe the reason we haven't found an answer yet is because "how did the universe begin?" is not the right question.

Greene, who wrote the critically acclaimed bestseller *The Elegant Universe*, is not just playing with words. "It's very well understood what we're driving towards," he explains, "but part of that is a fuller understanding of the question. That's part of what the problem is." It is an exercise that can be applied to any problem, in any aspect of life.

Some questions seem so basic that we cling to them even though they are not the right ones to ask. Maybe there is actually not a single question. Maybe we would do better to seek insight into a family of questions. Instead of "How can cancer be cured?" the family of questions might be "How can aberrant growth be contained?" Instead of "How can we build a faster, more powerful chip?" it might be "What kind of computing power will be most important in the future?" Instead of "What should be our next flavor of breakfast cereal?" consider "What do we need in the morning?" or "What flavor do *we* want to be?"

Instead of asking if people like a new product concept, a better question may be, "Do you see yourself ever *using* this product in the future?" For example, when Welch's developed a new concept for a frozen smoothie product, most people the company approached said they loved the idea. "The trial was great," explains Dan Dillon, Welch's CEO. "People loved the product. It was a hit. It was only after you gave it to them in the marketplace and asked them to go home and use it with their own microwaves that the problem became apparent." The problem was, no one wanted to bother with nuking a frozen drink in the microwave—they'd rather do without. As a result the concept was never fully executed, but it might be resurrected by asking another set of questions, such as, "Where might you enjoy drinking this smoothie?" It just might be something a 7-Eleven store might offer as a fountain product.

Sometimes the question is not *if* but *when*. Welch's currently has a $100 million business in refrigerated juices. They sit right next to Tropicana in the refrigerator case. "We tried that five times and failed because it was too early," explains Dillon. "The market wasn't ready for it." The category hadn't developed yet to be able to extend beyond orange juice. The category had to develop to where people went to the refrigerated section to do their juice shopping. Fortunately for Welch's, that time finally came.

Every successful innovation in business, the arts, science, and daily living results from someone finding the "perfect" problem to solve by asking the right questions in the right places. Even innovations that come by chance or by luck came from someone stumbling upon the right question/problem/solution set. Does this mean that there are some problems that are "better" than others to occupy our attention and become the focus of our work? Yes, if that work leads to a leap innovation as opposed to an incremental improvement.

Questions often appear to have hard and fast boundaries. They may seem straightforward. They address what you think you want to know. But what you might not know is that you might actually want to know something else.

A common analytical approach is to dissect a question, examining each of its visible components to try to find significant meaning. While this is an extremely useful exercise, I also like to take a question and "fuzz it out," blurring the edges of the definitions, expanding the scope of vision, stretching the issue into new territories, and exploring the "wrong" places.

Consider that on average only one in 5,000 drugs discovered in research labs ever make it through the development process, FDA protocols, and ultimately to market.[10] It makes sense that in the pursuit of new cures—and new ideas in general—we start by asking new questions and examining problems differently. Often it's not clear what the pivotal problems are. They can go unrecognized for weeks or even years—just ask anybody in therapy.

What is the "perfect" problem? It's the turning point. It's the gap, the disconnect, the aberration, the irritation, the potential for beauty that is at the heart of a negative condition or situation. It's why we are still where we are even though we know that is not where we want to be. It's the missing stepping-stone to the next level of success. It's the wall, the bottleneck, the logjam. It is the catalyst of successful innovation. It is the one where you say, "If I can nail this one, it will be very, very sweet"—it will have a major impact. Perfect problems are the ones that unleash new forces and open up new worlds when new solutions are found.

> You can't depend on your eyes when your imagination is out of focus.
> —Mark Twain

I am not trying to suggest that there is such a thing as absolute perfection. The word "perfect" is used here in relative terms to describe questions and problems that yield profound opportunities for significant advancement or leap innovation. Although the degree of "perfect" is reflected in the results of the solution—it is impossible to know for certain whether a problem is "perfect" until after the fact—discovering the perfect problem is as important as discovering the perfect solution. As you approach perfection in either case, you come to an insight—you can often feel that sudden burst of discovery and inspiration, the excitement, the *eureka!*

Edwin Land and his daughter went to visit the Grand Canyon many years ago. Founder of the Polaroid Corporation, Land brought along a camera to snap some photographs of his little girl in the midst of the great natural wonder. She was so excited by what she saw that she blurted out a question that took her father by storm: "Daddy, why can't we see the pictures *now?*"

The question set Land to inventing. From its beginnings in 1937, Polaroid had produced sunglasses (at the time called "dayglasses"), goggles, and synthetic polarizers. On February 21, 1947, the direction of the company was dramatically and completely changed. On that day, at the meeting of the Optical Society of America in New York City, Land presented his latest invention, a film that could develop its own image in an instant. For Edwin Land, his daughter's naïve question exposed a "perfect" problem. Its solution led to a giant leap innovation in photography and, for decades, an enormously profitable, virtually monopolistic business for Polaroid. Unfortunately, Polaroid never asked a "perfect" question ever again, and after a run of unbeatable success, the company has been in sharp decline for over a decade and has fallen so far behind in technology advances that it has hovered near bankruptcy.

The perfect problem asks the perfect question of the perfect person. If the little girl had asked a park ranger the question, instead of Edwin Land, her father, chances are that we still wouldn't have the Polaroid camera.

"It is also important to be looking for the opportunities, not just to say you have done something to solve the problem, because the innovative answers are most often going to come from a place where you have not been looking for them," says Dave Ditzel. What's important is the ability to respond to the right opportunities.

At Transmeta, people are willing to say, "Hey, that's an opportunity, let's do it." The answer is really attitude, more than anything they're doing. It is the willingness to do something about it when opportunity arises, and the judgment to know which is the best opportunity to take. As Ditzel puts it, "A lot of managers will say, 'Well, we found these five opportunities, and they're great!' I say, 'Yeah, but unless they are really compelling, you found the wrong opportunities.'"

The "perfect" question often lies out of the range of everyday vision, and it is endlessly changing. To see it requires searching through diverse bits of information after taking off the blinders. We can feel stymied by the number of alternatives and their consequences. The more data points and choices, the harder it is to figure out what the right problem is, much less what it will take to solve it.

What else gets in the way? What diverts our attention? What derails us? What leads us to focus on the "wrong" problems?

UNCONSCIOUS COMMITMENT

> To the man who has only a hammer in the toolkit, every problem looks like a nail.
>
> —*Abraham Maslow*

The first definition of an important problem is usually wrong. Yet, the first definition is often the one we work with. We have a tendency to want to narrow definitions. It's human nature. In fact, it's part of nature in general, as Louis Pasteur, the father of microbiology, observed: "We see what we are prepared to see."

We process much of what we take in with lightning speed within commitment to boundaries that limit our ability to see. Some scientists estimate that we process less than one billionth of what is going on in our immediate surroundings. Typically, if we don't have a preconception about a possibility, it spontaneously gets screened out—never entering the realm of our awareness. No blip appears on the radar screen. Each species has evolved to detect mainly what is most important for its own survival: Snakes see in infrared to sense the warm blood of living prey; bees detect only the colors of certain flowers; bats don't see much of anything, but use sonar to guide them in food-gathering.

While this hardwiring is a boon for day-to-day survival, it is a disadvantage to innovation. For a long time Bill Gates saw only software discs, choosing to ignore Internet browsers such as Netscape, which had the potential to trump Windows and undermine its core business. Gates's reluctance to enter that area of competition nearly cost Microsoft a place in the web browser market.

By some estimates, as much as 90 percent of the thoughts we have today are the same ones we had yesterday.[11] Much is force of habit, but we also often fall in love with our own ideas, charmed by our own beliefs. As such, there are gold mines all around us that most of us never see. Innovators, in contrast, see and mine the hidden treasure. An example to drive the point home took place during the California Gold Rush. While most people rushed out to find a fortune panning for gold, a lackluster apparel manufacturer named Levi Strauss made the *real* mother-lode fortune.

Scientists have done some fascinating and suggestive experiments with ordinary houseflies. If you capture and keep houseflies in a jar and then remove the lid after a few days, most of them will not fly away. In fact, they stay right where they are—inside the jar—even though they could escape if only they could see their way to freedom. But they seem "committed" to a lid that is no longer there. Psychologists have identified this phenomenon as "premature cognitive commitment." It is premature cognition in the sense that it occurs, more or less automatically, before we are aware of or fully understand the stimulus. It is "commitment" because we are locked into a specific set of thoughts. Like the houseflies, we give up the freedom to choose once we become committed to the nonexistent lid.

The first step in challenging a commitment is recognizing that you have made it in the first place.

KNOWING TOO MUCH

> There are two fools in every market: one asks too little, one asks too much.
>
> —*Russian proverb*

Dr. Philip D. Noguchi is afraid. And he's not alone. What if someone dies? What if people get seriously sicker than they were before? He shares his fear with all of his colleagues at the U.S. Food and Drug Administration (FDA), where he is director of the division of cellular and gene therapies. It is their job to make sure that new foods and drugs are safe before they are allowed to be sold to you and me. Remember thalidomide? And DES? And saccharine?

Nobody wants those kinds of disasters to happen again. And so, Noguchi and the other FDA directors have developed lots of ideas about how to make sure they are sure. Pharmaceutical and biotech companies must submit new drugs to a long, heavy chain of trials and tests, which typically take at least ten years before the therapies are allowed to come to market. The process can be prohibitively expensive: A company has only about seven years to recoup the hundreds of millions of dollars spent on R&D before its patent runs out.

The FDA has no incentive to promote innovation. The people who work there typically don't have corporate experience or perspective. Given their predilections, they often issue strong demands that don't always make good business sense. They are unconcerned with the path to profitability. Their primary responsibility is to keep us safe, not to keep corporate profits healthy. But if a company cannot perform profitably, it comes to a screeching halt, along with the potential cures it may have in its product pipeline.

Noguchi's fear is understandable. Fear can make us overly cautious—in this case, with good reason. We want to know more and more before we move. Fear can also keep us from opportunities to save lives. "Analysis paralysis" can set in at the FDA, as it often does at traditional organizations.

What is the right balance for progress? What about looking at fear differently? As with most things, it is a matter of balance and fine-line decisions.

We can require too much information, after which there are diminishing returns or even damage. The insatiable need to know more before taking action, coupled with the delusion that we can know it all, sabotages innovation. Thousands of drugs that might be good are stopped along with those that are not good. The cost of gaining additional substantiated evidence before we act can often be devastating.

In response to public pressure, in 1997 the FDA adopted guidelines for Fast Track designation for new products that address an unmet medical need. Applicants can receive priority, accelerated, or standard review timelines, the fastest being designated for drugs with the potential to cure life threatening or fatal diseases such as cancer or HIV, especially when there is no other applicable drug already on the market. Fast Track streamlines and expedites the process and moves the most important sets of decisions up to the front of the line. ImClone, for example, received a Fast Track designation for C225, allowing for submission of a rolling application, with data submitted for review as it is obtained as opposed to being submitted all at once at the end of development.

To avoid the hassle and the risk, many people choose to deal only with the "safe" problems, for which there is a preponderance of proof. Safe problems, however, are obvious to everyone, including the competition. Rarely do they yield leap innovations. Instead, they yield safe, but impotent solutions. In contrast, H^3s expect to screw up. In fact, they want to. They make sure they are not sure. It is not a blow to their egos if they don't know everything before they act. After all, too much ego stops inquiry, while too little stops aspiration. The ability to achieve a successful balance is critical to finding and solving the right problem. It is signaled by well-developed senses of humility, openness to truth, and empowerment.

NAÏVETÉ IS AN ASSET

I can't understand why people are frightened of new ideas. I'm frightened of the old ones.

—John Cage

"It would have been a handicap if it had stayed with me too long," says Sam Waksal, speaking of his own naïveté in starting his biotech company ImClone. "But it turned out to be an asset. If someone had said to me, 'In order to get a new drug on the market, it's going to take hundreds of millions of dollars and decades to do it,' I would have probably said, 'You know what? I think I'll stay where I am as a professor and let someone else do it.' I think the naïveté was that I could say 'I can do it,' without feeling that there were insurmountable barriers, as others felt."

As a child, Laurie Anderson began thinking about making art and music. Like many artists, she didn't care about a career path. She lived on little money, and that was fine. She believed that her groundbreaking art was all that mattered and that everything else in

her life—food, shelter, health care, and other vitals—would somehow fall into place. She had a certain naïveté about making a living. But she was making powerful art. "The minute I started worrying about how I was going to pay the rent, I dried up," says Anderson. Her naïveté gave her the freedom to keep pushing the edges of her talents and ideas. Her works exude an innocence that attracts and captivates a broad audience around the world, as well as an exceptional roster of collaborators.

Many successful innovations and hot companies were started by people who didn't "know it all." Many were amazingly young and inexperienced. They never learned that they couldn't do what they contemplated, so they went ahead and did it anyway. Bill Gates and Steve Jobs were in their early twenties when they began to build their empires. Nine of the top self-made billionaires in the '90s were under forty, including Michael Dell, Ted Waitt, and David Filo. A surprising number never even made it through college. While there is no substantiated proof, the correlation between their youth and their unmatched success appears to be more than coincidental. They never got the chance to learn fear. They never got far enough to become weighed down with rules. They never had to "unlearn" conventional wisdom or struggle to break free of bad ingrained habits.

What if you didn't know what to be afraid of? What if nobody told you, "You can't"? What if nobody told you how it should be done? What if you couldn't see an established path? You can't become naïve. But, you can pretend. You can set aside a space for innocence. You can pretend that you don't know what you know. You can "forget" who you are for a moment. You can pretend that you don't care. You can pretend to forge ahead with your visions with a devil-may-care toss of your hand. You can pretend for five minutes or for five months—however much time you want to slice out of your life's pie.

You can also recruit virgins—young people, neophytes, people outside of your core circles—to your territory and leverage their naïveté, just as John Seely Brown and researchers at Xerox PARC did when they invited a group of computer-savvy middle-school students to the facility to "play" at invention.

SWELL

If you naïvely expand a question, the question can become robust enough to embrace variations on its own theme. Brian Greene, for example, considers the question *How did the universe begin?* "If we need to change what we mean by 'begin' because we understand time better in the future, that will be OK," Greene says. "And if we have to accept one day that maybe the universe is eternal, that it's one of those things that doesn't have a beginning, the question of *where its beginning came from* is wrong. You can see it as part of a larger family of questions."

As that family of questions swells and shifts, so does the number of potential solutions. When a family of questions grows to a critical mass, entire industries take major leaps. The industrial revolution gave us applied engineering, mass manufacturing, and mass merchandising. The pharmaceutical industry has given us applied chemistry, mass screening, mass trials, and mass prescriptions. Now, genomics is the disruptive force, redefining old medical problems. If we shift to looking at causes as opposed to looking at symptoms, we see that the perfect problem may no longer be found in new blockbuster drugs such as Prozac and Claritin, which can each be used to treat millions of patients. We will stop trying so hard to find a new miracle drug that can cure millions of cancer patients.

Rather, the perfect problem might now be defined in terms of succeeding in a business where the introduction of new molecules becomes the equivalent of surgery, where new vectors carry engineered biological arsenals that narrowly target diseased cells, which are genetically specific to an individual, and stop their destructive power. One perfect solution might be the development and marketing of hundreds of custom-designed drugs—one for each patient, as opposed to a one-drug-for-all protocol that we now have.

As suggested earlier, one way to expand the view of a problem is to "fuzz out" the sharp demarcations around a term's definition or a set of desired outcomes. Whoever rules the definition of the problem rules its solutions. Nokia snatched market leadership of cell phones away from Motorola because it defined the problem space as being digital, size- and design-driven, whereas Motorola got caught with a clunky analog design and a fragmented product line. HMOs defined *the* big healthcare problem as the efficient management of costs, but they did not define it well in the larger scope of human care. Antibacterial soaps targeted cleaning problems, but didn't consider the whole system of germ evolution. Now after we have developed resistant strains, super-germs are getting even. While most computer manufacturers solved the design problem by creating a narrow range of nondescript, boxy gray desktops and laptops, Apple defined the problem as an aesthetic one. The company decided to offer hot colors and cool designs, a move that not only lifted Apple back up to a new platform of success but also helped raise the bar for the industry as competitors began to pay more attention to the "look" of their machines.

When vision swells beyond the boundaries of where others search, when passion overrides fear, leap innovation is possible. For Waksal, ImClone is poised to change the way cancer is being treated. This was Waksal's ideal of what biotech companies were meant to do. "We're not meant to create the fifteenth calcium channel blocker and the tenth erectile dysfunction drug. That's not interesting," says Waksal. "We were meant to do things that change the way diseases are approached, especially in areas that don't yet have anything available for people. That's what we're meant to do."

For Dave Ditzel, the breakthrough came when he looked beyond chip hardware and found expanded possibilities by merging hardware and software worlds. Similarly, Corning's universe magnified when researchers saw through glass to a sea of silica, from the potential of light bulbs to myriad high-tech, silica-based products. Whether it happens in insurance, music, computers, organic food, or any other industry, there is always a more expansive view. There are always new solutions, and new problems will always emerge, and H^3s are more than willing to take them on. For example, how do you market millions of customized drugs? How do you deal with new ethical questions? How do you patent? How do you get these through the FDA? What new diseases will emerge when people begin to live well past 100? What new viruses and bacteria will find ways to outsmart us?

It takes creativity to find perfect problems and create new sparks. It also takes creative talent to take a spark and set the world on fire. The next chapter, "Bubbling," presents new ideas about developing the sparks into successful innovation concepts.

₀ 2 ₀

BUBBLING

New Approaches to
Idea Development

Life is not a problem to be solved, but a mystery to be lived.
—*Thomas Merton*

"Why can't you accept that fact that you *are* eccentric?" Frank Gehry asked his good friend Peter Lewis.

"It was, like, *Ding!*" Lewis declared.

People who realize that they are creative or eccentric give themselves permission to create. It is not something they turn on when they are asked to participate. It is something that defines them. It's not a role; it's not an exercise. It's a way of life.

Imagine: You work for a cereal company and have to think up new cereals on a regular basis to keep the new product pipeline full. It seems as if every cereal that could ever be created has already been thought of. Then management hires some creativity consultant to come in, full of a "Come-on-guys!-Let's-go!-This-is-going-to-be-fun!" attitude. Your team then schedules a few hours in the afternoon to hang out in the conference room where the consultant conducts a brainstorming session, poking, goosing, and leading you to think of a pile of wild ideas. Or, even worse, managers think they can lead these sessions themselves, so there is not one drop of fresh blood, just the same old folks you know and work with every day, sitting around, trying to squeeze out new thoughts. The process is deceptive because you do end up with a lot of ideas. You may even think you're getting somewhere. You have all the symptoms of success. People are excited. They feel creative. You have reams of paper, full of thought-scribbles. But you don't really achieve the success you wished for. When all the brainstorming effluence loses whatever sparkle it ever had, you schedule yet another brainstorming session to try to think of some new cereal ideas.

BEYOND BRAINSTORMING

Many traditional companies have formalized the process of brainstorming, reducing it to an activity often characterized as the untrained leading the unwilling to do the unnecessary. However, many, if not most, successful innovations come from the "wrong" places—nonconformists with an obsession, individuals stumbling on new discoveries by accident, people finding new uses for products intended for different markets, and so on. After twenty-five years of studying IBM, General Electric, Polaroid, and Xerox, James Brian Quinn of the Amos Tuck Business School at Dartmouth College found that not a single major product had come from the formal planning process.[1]

Unfortunately, brainstorming, in one form or another, is often the only creative tool used today by most organizations. An unruly mass of new ideas is generated. A few are chosen, usually based on traditional criteria and old metrics. However, most brainstorming results in incremental "newness." More often than not, it becomes a trap, a waste of intellectual capital and time.

Another big problem lies with the people involved in brainstorming and in what they do with the ideas that are generated. In most organizations, those ideas are likely to collect dust, or they end up thrown away, right away. Many brainstorming initiatives simply fail to produce meaningful innovation. Companies need to engage in more creative initiatives before, after, and sometimes instead of brainstorming in order to generate and develop successful innovation concepts.

For example, a major household appliance manufacturer had a familiar routine of holding a team brainstorming session in each business unit three or four times a year, on average, to develop new models. Typically, the meetings would be called for a Friday afternoon. A brief memo stating a few facts about the situation was sometimes sent out to the participants, who would glance over the items five minutes before the meeting, if at all. Most of the time, no one really prepared very much for the session, but instead operated by the seats of their pants. When they finally admitted that the piles of ideas generated during the session were pretty baseless and useless, we were invited to help. We began by setting up a more robust and varied exploration to discover new hypotheses, and the development process shot off from there. We helped them to define a new set of parameters, working both within and outside of these, in total freedom, generating and helping the teams to develop new ideas for washing clothes and dishes. We then helped to evaluate and prioritize the ideas with a new set of scales, including some measurements they had not considered before. Together, we then developed a medley of both top and fringe ideas into substantial concepts, including a diverse array of inputs from experts, customers, and select outsiders. We brought our own personal creativity in our approach to research, strategy development, idea development, and execution throughout the development process—as we do to every client's projects—as is discussed in further detail in this and following chapters.

Creativity is not a discrete event. You can't schedule it. However, you can try to become a creative person. You can try to create a creative organization, through and through.

Look at the creative people you know. How do they operate? How do they connect? Do they study creativity techniques? Do they don different hats or seek inspiration in Koosh Balls? Do they set aside times in their lives to think of new ideas? Do they go through extensive analysis to decide which ideas to toss and which to ride? Probably not.

Look at where they live, what they eat, the way they dress, the people they hang out with. Look at how they work, how they schedule their lives, how they play. Look at their toys, their art, their joys, and their fears. Look at how they keep riding the edge.

Creativity is a way of life for these people. Typical H³s are both thrilled and comfortable with change. They see life as a series of episodes rather than as one long story. "My life winds up being very episodic," says Nathan Myhrvold, former CTO of Microsoft, now co-president of Intellectual Ventures, an entrepreneurial investment firm and think tank, which he co-founded and which is focused primarily on technologies, computer science, intellectual property, and biotech. "I don't have any intention of picking one single thing I'm going to be doing for the rest of my life."

This is a recurring theme among the most innovative leaders. David Cole, the former president of AOL Internet Services and now chairman of the board of a new organic food company, Acirca, has a personal system in which he has committed to change what he's doing every three years. For people such as Myhrvold and Cole, the creative way of life paradoxically requires both total immersion in their work and dramatic separation from it. To stay creative and fresh, both leaders crave tension and freedom. They have both a strong inner voice that distinguishes itself from others as well as a strong ear to listen to others' voices.

There are big psychic differences between people who live creative lives and people who try to be creative when called upon to do so.

You can sense it. It feels different to be in their presence—an energy you don't normally feel with others. "Occasionally, I get to shoot someone I really admire, someone who's just wonderful to be with," says Timothy Greenfield-Sanders, world-renowned portrait photographer. "I love to be with them." Greenfield-Sanders attributes a big part of his creativity to his inspirational subjects, artists such as Andy Warhol, Robert Rauschenberg, David Bowie, Philip Johnson, Erté, and hundreds of others. "'When you meet people like that and they are very accomplished, you know why. . . . It's because they *are* special," Greenfield-Sanders explains. "They are so talented and so full of ideas. . . . So, it's a big charge. That's how I charge myself."

Neither Greenfield-Sanders nor his subjects sit down and say, "'OK, now I have to think of a new idea." Or, "Now, I have to be creative. Let me conduct a brainstorming session." They simply *are* creative. Like his subjects, Greenfield-Sanders surrounds himself with creative people.

We don't simply need compartmentalized creative processes such as brainstorming sessions. We need to live creative lives. We need to *be* creative people. We need to eat, sleep, and breathe creatively. We need to become what we want to produce—fountains of innovation. That is H^3.

> Creative pursuits are important. It's similar to breathing. If you don't breath, you die. If you don't create, you die—or at least a part of you dies. I can't imagine living a day without it.
>
> —Annette Lemieux

LIVING COLOR

Whatever you see, you automatically name it. Try this: Look around the room you are now in. Let your eyes scan. As you see an object, in a nanosecond, your brain calls it *chair*, or *table*, or *window*, or *Fluffy the cat*. You can't help it. Since infancy, you've learned to shortcut by developing a set of symbols to help you process what you see more quickly. Ball = round circle. Person = stick figure with a smiley face. As you grow, you develop more and more symbols to reduce what you see to visual bytes and what you hear to sound bytes. The symbols you adopt relate to how you see the world and its many parts. But often, the minute you name something, you stop looking for what else it might be. You are tricked into thinking that you know what something really is, and then all of your subsequent thoughts get piled on top of that narrow view (see sidebar, "Seeing Red").

Names, words, and symbols give us speed but reduce our vision. They are classified thoughts. We mainly think in words, not images —the very opposite of what many cognitive scientists might prescribe for increased creativity. A picture, whether it is physical or mental, has myriad data points, which have the potential to create new sparks. Einstein often visualized a concept before verbalizing it or scribbling a formula. Philip Glass's inner audi-

---

SEEING RED

You may call it "red." An artist may see crimson, scarlet, vermilion, oxblood, maroon, burgundy, madder-lake, pink, lipstick red, fire-engine red, beet-red, blood-red, ruby, cherry, candy-apple, blush, flush, as well as varying degrees of light and dark possibilities within each.

---

ence heard the music first, before a pen was touched. Creative people tend to respond more to visual triggers.

If you are sensitive to variation and nuance, if what something "is" is somewhat open in your mental picture, you see a lot more possibilities.

Frank Gehry saw silver fish writhing and buckling in his bathtub. Their shiny bodies undulated into beautiful bends. His mother went to the fish market to buy live carp, carefully choosing each one from the bubbling tank. At home, she kept them in the bathtub until the moment she was ready to turn them into gefilte fish for the Passover Seder meal. This image triggered a vision Gehry would actualize sixty years later as he designed the magnificent titanium curves and twists of the spectacular Guggenheim Museum in Bilbao, Spain.

Images and sounds in the arts inspire, impassion, sensitize, and open doors of perception. Art helps us to see differently and find new meaning.

"Art keeps my mind constantly open," Peter Lewis says. Lewis, chairman of the fourth largest auto insurance company, Progressive Insurance Corporation, points to a large abstract painting, "Samba School" by James Rosenquist (1966), which punctuates his living room: primary-colored shards, layered against sheer iconic figures in a white space. "To look at that image and to understand that there's a lot going on there, a lot of which I still don't understand—I can't explain, exactly—it is mind-opening. The attitude of the people who create the images, even the attitudes of the people who appreciate the images—they're much less tight-assed," Lewis remarks.

"I have no doubt that my intense admiration for creative people, in part, shows in the art we hang around the office," says Lewis. "It manifests in our art-filled annual reports, and in my somewhat offbeat behavior, which gets a lot of attention. In part, it is evidenced in our joy in doing things differently."

EMBRACING FOG

Larry Witte likes to fish—for genes, as opposed to trout or marlin. A research scientist at ImClone Systems, a maverick biotech company, Witte uses bait and hooks from a process called polymerase chain reaction (PCR). He fishes genes out of DNA and RNA soups made from the liver cells of mice fetuses. It is hard to see what is swimming around in the fishing hole, but Witte is happy with anything he pulls up. "Whatever you get, you look at," explains Sam Waksal, chairman and CEO of ImClone. Waksal and his team of scientists love to go fishing in a sea of molecules. That's how they hooked C225, their new hope in curing cancer.

"Some of the things are already known. Those you can toss back. But other things are truly new," Waksal says. It is the opposite of how most people operate. Most people cling to the railings of old ideas, but H³s cast them aside. It doesn't matter what the new things are, they are valuable just because they are new, if not now, in some future initiative. Ideas are not thrown away, but set aside carefully to rest for some prospective future awakening.

Witte was messing around with a novel gene when he found chemical receptors that turned out to be on the surface of all growing blood vessels. He called this receptor FLK1 (Fetal Liver Klonase). Then he identified a second receptor, which he called FLK2. ImClone initially looked more at FLK2 than at FLK1 because it seemed the more promising. But Witte and his team kept working on the FLK1 gene and discovered that it was the receptor for VEGF (vascular endothelial growth factor), a substance made and secreted by tumors that causes blood vessels to form that, in turn, feed the tumors so they can grow. The breakthrough discovery came when ImClone researchers found a way to block the VEGF receptors, thereby cutting off the tumors' food supply.

If new opportunities and solutions were crystal clear, everyone could see them. But that is not the case. Instead, they come out of primordial fog, just as the rest of the universe did. Instead of fearing it or steering clear of it, fog is a friend to innovators. It can be just as good to get into that fog as it is to clear it away.

Sometimes when I'm painting, I'll make a "mistake," a mark that I didn't intend. Either I can trash the painting and start over, or I can think of how to use the mistake to create something new, often even better than my original intention. I started thinking this way as a very young child, looking at random marks and visualizing ways in which I could turn them into new images with a few more strokes of my crayon. When I was four years old, I invented a game called

Sanders declares. He plays well with others. He invites them into the game. He knows how to manage the mêlée.

Beyond the joys of play and discovery, when you grope around in the fog, you are bound to stub your toe. Fog is dangerous—especially when the stakes are high. But H³s take it on and celebrate failures. They use fog as a building material. Removing the threat of punishment for failure and pushing back judgment makes the experience of playing in fog more fruitful. "For every new idea that succeeds, ten to twenty fail," says Roger Ackerman. "At Corning, for example, we developed a material for hard-drive memory components, but totally missed the innovations that occurred elsewhere. At the time, we didn't have enough knowledge. There was a lot more to aluminum's capabilities than we realized. We blew \$50—60 million." Ackerman doesn't mind taking the hits, however, because he knows failure can be a success tool.

Corning has had a stellar performance at turning a failure into a success. "At one time we thought we had invented a new way to make auto glass," Ackerman recalls. "Then along came float glass, and it blew everyone away. We didn't see that coming. We were looking in the wrong place. Twenty-five years later, we used that failure to make the most advanced screens for LCD displays." Today, the company owns over 70 percent of the LCD display market. Among other things, this screen is on practically every laptop computer today. "We can't keep up with demand, and no one else is even coming close to us," John Loose, Corning's CEO, says proudly.

SPARK SPACES

Large spaces have one kind of fog. Small spaces have another. There are opportunities in both. When an opportunity set is large, there are inherently more prospects for discovery and development, although it is easier to get lost in the possibilities. When working within a small, narrowly defined universe, options may seem frustratingly limited. But these little spaces offer hunting grounds that others miss.

BIG AND BOUNDLESS

"You can't be too late to exponential growth," Nathan Myhrvold points out. He has enjoyed an exponential glory ride as one of the original architects of Microsoft and, until 2000, as its chief technology officer.

Myhrvold left Microsoft to take advantage of another space growing at an exponential rate, namely, biotech. New technologies from genomics, proteomics, and other areas have opened up all sorts of possibilities, which his investment firm, Intellectual Ventures, is taking advantage of. According to Myhrvold, the biotech industry is a hotbed of innovation and expansion, which will increasingly and profoundly impact many other industries. And he still believes in the New Economy.

The New Economy is all about exponential economies. Far beyond the scope of the Internet, there is a collection of industries that are experiencing exponential growth. The most famous example is the chip economy, illustrated by Moore's Law, which states that computer chip power doubles and price halves every eighteen months. We can do more today with an inexpensive laptop than we could twenty years ago with a room-sized mainframe. In software, as another example, the lines of code written for Windows have been increasing at a rate of 39 percent a year. The code-lines for Netscape have been growing by 221 percent.

As EMC^2 Corporation, the leading information storage systems company, can attest, the digital storage economy exponentially stuffs gigabytes of data into increasingly smaller devices. Currently one gigabyte fits on a coin-sized disc—that is 1,000 times more infor-

mation than it once took a closet to hold. The optical fiber economy is predicted to increase by 150 percent per year, moving towards all-optical switches and networks, thereby increasing communications bandwidth by 48 percent per year.

Biotech is an exponential economy in which the information we
gain access to doubles every year or so. As new genes and proteins
and their functions are discovered and deciphered, the data bank
swells exponentially. Observing societal and related technological
trends, Myhrvold sees five forces converging that are driving this expansion:

1) Demand

- **Potentially, every human being on the planet can be a
  biotechnology customer.** Human DNA consists of 30,000
  genes—each a potential beneficiary as new cures are found and
  new diseases are prevented. As the global population grows, so
  does the opportunity space.
- **Every disease organism can be fair game.** Each organism has
  its own set of biocode, making the opportunities for drug discovery virtually limitless. Many illnesses involve viruses, bacteria, or mutant cells. With gene and protein mapping, scientists
  can decode the destructive instructions of these disease organisms. The code can then be rewritten to nullify the threat.
- **Every plant and animal can be affected.** Beyond the tremendous help these new technologies offer human bodies, they
  can help to cure and prevent disease in cultivated crops and
  animals.
- **In sum, everything in the biosphere can potentially benefit
  (or suffer) from a new biotechnology.** If something is or has
  ever been alive, it is made up of genetic and protein materials.
  Each is a possible candidate for a new solution. Granted, this

prospect has some worrisome implications as one company's idea of a biotech solution can potentially cause devastating consequences if it fails to consider the whole body or the whole ecosystem.

2) Virtuous Cycling

The more we know, the more we need to know. Many think that now that we've mapped the human genome,[4] we have found the answer to our questions about disease. But the genome is not the answer. It merely raises more questions, opening up entirely new fields of study such as proteomics, the study of proteins, which far outnumber the number of genes.

3) Standards

Genetic code is a standard that every plant and animal uses. DNA and RNA are a common language. Once this standard was identified and understood, it set off an avalanche of discovery.

While the biotechnology business has been populated with thousands of mostly small companies, working with hundreds of different technologies and processes, standards are beginning to emerge. These standards allow new technologies to plug into existing systems, and allow experience bases to build upon themselves, exponentially increasing the rate of innovation within the field.

4) Competition

With little or no competition, development tends to move slowly. Twenty years ago, there were a handful of biotech companies, and the industry made relatively little progress. Now there are over 3,000 biotech companies racing each other. More developments happened in 2000 than in the first decades put together.

5) Physical Laws

Biotech and other high-tech areas can grow exponentially because they are not subject to physical laws that restrict the development of many other products. Today's automobiles and airplanes, for example, are much faster than their counterparts created by Henry Ford and the Wright brothers, but not by a factor of thousands. Biotech and chips, on the other hand, keep growing by increasing leaps and bounds because the same physical laws do not apply to them. While there may be other laws of physics to restrict them, it may be many generations before they are applicable.[5]

What? You say you manufacture soap or grape jelly? Your technology isn't that phenomenal? Conditions are not particularly hot? How do Myhrvold's observations relate to you?

Your situation might not have all of the exponential conditions necessary, but it might have some. The first step is to look outside of your own universe and find evidence of trends and forces, then to find connections. Look outside of your company, your industry, your culture, and your comfort zone (see sidebar "Threads" on the following page).

There is no cap on ideas. They can keep sparking, flowing, and growing. As long as they do, if the pool keeps expanding, as is the case with biotechnology, there is no limit to opportunity. Society can provide the kindling for the spark. With high-quality education, we can produce a critical mass of people who know enough and think enough to be able to work with new possibilities. For example, the more people know about computers, the more opportunities we find to expand the use and capability of computers.

THREADS

Imagine that you own a thread manufacturing company. You supply threads to fabric-makers and apparel manufacturers, among others. Thread isn't all that sexy. In fact, it's a veritable commodity. And the industries it supplies are in a downward flow.

The threads that spiders spin, however, are another story. Spider silk is the toughest natural fiber material in the world that we know of. It is also one of the most beautiful materials. No one has been able to synthesize it, though many have tried. If, however, you could leverage the technology developments of genomics, you might finally find a way to make silk leap onto a whole new platform.

Spiders don't produce enough silk to supply anything useful. And you can't farm them because they eat each other. But what if you could find a way to manipulate spider genes to get the silk you want? What if this approach gave you higher volumes or superior strength? You could sell silk in ways and to markets that you never imagined before. Maybe as suture material? Maybe woven into a fabric to produce a barrier that even bullets couldn't penetrate?

Nexia Biotechnologies figured out a way to add a spider gene to goat chromosomes to make goats that spin silk in their milk. Goats have advantages that spiders don't: They are "farmable," and they make lots of milk. Jeffrey Turner, Nexia's CEO, got the idea as scientists isolated the spider genes behind the silk. He then found that the silk glands of spiders and the milk glands of goats are, genetically speaking, practically identical. Here was commercially viable spider silk production—new threads, born of a low-tech, mature industry (thread) and an exponential trendset (genomics). Nexia, along with a sparse handful of competitors, including Genzyme, are pioneering in the world of transgenics, cutting and pasting genes among species. Beyond silk, they hope to mass-produce drugs and super-engineered materials more efficiently, using animals as manufacturing plants. Thread is definitely looking bigger and sexier now.[6]

If There Are No Physical Limits, There Are No Limits

As new technical capabilities are developed, new knowledge bases develop, which in turn pave the way for more innovation. Technology can unleash exponential demand, giving us access to things we never knew we could have before. As competitors experiment with different approaches and models, the universe of possibility expands. Considering the fact that biotechnology is mostly about increasing access to information, we still have plenty of room for discovery and innovation before the laws of physics constrain us. If there are no physical limits, there are no limits.

People and organizations who choose to play or link with others who play within an exponential market space enjoy ever-increasing opportunities for new ideas and innovation success.

TINY PORTALS

Small opportunities are often the beginning of great enterprises.

—Demosthenes

Most people think that they need to do something radically different to affect a big change or a leap innovation. That's often true, but not always. Sometimes an incremental, small movement can unleash a massive eureka. A tiny virus goes into a cell and changes everything. A pinch of spice transforms a dish. A universe resides in a grain of sand.

Large shifts have their own set of difficulties. People resist radical change. It tends to be radically more expensive to pursue. It's difficult to see the leap opportunity because it is so different from what we know. Most people and organizations are not able to see or make a leap initiative happen effectively, if at all. Many have to work within tight boundaries and small spaces. Often, because of those restrictions, they believe that leap innovation isn't possible for them.

Medical researchers are dealing with infinitesimal variables, particularly tight regulations and high stakes. It is achingly hard to see new potential in their microscopic portals. And it is even harder to convince their community of peers that they have made a new discovery or developed a new solution, or that there is new potential. Often the portals appear opaque. No one can see the universe that lies on the other side.

But slight modifications can make big differences.

Hodgkin's lymphoma has been classified as either Type A or Type B. The variations, however, were thought to be so slight that for some time physicians treated both in the same way. Their results were not great: 45 percent of patients with Hodgkin's lymphoma were cured, whereas 55 percent died. Then someone proposed that the miniscule difference in types might really be a bigger deal. Researchers separated the two types from each other in testing and treatment. When they tested against Type A alone, their success rate skyrocketed. It came down to a tiny, seemingly insignificant variance.

Six Sigma, an increasingly popular quality-control methodology known for its attention to seemingly insignificant minutiae, was developed in the late 1980s at Motorola and won the Malcolm Baldrige National Quality Award. It is a process-focused intervention for improving productivity, operating margins, and profits and for reducing defects. Because it is so detailed and painstaking, it takes a long time to learn. Yet companies such as GE, DuPont, and Allied Signal sing its praises. It reduces their realities to small margins of error or deviation. Six Sigma is tough. It's no-nonsense. In a sense, it seems the antithesis of creativity. In another sense, you have to be creative to do it well because it is very focused on eliminating variance and it is therefore tempting to succumb to monochromatic thinking. Even at a miniscule level, creativity is possible. Hypothetically, it may even be gratifying to change something as seemingly insignificant as the size of a paper clip—if doing that triggers a leap.

A common perception about artists is that they are loose and unfettered, free to create whatever they want to, with no boundaries—and that because of these characteristics, they produce more creative works than the average person. In fact, many of the most successful artists impose tight restrictions on themselves, which demand even more creativity. "I lead a very disciplined life," says Richard Serra, a prominent sculptor who uses space as a sculptable material. "My schedule is tightly controlled and organized, in some cases, with some projects as far as four or five years out." Serra restricts his work, by using only a specific type of steel, by designing only in super-large scale, and by focusing only on a narrow range of shapes. Yet these tight parameters are tiny portals to an expansive body of thought, as Serra explores within them. Out of these small openings come big ideas.

Timothy Greenfield-Sanders works with changes so small that most people would not even be aware of them. But he leaps with the "little bits," and they make all the difference. Tiny changes in a subject's mouth, limitations of only looking at somebody's head, no propping—the same, simple lighting—and yet his work looks different from work by Avedon, Annie Liebowitz, and every other great portrait photographer.

"I created a look that's just mine," he says. He did it consciously within an extremely narrow range of variables. It is a form of branding. He and other artists present brands of tiny subtle nuance in big and powerful ways: A Rothko is instantly recognizable, taking the same approach to images in each painting, and Philip Glass compositions, with their minimalist phrases and super-subtle tone, sound like no other. Each artists' "signature" is evident in the tiniest of traces.

"I try to make iconic portraits. And part of that is making someone a little bit better looking, a little more dignified, a little bit more pulled together than they really are. And that's what my look is," Greenfield-Sanders explains. It is little bits. He finds a universe within the person in front of him. "What I try to do is then bring out the person inside—the person who is not in front of my camera, the person who is upstairs having coffee with me. That's the person I want to show. If I analyze how I work, it's small, subtle ways of making someone feel comfortable. There are about fifty different little things that I'm thinking of at once: Is the light right? Is the subject falling asleep? Can she hold that pose?"

Greenfield-Sanders doesn't shoot a lot of film—another constraint he imposes upon himself. He has to nail it within a small number of tries. Most photographers shoot ten rolls of 35 mm film, with thirty-six exposures each—360 shots over the course of a long day—against his seven shots knocked off in fifteen minutes. It is a very different way of shooting.

"In a sense, anyone can take a photograph. How can I make it really difficult?" Greenfield-Sanders asks. "I shoot in large format, ten shots, and I have to do it in a very short time. But, boy, it's fun."

Seeking to make it difficult is an interesting quest. "It's a great way to learn," says Greenfield-Sanders. Through tiny portals, his portraits are grand and distinctive—everyone from Lou Reed to Aaron Copeland to Dennis Hopper to Madeline Albright to Bill and Hillary Clinton to Monica Lewinsky to Orson Welles—over 5,000 portraits of people you know, over a twenty-year career.

However small your space, there is always an opportunity to innovate—no excuses. Whether you are aiming for a big leap innovation or simply trying to creatively solve a small problem, even if a small idea is all you need, more creative sparks come from expansive thinking. "I think it's clear that you get many more small ideas by thinking big than by thinking small," says Nathan Myhrvold.

VOICES AND VISIONS

New voices saved the life of one of the top commercial baked goods companies. The company's core business, white bread, was tanking industry-wide. People weren't buying it anymore. Unfortunately, white bread accounted for 70 percent of revenues. Lots of new breads were entering the market—fancier, grainier ones, with tooth—but management thought that if they stuck to their knitting and just made their white bread better, they could hold on to a substantial number of customers.

What is the main problem with white bread that everyone wants to solve? People who eat white bread like it for its softness. They like the feathery lightness on their tongues, and they don't want to startle their incisors or disturb their molars. But after a couple of days, these whispery slices turn stale. If someone could solve that problem, these people would love it. And so, the managers of this baking giant hired an outside lab to tackle the staleness thing. They found their savior in a new custom-designed enzyme that would keep their bread fresher longer—two weeks would not be too much to hope for.

The company called us at SPWI for help in positioning this new benefit to its customers. In every project, we talk to at least a couple of dozen stakeholders, including, in this case, the lab scientists in Australia. Yes, the enzyme was a real coup. It worked: I pressed sixteen-day-old bread between my fingertips and felt only soft cushions, and when pressed hard, the bread mushed down to a thin sculptable sheet—just like

> Customer voices can move you forward. They can also hold you back.

the day it was born. What else could this fabulous enzyme do? We probed and poked. "Oh yes," one of the scientists said, "it also allows the recipe to eliminate preservatives. And it results in a bread that's more fat-free."

"Don't worry about those other things," the marketing group said. "We know the problem. It's simple. The main thing our white-bread eaters care about is staling." Every time they listened to their customers, they heard the same thing. "And now we have the new solution. Just help us to position it, and we'll be fine."

We explored all three benefits anyway.

The new bread might as well have glowed in radioactive green. People hated it because they couldn't imagine how a bread could stay fresh for that long without being full of scary, nasty, carcinogenic chemicals. They didn't believe that it was all natural and chemical-free, without even the usual preservatives. They just refused to believe it. And, no, they would not be buying it any time soon.

"But white bread eaters don't care that much about nutrition," we were told. "If they did, they would be eating whole-wheat bread instead. They don't care about a few preservatives. And the fat content was reduced only about 5 percent—not a big deal."

We were able to look deeper and wider at the emerging trends, and we predicted that even white-bread eaters were changing their attitudes toward food. The important problem here was that white-bread eaters like white bread for the taste and texture, but they do wish it were a healthier food. If they could get 99 percent fat-free bread with no preservatives and if it could still taste exactly like their old favorite, they would love it. Customers originally said the problem was freshness. Solving that one, in this case, would have been a disaster.

The results stunned our clients. We developed a new brand, a new package, and a new positioning for the bread that was so successful, it was extended out over the rest of the product lines.

Customer voices can move you forward. They can also hold you back. Listening to customers too much narrows the perception of problems and solutions to a set of alternatives very close to a company's starting point. Most customers do not make creative leaps; rather, they think in terms of slight modifications of present solutions. Very few innovations ever come from customers' voices. To get the best picture, you have to listen to lots of voices. How many computers do you have in your briefcase? That would have been a ridiculous question to ask a customer just twenty years ago.

Fresh Songs

A supernova exploded with the release of *Supernatural*. After decades of quiet, Carlos Santana's star rose again, bigger and brighter than ever before, in large part because he brought together an unlikely catch of new voices. Santana's plan was, according to *Time,* to "reconnect the molecules with the light."[8] Santana's *Supernatural* CD sold over 3 million copies in eighteen weeks and ranked #1 on the *Billboard 200* albums chart. *Smooth*, featuring Rob Thomas of Matchbox 20 on vocals, was a #1 holder on the *Billboard* singles chart. A kaleidoscope of unexpected voices from unexpected places, such as Thomas, Lauryn Hill, Wyclef Jean, and Dave Matthews, poured reggae, rap, retro, and other sounds into the cauldron.

Mixing a broad range of voices has helped Corning throughout its history—it has become a common practice. "We dialog with customers, potential customers, and people in the industry," says CEO John Loose. "We have a lot of radar equipment. We're always out there looking. We look for game-changing trends. We work with a lot of start-ups. We triangulate. We work with outside consultants. We are forward-looking. That's a key part of who we are."

SPWI project palettes often include voices from the Leading Edge Expert Network[sm], the fringes, a deep and wide range of stakeholders, and New Idea Development Groups[sm] (see sidebar "The SPWI Mix"). We listen to customers, but we listen at least as much to non-customers. We bring together many knowledge and experience bases. In developing a new television network for Viacom, for example, we talked with children who were too young to watch Viacom's current offerings. We invited anthropologists and poets to weigh in. We talked with experts in other industries, artists, and sociologists. These people gave us glimpses of what a new network might want to serve up. These voices mixed with our clients' voices as well as our own to produce new channels.

> I'd rather have people look at my works and see what they want to see in them. It's better than telling them what to look for.
>
> —Dale Chihuly

The convergence of two or more knowledge sets is necessary for innovation. A new idea happens when two or more separate thoughts come together in a unique way. Imagine the possibilities that could be unleashed with a convergence of different kinds of voices—of people who understand science, those who understand business, and those who understand art.

Listening to Your Own Voice

> Care about people's approval and you will be their prisoner.
>
> —*Tao Te Ching*

A lot of people at America Online listened to frequent complaints about the difficulty customers had logging on and staying connected. How could AOL reduce congestion and improve line quality? Many called for the company to halt its marketing efforts until the problem was resolved. AOL, however, pushed for an even bigger marketing blitz to sign up even more members and invite even more traffic. The company believed that the most important goal was to amass scale fast—before anyone caught on or caught up—although even inside AOL the voices were often contradictory. The company used a variety of tactics to build scale at unprecedented speed, and the landgrab paid off richly in profits and power, solving the log-on/bump-off hassle in the process.

> Listening to other companies' customers is the best way to gain market share, while listening to their visionaries is the best way to create new markets.
>
> —Esther Dyson

We often get trapped by our beliefs that customers know better what they need, or that competitors know better paths to success, or that Father Knows Best. We don't trust ourselves. If it were a good idea, they'd be doing it. If they react negatively to our ideas, we must be wrong. If they like our ideas, we must be right. These assumptions keep us from innovating.

THE SPWI MIX:
BEYOND REGULAR CUSTOMERS

Competitors' Customers
New Users
Next Users
Former Users
Lead Users
Non-Users
People from Other Cultures
Leading Edge Experts: Industry, Arts, Sciences, Parallel Industries
Influencers
Children and Other Innocents

H^3 inner voices are louder and stronger. They inspire more confidence. Sometimes, they just "don't get" why others "don't get it."

Innovators listen to themselves. Once they find their voice, they find their power. They can hold onto it in the face of dissension. There is a delicate balance between the wisdom of following your own voice, despite what others say, and keeping an open mind to other voices. It comes down to vision and talent. If all you are is self-absorbed, if you think no one else can have a good idea or a valid point, then you will not move innovation forward. But if your vision is strong, if you have ideas burning inside you, if you've heard from others and you still believe in yourself, tenacity has its rewards.

> Democratic principles
> don't apply to art.
> —Richard Serra

Everyone told biotech researcher John Mendelsohn that he was going down a fruitless path. As Sam Waksal recalls, "John was talking about utilizing the EGF receptor antibody as a diagnostic: This kind of approach is a huge waste of time half the time. But sometimes it's interesting. John had used it with a chemotherapeutic agent in an animal. The chemotherapeutic agent alone didn't do very much, and the antibody alone did very little. But when he used them together, the tumors died. It was an *aha!* moment."

Mendelsohn wasn't expecting that. "I don't know if anyone really understood what it meant," admits Waksal, "but we very quickly understood during his presentation that it was acting like a drug, not an antibody. It was synergizing to send cells down a death pathway." Mendelsohn's inner voice was finally moving his colleagues, although the rest of the world was still not listening. Waksal recalls, "We suddenly said, 'That's what it is!' Right then and there, we said, '*Bang!*'" Waksal got very excited. He predicted that this was going to be a great drug. Not everybody agreed, and at the time nobody else in the pharmaceutical world thought this was an interesting area. Waksal marveled at how such smart people didn't "get it."

Your own creativity and intelligence have to be main ingredients, using your intuition as a guide. Your own inner voice is as valuable as all of the others. Play with the volume of your customers' voices. Mix in new tracks. Play with the volume of your own voice.

CLEARING A PATH

Fog can be fun, but you still need to set upon a path to a clearer concept. The "gut feel" is one indicator of the right idea. It cuts through the fog, if you let it—and often gives you a clearer view of the opportunities. Check out how you feel about them. You are a sum of your thoughts and experiences, a rich bank of data. All of these data contribute input, some of which you are well aware of and others which you don't consciously know yet. This amalgam is what forms your gut feel. There are reasons behind your intuition that warrant investigation. The more diverse your knowledge is, the broader your base of intuition is, which leads you to new connections and, ultimately, new ideas. Sometimes, you have to clear a path to your own center to listen to your own voice.

When I moved back to Manhattan, after living full-time in my country house in the Hud-
son Valley for about seven years, I was happy to
be back in a creative hotbed, with easy access to
some of the finest museums, galleries, theater,
and performance centers. I was excited to be in
a cachepot of inspirational architecture, bril-

> In small matters, trust
> the mind. In the large
> ones, trust the heart.
> —Sigmund Freud

liant restaurants, and beautiful boutiques. One day, about four
months after I arrived, I was sitting in my office, gazing past my
pale-gray desktop monitor at the big sky and the treetops in Central
Park. I had been working incredibly hard, so intensely, logging in
long hours, with few breaks. Feeling overwhelmed and exhausted, I
liked my work less and less. Then a phone call from my friend Larry
interrupted my ruminating.

Larry immediately saw a way out of my funk. "You should practice
what you preach," he said, since I helped companies find creative
ways to solve *their* problems. "You should get out, go see some art,
take a break, refill your well." I heard the echo of my own voice ad-
vising the same things to my clients. "But, I can't," I complained,
naming every excuse I could think of: "I have too much to do. I have
impossible deadlines. I can't afford to do it right now." I sounded
just like my clients.

"Here's your creative strategy," Larry said. "Once a week, pick
one cultural event or exhibition, and go to it. Eat one meal a week
with a friend, old or new, at a restaurant you have never been to before. It will take maybe five or six hours out of your entire week."

"But, I don't have time," I protested. He advised, "Do it, and it
will give you more time in the process."

The strategy worked. I felt renewed and inspired. My own creativity got released. And, believe it or not, I found more available time
and more creative output because my mental load was lightened and
my senses were sharpened.

H^3s have some kind of creative strategy—a strategic direction for
creative thinking and development. It can be an implicit or explicit

path. Creative strategy can be applied to a new product development initiative, organizational development, and life in general. It doesn't need to be a tight, intricate plan. It can be loose as it guides people toward a particular goal. It gives a framework for understanding innovation potential in an organization and in specific projects.

At Lend Lease Corporation, the Australian-based international real estate conglomerate, the creative strategy is to develop the impossible: The company intentionally takes on projects that appear undoable. It excels in the architecture of futuristic buildings. For example, every project starts with a challenge from the chairman, Jill Ker Conway: "How can we do what's never been done before?" Builder of the Trump Tower, the Sapporo Dome in Japan, Chiswick Park in London, the Newington Olympic Village in Sydney, which housed over 15,000 athletes during the Summer 2000 games, as well as a participant in the renovation of Grand Central Station and the construction of the Sydney Opera House, Lend Lease has managed to create sparks of innovation wherever it turns—whether in real estate, financial management, union contracts, or construction of public buildings and gardens.

CREATIVE PRESSURE

> What seems mundane and trivial is the very stuff that discovery is made of. The only difference is our readiness to put the pieces together in an entirely new way and to see patterns where only shadows appeared a moment before.
> —*Edward B. Lindman,* Thinking in Future Tense

It could be a wrinkle in the velvet comforter in the afternoon light. It could be the pattern of buildings against the sky. It could be the shape of a letter on a page. It could be a memory. It could be a vision. It could be anything. New ideas have magic triggers—some hidden, some unlikely. A new idea won't be found where you look.

It will surface when you look away at something else. It will come from a new voice in your ear. There will be a new configuration of data points and pressure points. It will result from new synapses.

If you take two pieces of music, such as Beethoven's *Ninth Symphony* and Santana's "Smooth," and you chop them up into individual words and notes and feed them into computers, the machines will count the frequency of each word and each note in each piece. But what will this tell you? It won't tell you much about the songs. It won't tell you of the beauty and the emotion within the compositions. You won't be able to tell one from the other. You still need to find out what the words and notes are doing, and how they string together, at different levels of tension, to form each masterpiece.

Tension

> One of the greatest pains of nature is the pain of
> a new idea.
>
> *—Walter Bagehot*

"To suggest an idea was like causing a fight," reported an Aetna refugee upon his grateful return to his former employer, the Progressive Insurance Corporation.

There has always been tension between the status quo and the new idea. In lots of cases, the tension is so strong, it's painful and destructive, as appeared to be the case with the former Aetna employee. The status quo pulls harder, offering the illusion of safety and comfort. Rather than experience the discomfort, many people acquiesce to stagnation. Creators, however, know that they need friction, tension, and conflict to make a spark. They actually like those dynamics, up to a point. New ideas come out of the rub between at least two different positions or points of view. Tension can cause you to reach a new height or better place. Creative people find ways to optimize tension—not enough and you go nowhere; too much and you go nowhere. If you get it right, tension becomes a creative tool.

Where there is tension, you can harness it. Where there is none, you can create it.

You can get new ideas out of the dissonance found in opposing or contradicting circumstances or arguments. Many H[3] companies purposefully design creative tension by doing things such as introducing "trouble-makers," putting people with contrasting skills and personalities together, and inviting controversy. The sparks of creativity are always flying because their recruiters have begun hiring people in opposing pairs—the more divergent in their views and experiences, the better.

"I like to make trouble and upset apple carts," says John Seely Brown, chief scientist at Xerox and former director of Xerox PARC. "We invited tension by bringing in contrasting groups of new people, new brains, new thinkers." Within PARC itself, creative tension was mined and managed well. "If it's too smooth, you're probably not colliding with reality as quickly as you need to, to change a company," Brown says.

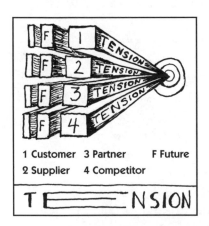

1 Customer 3 Partner   F Future
2 Supplier 4 Competitor

It has not always been easy to tip over the cart, however, as people in Silicon Valley are fond of pointing out. Among other innovations, PARC researchers came up with the graphical user interface (GUI) and the Ethernet, but were unable to persuade Xerox management that these inventions were worth pursuing. The tension among Xerox managers was so strong and intractable that they could not see their way to market PARC's discoveries, thereby giving them up to the competition.

Tension between current realities and future visions needs to be mined and managed. Tension encapsulates energy, both for you and for your customers. Our first instinct is to rush to relieve those tensions because they're uncomfortable. It hurts . . . here's an aspirin. It's too slow . . . here, now it's faster. But there is major difference between the desire to relieve tension and true aspiration.

If we delay our attempts to relieve tensions, if we feel them and live with them, if we strive to understand the less obvious, peripheral dynamics of those tensions, we can release new energies to fuel new ideas.

If you ask people how they feel about car insurance companies, more often than not, they'll tell you, "Insurance companies suck." They don't like their agents, they don't like their carriers, and they don't like any part of the system. They feel generally ripped off, inconvenienced, and aggravated most of the time. Insurance companies are necessary evils. Nobody seems to trust them and few feel well served by them. After losing tens of thousands of dollars and countless hours trying to get claims paid on two car accidents a few years back, I happen to agree with that sentiment.

Peter Lewis asked, "Why do you have all of those problems when you get your car fixed?" He looked at all of the players, from the agents to the adjusters to the mechanics to the replacement-car renters to the drivers and the tensions among them. "Why is it so dysfunctional?" he wondered. "What became clear to me," says Lewis, "was that there had to be a real opportunity to do one big insurance and repair process that would be consumer-friendly, much more efficient, and much less expensive."

By mining the tension in the auto insurance world, Lewis developed a big new idea with Glenn Renwick, the man whom Lewis later chose to succeed him as CEO. "We started to think about why this would save costs," Lewis explains, "and we were worried about things such as 'Would people just give us their cars? Would they give up control of their cars so easily? How would the body shops react to our being the buyer instead of the customer being the buyer?' It was a whole new idea for the owners of body shops. Will people come back and pay the deductibles after they get their cars fixed? And how would that happen? Can we make the trade-off of the damaged car easy and confidence-building?" Lewis had to figure out how to navigate the new space, mine the tension, and reap its rewards.

The idea was well received and, interestingly enough, the body shop people loved it. They don't like hassling with insurance companies and customers—the better ones would much rather fix cars. Progressive began to see even more benefits in terms of service, savings in storage and parts acquisition, and the ability to get cars fixed faster by managing garages' capacity. Eventually, the company could take a picture of your car, put it on the Internet, and send it out to its network of nearby body shops to query availability. "We'll get this work done even better, even faster," says Lewis.

Tensile Strength

Lewis and Renwick plan to shift all of Progressive's business to this model if testing continues to yield successful results. "All of it. It's irresistible," Lewis delights in saying. "It's easier. All you have to do is take this shiny-new rental car, sign the rental slip, and you're out of here." Lewis has envisioned all the parts knitted together. "When you come in with your banged-up car, you will receive a big box, embossed with the Progressive logo, in which we will put all of the personal shit that you have in your car. Next, we'll give you a beeper so you don't have to worry about when it's done. After we've certified the repair, we'll beep you. It will have our warranty on it, which is much better than you would get otherwise."

It almost makes me want to go out and have an accident.

But how good is it for Progressive? Lewis says it is good and strong. It will suck out cost. "There are all kinds of estimates. Some say that for every dollar we spend, we'll save seven dollars. It's huge. It's almost too obvious to worry about," Lewis boasts.

In the current process, according to Lewis, body shops see customers as an opportunity. "You come in with your damaged car and an insurance check for $2,700," he supposes, "and you're thinking to yourself, 'Gee, I wonder if I can get this guy to do it for $2,500 so I can save $200 of my $500 deductible.' And you're flappable because you're upset and you've never been through this before." Lewis knows how the conversation usually goes. He fills me in, "The mechanic says, 'Look, Blondie, you've got that god-dammed Progressive. They screw everybody. They sent you in here with this low-ball estimate, which is crazy. They didn't see this or include that. They're god-dammed thieves!'"

Lewis continues, "So now he's destroyed the confidence you have in us. So now he says, 'Look, you've got a $500 deductible. Most people do.' And you say, 'Yes.' And he says, 'They gave you $2,700. That means that they think it's a $3,200 job. I can make this a $4,200 job, if you'll just sort of be insistent with the company, you won't have any deductible, and I'll make $500 extra.'" There's negative tension between you, the mechanic, and the insurance company, and it often goes from bad to worse.

"That's what happens," Lewis says. "And then he dicks around because he can't get parts, so the car's sitting out there and the storage charge is building up while he waits to get parts. And you've got to go out and figure out how to get a rental car for yourself, and then we've got to send a guy back out there to re-estimate and negotiate him down to some real number, but he always beats us a little bit. And he's much smarter than our guy, and he's a lot smarter than you."

Now, change the world. All of those costs go away! "We look at the car fast. We go to garages that aren't busy and we pay them very fairly," says Lewis. "We will probably wind up with our 'own' shops— our preferred suppliers—because we'll get people who won't tell us they can do it if they can't, who will deliver if they say they will deliver, who will have consistently high quality. We will pay them extra because they're not getting anything on screwing the customers or screwing us otherwise. We want it to be easy for them to make a profit doing business with us. And while his neighbor is going to have to wait three weeks to get his car back, our customer is going to get his back in five days." That is hard to beat. "So, what we'll wind up doing is re-rationalizing the whole auto repair process." Lewis expects his competitors to follow. "They have no choice," Lewis exclaims.

In a healthy creative environment, tension produces creative sparks, yet a spark needs oxygen in order to burst into flame. Metaphorically speaking, the breath of fresh air can come in the act of separating oneself from the problem or even the noise and distractions of the workplace. Separation is every bit as important as tension, as many artists and scientists will attest.

Deep Think

"I've solved most of my problems at the end of the workday, in a somewhat altered state of consciousness, which removes them from the concerns of eating, drinking, sleeping, and fucking," Lewis explains. He is serious. It's sort of like the great-ideas-in-the-shower phenomenon. Lewis swims, with a tape recorder poised at each end of the pool to capture his flashes of brilliance as he makes each turn. He has a whole repertoire of mindset-altering methodologies that allow him to get to a deeper level of thinking. And he delights in them.

Lewis hopes his employees get to altered states too. "I hope they do something to change their minds—to get creative. If you can't do it, you can't succeed. It just doesn't work. You can't achieve the performance standards we demand unless you improve constantly. And you can't improve constantly unless you're creative."

The concept of altered states and separation is one that appears over and over again in H³s. In order to create something new, they create a detachment. It can be a physical, emotional, or intellectual separation. They are in altered states—undergoing hypnosis, medi-

SEPAR ATION

tating, running, working out, going off on a retreat, or taking a sabbatical. Distance and disconnection help us to get a new perspective and see new possibilities.

As we sat, playing with ideas over breakfast at Lespinasse, John Seely Brown kept closing his eyes. The sparks had been flying at our table, flashing and popping through the air over our omelets and muffins. Sometimes, when I asked him a question or shot out an idea, he closed his eyes, in deep thought, as if to shut out all distractions to his thinking. He seemed to separate himself for a moment from the dialog as well as from the room in which we sat in New York City. And then he came back with his answer, comment, question, or next idea.

> I close my eyes
> in order to see.
> —Paul Gaugin

Separation, virtual or actual, is a tool many H³s reach for.

David Ditzel removes himself from the outside world. "I tend to hole up, usually at home, over a weekend," he tells me. "I get up about noon on a Saturday. Then I procrastinate, but then by about 10—11 P.M., I really get cranking. I will blast through about seven—eight hours. At 2 or 3 in the morning, I am really going full steam. I've gotten things out of the way by then. The phone isn't going to ring, and nobody's sending me an e-mail. I get worked up into a creative mental state. I was doing that last night until 4:30 A.M. Being very intense about a particular idea—not having interruptions and getting a chance to think clearly about a topic—lets me get into more depth about a subject."

Violin virtuoso Joshua Bell does the same thing as he practices through the night in a creative zone, without stopping to eat, drink, or sleep. "It's how you get to the truth of the piece," he explains. He does the same when he gets into video games, racking up amazing world-champion scores.

At one point, Ditzel needed so much separation from the noise that he quit his job at Sun Microsystems. "I didn't like where things were headed, and I didn't believe in the vision, so I became de-motivated," he recalls. "I had to force myself to go off and think of something new. I had been in a senior position at Sun, so I was spending most of my days in meetings. I couldn't innovate. I basically quit my job, so I could go and try to think of something differ-ent. I didn't really know what that was going to be when I left. I locked myself up in my house for a couple of months. I went through this torturous process of thinking about the industry prob-lems and what I wanted to do next."

Ditzel proclaims, "Quitting my job and going off to have the 'deep think' let me think about why things are hard and how they could be different." Letting yourself think in a non-evolutionary form, get-ting bigger separation from your current state is what is important. That's how Ditzel came to the idea of building Transmeta.

There are certain objects in the night sky that you can't see by looking directly at them because that focuses the light on part of the retina that is not sensitive to the particular light that you're observ-ing. It is a very faint light. So, what you need to do is look a little away from it, and then you can actually see it by looking slightly off of it. At the corner of your eye, you've got the right sensitivity to see the object. Rather than staring intently at the problem, harder and harder, making it more difficult to see the solution, you need to look to the side, and allow the problem to come in from the angle.

"You create your own rut by virtue of trying to beat down a par-ticular path that may not be fruitful," says physicist Brian Greene. "Finding a new path is not a matter of thinking hard or thinking more intensely. It's usually a matter of looking away, and allowing that new path to come to you in a more gentle way. If an equation or an approach is not working, oftentimes, you set it down and just let it go. You go running, or go play basketball. You just remove that as the focus of attention."

The way you get to the solution is by not looking for it. It's not by removing an obstacle. It's by releasing yourself and looking in a direction that is counterintuitive. If you want to see something, your brain says, "Look at it." But here, in order to see something, you *can't* look at it.

The space and time for reflection or incubation allow people to leap over the barriers of premature cognitive commitments, myopia, inertia, introspection, and HWDTAH ("how we do things around here"). Bill Joy, chief scientist of Sun Microsystems, physically removes himself from company headquarters in San Francisco and operates from his own office in Aspen, a thousand miles away. His purpose is to get away from the numbing effects of day-to-day exposure to the company to create new sparks. He attributes the birth of the JAVA programming language to his separation.[8]

Some people try retreats. Although the physical space is different, the same people are there with the same old baggage. Solo deep-thinks are really about getting to a blank piece of paper—a tool we can learn to use often—even every day.

Zigzag

Everybody always wants the back-of-the-napkin story. Everybody wants to think that all of a sudden an idea goes on like a light bulb. There certainly are moments of inspiration, where things come together, but it's usually after a substantial amount of zigging and zagging. As Dave Ditzel explains it, the idea for Transmeta, for example, came out of a few ricochets between different ideas that might be done. Then all the pieces clicked. That's where experience, art, and judgment come together. "People want to hear, 'When did

THE idea come to you?' But, they don't get it. It doesn't work that way," explains Ditzel. "It's really the last twenty years of my life."

Corning zigzagged its way to command the LCD screen market. Ackerman remembers their trumped auto glass quest. "Somebody started looking back in the database and three people put things together to make the discovery. It's about connecting two or three dots, or even more dots, and it's not in a straight line. Then iterate, iterate, iterate!" Ackerman exclaims. Optical fiber came out of a zigzag also. Its source was a vapor technology process that Corning invented in 1933.

OUTLIERS AND OPPOSITES

> The best armor is to keep out of range.
>
> —*Italian proverb*

"I was sitting in one of our daily conferences where everybody came in to have their coffee with the chairman," Peter Lewis says, recalling his first big leap against the odds. "Because I was the late chairman's son, I got to sit at the coffee table. That morning, one of our guys was mad because for the first time in history, some companies were refusing to write certain risks."

Things had started getting tight for the auto insurance industry in the early 1950s. So insurers pulled back and began to get picky about whom they would insure. If you had a fender bender or two, or a couple of tickets staining your record, they began to drop you into insurance never-never land.

One of the more experienced employees in Lewis's company sounded the alarm. "Agents are calling up fast and furious. Their companies won't write the risks, and they want us to write them," he said. "These are agents who never talked to us before, those sons-of-bitches!" Lewis was twenty-one at the time. He recalls, "I'm thinking to myself, 'The guys want to do business with us! They're begging to do business with us! There must be an opportunity somewhere in there!" Lewis asked, "Why can't we do this?" He was told by the more senior, more seasoned executives, "Because we'll lose money. That's why the other guys don't want to do it." Lewis considered the opposing possibility for a moment and then asked, "Why don't we just charge them more?" And that was the beginning of the business. There was no answer to that.

It was one of those "Duh!" moments.

This idea was born on the fringe: high-risk drivers. It went against common sense. But it made perfect sense. Even so, it took three or four sessions over the period of three weeks to gain approval. Finally, Lewis challenged the company cognoscenti. "I'll bet you that my pals Earl, Marvin, and I can sit down in three or four hours on a Saturday afternoon and figure this out," he said. And that's what they did. "In 1956, we did $83,000 of what we call non-standard auto insurance for people canceled or rejected by another insurance company due to their less-than-perfect driving records. And in 2000 we did $4 billion. So, that was a good idea. And there may have only been one or two years, in forty-five, that we didn't make money on it."

> When all men think alike, no one thinks very much.
> —Walter Lippmann

The success zone seems obvious on a typical cluster graph of customer preferences—it is in the densest constellation of data points. But the potential for successful innovation is more likely to be found in the outliers. It is there, out on the fringes, where renegade preferences reside, where competitors are unlikely to be concentrating: the potential for the next light bulb, the next computer, or the next String Theory that turns scientific knowledge on its head.

It is taking more and more for things to move us these days. We have seen so much. There are fewer surprises. The force has to come from another strange and contrary place, to create new success.

H³s prefer to live on the edge, at least in some aspect. They like going against the flow of traffic. They like going where no one has

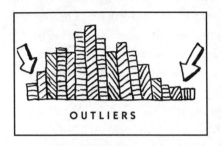

OUTLIERS

gone before. They don't want to be mainstream. Doing the impossible excites them. These appear to be parts of a personality trait they share. The opposite path often leads to discovery. While this fact is not news to most of us, few of us are creative and brave enough to do anything productive with it.

Genentech, once the renegade and now one of the largest and most profitable biotech companies, is making a monoclonal antibody that is targeting the growth factor. Now ImClone is the rebel as it takes the flip side. "Here's the difference," offers Sam Waksal, ImClone's founder. "It's like having an auditorium full of 1,000 people and each one of them has a key. The key is the 'growth factor,' which fuels tumor growth. Genentech's antibody has to go around and grab everybody's key. Instead, what we do is stick gum in the lock. That's much easier. So it doesn't make any difference if there are 1,000 keys out there, if it can't get into the lock anymore." ImClone's C225 is making the antibody against the tumor's growth factor receptor. "We think that's the most important approach in anti-angiogenesis. It's going to be a big product!" Waksal is proud to say. "And that's a discovery we made, by going the other way."

Fringe Benefits

In his book *The Innovator's Dilemma,* Clayton Christensen shows how low-end technologies can come in and disrupt an industry. So it makes sense to look for new ideas there. In the low end, you can find new ideas about how to solve problems more inexpensively or simply. In the high end, you can find new ideas that you can borrow from and produce at your own price points.[9]

Beyond this, in the outer fringes we can find the strange and un-familiar new ideas we would never ordinarily consider, but that contain seeds for the future. Consider yogurt: For years no one in the United States ate it, except for hippies and health nuts. Now it's one of the most important products in the dairy business. And just where did snowboards and lattés come from?

Many H³s regularly expose themselves to a wide range of creative stimuli. Some, like Corning and Progressive, maintain impressive art collections so that employees "live with the art." SPWI often brings in people from the fringes to co-develop concepts and takes clients on creative journeys, through galleries, museums, bou-tiques, international food markets, and neighborhoods, to name a few. It is immersion and separation at the same time. After such trips, a group of cosmetics company executives were inspired to de-velop new color themes. A frozen foods marketing team got a fresh perspective on packaging. An office supply manufacturer saw op-portunities for new distribution channels. An information services company responded to triggers for new content. These experiences enabled the teams to operate with new definitions.

The innovation project portfolio for H³s often includes some high-risk, some low-risk, and some medium-risk projects, similar in concept to diversified financial portfolios. Projects often vary by time horizon as well. Some reach out into the fringes.

The best ideas are the ideas out on the edges of our perception, the thoughts that contradict what we "'know." It is the first drops of wine we have ever tasted that have the power to move us to new places. When we reach for the outliers, opposites, and strange fla-vors, they can shoot us into the future. They are our leaping points. That's where genius begins.

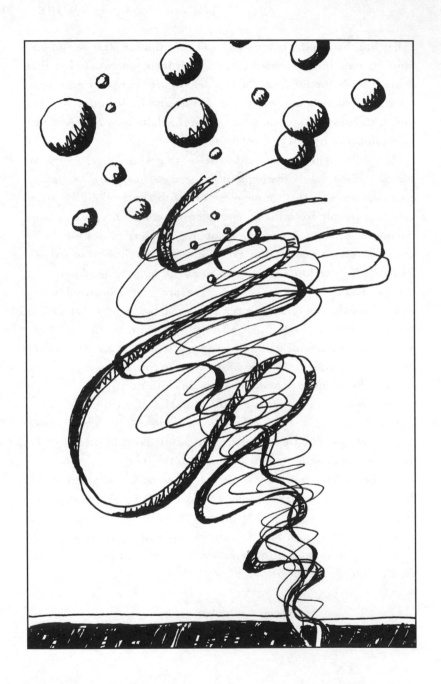

. 3 .

BARGAINING WITH THE FUTURE

The Valuation Struggle

Our beliefs determine our measurements.
—*Albert Einstein*

I *really* hate airline food. I've either gone without a meal or lived on peanuts. I've ordered the kosher, the vegetarian, the dairy-free, or some other special meal, hoping it might be a cut above the rest, but it wasn't. One day, as I was preparing to catch a noon flight to Minneapolis, I had an idea. I decided to order takeout from Mangia, a nearby gourmet shop, and take my brown bag with me on the plane.

Soon to be the envy of my fellow travelers, I ordered a fresh turkey sandwich on a homemade sourdough roll, with arugula and lemon-thyme mayonnaise and a great roasted baby red potato salad in an olive oil and mint vinaigrette. I got a mini chocolate pecan tart for a treat and a Granny Smith apple in case the flight took longer than expected. None of that pressed and molded turkey for me. Let the other passengers eat what they could find.

When people on my flight commented on what a great idea I had, an even bigger idea came to me. Why not start a travel-food business? Although I was only nineteen years old and just beginning my first job as an art director at a Madison Avenue ad agency, I didn't think this new business sounded all that difficult for me to handle. Airline travelers could order their extraordinary meals when they ordered their tickets, or, if they ordered their meal far in advance, our customer service team could call them two weeks before their flight to take their orders. We would deliver the meals to the airline food service operation, which in turn would merge them into its system so that flight attendants could hand them out to our customers at the same time they served up the icky stuff to other passengers.

Friends all thought it was a stroke of genius. Two even joined the cause. At various airports, we conducted surveys, asking passengers for their opinions and suggestions. The response was overwhelmingly favorable: 80 percent of respondents loved it. My partners and I worked out the logistics, designed a model, researched suppliers, calculated costs, studied the airlines to get a deeper understanding of their operations, put together a business plan, and—with great anticipation and excitement—went out to sell it.

Since you know that this service does not exist, you have probably inferred that my idea "failed." It never got off the ground because the airlines didn't think it was worth much. At the time, the airlines were spending between two and four dollars on a passenger's meal, including packaging and flatware. These companies are always on a tear to bring those costs down even more. In contrast, we discovered through our surveys that most passengers were willing to pay up to ten dollars more to get a fresh, delicious meal delivered to them.

Even though my idea would have saved the airlines an expense and brought in additional revenue, it did not fly. We studied other mechanisms—delivering the meals ourselves to the planes, bringing brown bags to passengers at their gates, setting up kiosks in the airline terminals. Each time, the gatekeepers said "No." They didn't see the value their passengers saw. They didn't see the value of a better experience for the customer. They didn't see the value of improving the customer's perceptions. They didn't even see the value of the positive effect on their bottom line. They believed there was more value in the status quo.

I never made a dime off this idea, but it was worth a lot to me. It showed me the significance of seeing differently. It changed my vision of the future. It expanded my awareness of the value of ideas. It became a catalyst that helped spark the creation and development of a successful consulting practice in new product development and innovation management. It propelled me to get the education, resources, and connections I needed to make ideas happen—for real. The value I thought this idea had at the beginning differed greatly from the value it ultimately delivered.

This venture was the beginning of my experience with the value struggle, not just in the business world but everywhere. Whenever there is more than one vision in the mix, there is a struggle: Whose vision will lead the evaluation? Whenever there is a buyer and a seller, there is a struggle: Who has more power in setting the price? Whenever there is uncertainty or change, there is a struggle: What are your bets and where will you place them? Whenever there is a gap between expectations and results, there is a struggle: Your evaluation was incorrect, now what? Whenever you have options, there is a struggle: Door #1, Door #2, or Door #3? Whenever you step back to see a fuller picture, there is a struggle: You discover more factors that must be considered, but you don't know their economic impact and you don't know how to attach numbers to them.

Many H^3s have developed new insights and approaches to practical dilemmas in valuing new ideas, enterprises, and our lives. They begin with the relationship between vision and value, a relation complicated by the fact that changes in one lead to changes in the other. The term "vision" includes foresight, dreams, imagination, mental images, and goals. In essence, all these get down to your view of what will happen and what you will try to make happen, whether it is in the next second, the next year, or the next decade. Likewise, the word "value" should be taken in its broadest sense, including worth, ideals, ethics, and priorities—in short, the essence of subjective meaning and the ultimate gauge of what we hold dear. Finally, the chapter offers a basket of new metrics and factors to consider in any valuation.

VISION JAM

> We don't see things as they are; we see them as we are.
>
> —*Anaïs Nin*

"Numbers don't talk to me," says Peter Lewis, chairman of the Progressive Corporation. "People and ideas talk to me. If somebody comes to me with an idea, my main criteria are: 1) Will it enhance the customer experience, and 2) Can we make money at it? That's it really. It's that simple."

But, of course, it's not that simple. The answer to the questions is "It depends . . ." It is all a matter of perception. Value is inextricably linked to vision.

Language affects our perception of value. The language of business—a language that forces us to perceive the world in terms of balance sheets and to predict the future as a function of the past—serves to limit our abilities to fully appreciate the value of ideas. Nascent ideas may get discarded long before they reach their potential because we are trained to evaluate them through a lens that devalues them. The language of business is full of ratios and equations—it is a numbers-based language. And numbers are simply not enough.

We conduct research to point us toward the "right" choice. We try to quantify our prospects and validate our choices, using various numbers and criteria as guides as we sift through a pile of ideas. It is all very logical, often very thorough and organized. But why, then, do 90 percent of all new products fail despite our best efforts? Why do many of our most exciting ideas drift off and fade in our wake?

There is a gap between traditional valuation analysis and today's market-set valuations. Investments are never solely about dollar outlays. In most of life's situations, we make decisions using a combination of hard data, soft considerations, and gut. Yet, in traditional business valuation exercises, such as assessing a potential acquisition, most key decisionmakers will look only at the hard numbers. Balance sheets include only hard assets and liabilities. Profit-and-loss statements show only the accounting of past revenues against capital expenditures. To traditional assessors, these numbers are the best proof of value. But if these metrics are so great, why do most acquisitions hurt shareholder value? Why do so many big, smart companies desperately shed their once-touted additions at firesale prices, writing off billions and billions of dollars in mistakes?

Mattel blew it big time with its acquisition of The Learning Company. Quaker Oats could not handle Snapple any better than Conseco handled Green Tree Financial or Eli Lilly handled PCS. These companies misjudged their ability to extract value from their purchases, for which they paid dearly. Their future-vision was distorted because their traditional valuation methodologies were about the past.

Traditional measurements and allocations are not linked to future innovation objectives. Generally accepted accounting practices can recognize the value of some intangibles—goodwill, R&D expenses, patents, and the like—so long as a transaction is involved. Balance sheets cannot show such expenses if the transaction is "internal" to the enterprise.[1] Furthermore, it has been estimated that the typical balance sheet can misstate the market value of a company by as much as 50 percent because soft assets are not accounted for.[2] The typical budgeting process is devoted to noodling small differ-

ences, not to supporting creative visions. In contrast, many H³ innovators incorporate art and uncertainty into their designs and
metrics. They don't hesitate to swirl in a thick fudge factor. Profits
are not the only measurements of their successes.

Roger Ackerman, former chairman and CEO of Corning, got
jammed between conflicting visions of the future. The stock market
was softening, and Corning's performance was melting. He watched
his company's stock price take a dramatic dive. Corning wasn't alone

in the meltdown. Everyone started to retreat and hunker down until they felt
stronger again. Ackerman struggled with
his board of directors and Wall Street analysts who wanted him to trim costs as
everyone else was doing.

It wasn't that Ackerman didn't understand that the ice was getting thinner. He
just didn't want to pull back. He saw what
Corning's scientists saw, and they all believed in the future worth of innovative
products and businesses that were still in
the experimental stages. Ackerman
pushed for more investment in R&D to
support his vision, despite objections from many investors. They
didn't believe in his capacity to create the enormous value that
Corning was aiming to create. "It was our own conviction that we
knew what we were doing," Ackerman says. "We understood that
there would be a rebound based on our own ability to innovate and
in what we saw coming down the pike. We weren't focused just on
our current profitability. We were focused on the future."

As a result of this kind of thinking, Corning not only transformed itself from a housewares company to a high-tech company,
but also transformed the world, by developing the leap innovations
of optical fiber and optical networks. Investors responded and

Corning's stock soared in the 1990s. In 2000, it reached a new high of over $113 per share (after a stock split), but like most other tech stocks declined sharply in 2001.

Because Ackerman believed that the future holds tremendous opportunities for the communications industry and that Corning had the resources to go after those opportunities as no one else could, he valued R&D more than his analysts did. For Ackerman and other H³ leaders, value is ultimately dependent on their view of the future.

What we believe about risk, uncertainty, fuzziness, and intuition influences the price we are willing to pay and when we are willing to pay it. Traditionalists say an idea is worth nothing unless and until it is successfully implemented. In H³ organizations and for creative individuals, even ideas that are not actualized are worth a lot. They add to the creative treasury; they trigger new ideas; they provide points of departure to realms far beyond even the narrowest imagination. They can take a nineteen-year-old ad agency novice and direct her to her own successful consulting practice.

MÊLÉES OF MEANING

> What you see is what you see.
>
> —*Frank Stella, painter*

Contemporary art triggers passionate, sometimes extremely polar value assessments. Many people will view a contemporary piece such as Jackson Pollock's *Lavender Mist* or Rothko's *Yellow Band* in a museum and, with a flip of the hand, declare that they could have painted that painting themselves. What's the big deal—a bunch of paint drips on a white canvas or the simple swash of yellow across a red background? Some say, "My six-year-old can paint better than that!" as they gaze upon a chaotic jumble of streaks or broad swaths of color. Yet, someone else would pay many millions and feel she got a bar-

gain. Some viewers can see intricate expression or profound message—they interpret the spatters, smears, and scribbles as expres-
sions of insight and soul. The irony is that with such simplicity,
there is such controversy. People don't argue as much about the
worth of a Renoir. What you see is pretty straightforward, but with
minimalist and abstract works of art, a tremendous amount of their
value lies in the fact that within apparently straightforward objects
and simple forms, there exist multiple levels of experience. The
more you see in something simple, the more it's worth.

The converse of this rule also holds in both the art world and the
business world—namely, that the more simplicity you see in something complex—a Rauschenberg, for instance—the more it's worth.
If you can reduce the complexity to essential concepts, you can see a
much broader potential for them. You can see how the fundamentals can be leveraged. Once you see the essence of a complex idea,
system, or form, you have the key to unlock many doors. That's the
genius of binary code, of eBay's business model, and the elegance of
String Theory. What is the essential value? Again, it depends on
your point of vision.

We all start out making sense of the world by relying on our conscious sensory data. If we can see it, feel it, touch it, hear it, or smell
it, it's real. If we can't, it's not. But that's only a part of the story,
and by itself it's inaccurate.

We can feel as if we're standing still while we're actually flying 500
miles an hour in a jet or, for that matter, spinning and zooming
through the cosmos with the rest of our planet. We can be in a room
that seems odorless until someone else, whose olfactory sensors have
not been dulled as a result of being there, enters and smells noxious
gas. We get fooled by mirage, by subtlety, by limited experience, by
limited or dulled sensory systems—by limited consciousness.

If consciousness had no limits, we would be overwhelmed by the
billions and billions of assorted stimuli that surround us. We could
not decipher and respond because there would be way too much to

process. Screening out most of these stimuli, we attend to the most important and most relevant—imminent dangers or the essentials of life—often at the expense of creativity.[3]

Creative people tend to have a heightened sensitivity to intricacy, subtlety, and nuance. They have a superior capacity to sense, process, and find value in quiet, tangential, and distant beeps, blips, and flashes. Expanding our consciousness to take in more diverse and faint tickles and proddings can increase our acceptance of new ideas (our own as well as those of others). As discussed in Chapter 2, often the ripples from the edges of our data pool become the tidal waves of innovation. That's how Brian Greene saw strings within every particle in the universe. It's how the poet William Blake saw heaven in a wildflower. It's how Corning's scientists, who developed the innovation of fiber optics, created billions of dollars of value—out of vapor.

Value is deeply affected by context. A glass of orange juice that costs two dollars in Des Moines can cost eight dollars in Tokyo, and it's not because oranges are cheaper in Iowa. Each country has its own currency and its own value system. Traditional enterprises have one currency (usually monetary), whereas H^{3}s also have another—the currency of ideas. Sometimes, you need to change the context to close the gaps and extract more value.

The more diverse our experiences, both in breadth and in depth, the broader our view of the future. No matter what lens we use—wide-angle, telescopic, or macroscopic—each lets in a certain amount of light and produces a different image on the film of our consciousness. The point is to look through as many of these lenses as possible. A diversity of perspectives adds value. In short, how we see affects what we value. How we see is itself affected by where we look and what questions we ask, with whom we are looking and to whom we are connected, our future orientation and our past experiences, our fears and our aspirations, our templates and our fences.

Many H^{3}s—whether large organizations or single individuals—see the future as fast, big, and leveling. They tend to value speed, scale, and creative leaps more than their traditional counterparts do. Many H³s view uncertainty as a good thing. They value both sides of the blur. They see opportunities and embrace risks that others won't touch. AOL was one of the pioneers in the high-speed landgrab, a leap-before-you-look adventure into the unknown.

The value of a dollar earned from core operations means more than the value of a dollar from other income sources, just as the value of a dollar from topline growth means more than the value of a dollar earned from cost reductions. Cash flow can move in different directions from earnings for a variety of reasons.

If new customers buy, more dollars will drop to the bottom line. If capital investments squeeze cash flow but lead to new sales, operating cash flow trails earnings, which for a while can be a good thing. The big meaning in the message here is that typical assessments, using traditional financial analyses, do not always reflect true value. The struggle that investors go through is a matter of vision and faith. If they share the vision of those leading an innovation initiative and have faith in the leaders' abilities to make investments pay off in the long run, they are less demanding of short-term earnings. They'd rather get a dollar from growth than from trimming, and they are willing to risk more to get it.

ROOTS OF THE STRUGGLE

> Reality is nothing but a collective hunch.
> —*Trudy (Lily Tomlin)*,
> The Search for Intelligent Life in the Universe

What is the relationship between speed and perfection? How fast can you get a new product out? How "right" does it have to be? How fast can you improve it? How will people feel about it? What will it all mean in dollars and cents? Who knows?

If you think you're sure, you are handicapping your ability to innovate. You won't look for risks beyond what you see now. You won't see new opportunities. And you won't understand what really matters—the root causes of the problem and opportunity .

It's not only how much it will cost to sell, how much customers will be willing to pay, how perfect it is, and what might happen if you screw up. These measurements are important. But even more important is understanding what drives these measurements and what could make them change. How satisfied are customers? How happy are employees and peers? How much is being learned? These are the drivers of the future. These affect creative output.

H^3s such as Macromedia aim to get a handle on the sources of the risk, the drivers that will ultimately affect sales and profitability. What can affect how well a product or service will sell? What will influence the amount different groups of customers will pay? How efficient can channels be? How much talent will be on your team? How will the people you care about feel about you? What will they do? What is the sweet spot? What potential disasters lie in wait?

THE DCF TRAP

> You don't know what you've got till it's gone.
>
> —*Joni Mitchell*

It's better if you're not sure. And that's good because, as Heisenberg's Uncertainty Principle pointed out, the minute you are precise (or think you are), you are uncertain.

You can never see the whole deal. Betsey Nelson, executive vice president and CFO of Macromedia, was entering into the fog more often, with more and more at stake. The company had to constantly develop high-quality, cutting-edge products fast enough to lead the web design industry. She had to buy more companies, more capacity, and more competence. She couldn't grow enough of what she needed fast enough.

"I take exception to the premise that you can even try to assess value with things that are called 'hard numbers.' I've studied all those methods for probability distribution," says Nelson, "and the truth is that at the end of the day you end up using something called the discount factor." She explains, "What that is is a black box that acknowledges that you have some uncertainty. It just applies it in the form of a number. No more scientific, frankly, than any other method. If I think the discount factor here is 20 percent versus 25 percent, it's just the numeric way of capturing my risk assessment. I'm assuming a certain degree of risk, and I acknowledge that. But that doesn't mean that I've answered the valuation question."

Nelson argues, "People do gain too much false comfort from applying methodology like that. What I think is more interesting than just assigning a discount rate, assuming that I've now captured my risk, is to get down to the heart of the matter by asking, 'Where does my risk come from?'"

What are the numbers behind the numbers? And what are the numbers behind those? And what is important in all of it that can't be reflected in numbers?

Of course, managers still run the numbers, altering assumptions about things like inflation, taxation, the cost of money, projected market growth, and projected sales. That is what sensitivity analysis is supposed to do. But Nelson takes her analysis deeper and further. She's looking at various possibilities and asking, "In this scenario, does my risk come from a change in the competitive environment? Is it a change in my pricing? Is it a change in the talent pool?" She attempts to humanize the numbers and to find their motivations. "I feel that I get a better handle around my risks when I put names or labels like that on them rather than just assigning a particular number. I appreciate having the grounding in statistical and financial techniques, but at the end of the day, we really deal more with things like 'Am I going to lose a key engineer or not?' That's a *real* risk. And when you're talking about it that way, you can talk about what might be some of the solutions and relative value, I think, more meaningfully."

DigitalESP, an e-commerce services firm based in Raleigh, North Carolina, estimated that it had to forgo about $1 million in revenue each month in 1999 because it couldn't hire enough technical talent to handle projects—there simply weren't enough geeks available. The company's clients, including IBM and Ariba, had to wait way too long to get their needs met. In essence, for DigitalESP, the value of thirty programmers was far in excess of $12 million in that one year alone. The lost revenue, the lost opportunity, the relation-ship damage, the strain on existing resources, among other things, represented many millions of dollars in value lost not only for Dig-italESP, but for its clients as well. None of this showed up on finan-cial statements, none influenced discounted cash flow (DCF) analy-sis, yet it all greatly affected worth.

If a soft asset, such as a contented workforce, can reduce your time demands and help you get on the road to profits faster, its worth is relative to the advantages you gain by being first to market. If the soft asset can reduce your time, money, and emotional costs, it is worth at least the amount of the cost savings.

David Ditzel knew the value of his own innovation abilities better than his original employers did. Many talented engineers left Bell Labs while they were still quite young, including Dave Ditzel. Bell Labs did not factor this potential loss into its DCF calculations, thereby forgoing many millions of dollars in value creation.

The value of the talent asset becomes even more apparent when these people leave to form a company on the outside. They'll go to the venture capitalists, get an idea started, and then they're off and running. Ditzel estimates that talent jumps ship to go off on their own in 90 percent of the cases in traditional companies. That's a whole lot of value walking out the door.

If Bell Labs had attempted to figure out a way to value its budding talent more, the organization might have been better able to keep those talented people from leaving. "If you have technical and business visionaries who are willing to push a long-term work with their vision, then try to figure out how to support them financially and trust them," advises Ditzel. This is one key way innovators have learned to capture value.

TO HELL WITH CERTAINTY—GO FOR IT!

> You can only find truth with logic if you have already found truth without it.
>
> —*G. K. Chesterson*

Peter Lewis puts it this way: "We've got a lot of stuff going on right now, and we don't know what we're doing with it . . . like selling on the Internet. Whenever you enter a new domain, there's a huge price of admission, no matter how much research you do. When you get into the business, you find out things you didn't know." Although they need more as they continue to grow, Progressive moves with less data behind decisions than most companies normally require. The price of admission is paid along the learning curve, in dollars, sweat, and emotional energy. And it seems to be worth it. There is something to be said for the value of leaping without even trying to look at all the details beforehand. That's what H³ talent says when they bolt. That's what entrepreneurs say when they take the plunge. That's what H³s tend to say and do, much more often than traditionalists.

Uncertainty and volatility are necessary conditions for innovation, but so is action. If you're landing a jet plane, there are only so many iterative evaluations and adjustments you can make before the wheels have to meet the runway. At some point, Betsey Nelson has to hire or fire the programmer. A sculptor has to take a chisel to the marble. You crash and burn if you delay decisions and actions until you reach perfection—perfectionists always fail.

EMBRACING FEAR

If we are unwilling to be aware of the dark, we cannot see the light.

—John Cowan

As part of its mandate, Genzyme focuses only on projects and products that can produce radical change. These, of course, come with the least amount of certainty.

"The way it works is in steps at a time, but the division that we make early on in choosing which initiatives to support is between those where we can create a big change and all the rest," explains CEO Henri Termeer. He offers the example of experimental procedures for treating Parkinson's disease. "We can treat it somewhat with existing therapies, but eventually those don't work, and patients become prisoners within their own bodies, in the most awful sense. If you could replace what goes wrong in the brains of these patients, that would be great."

Genzyme is working with neurocells taken from fetal pigs, the same kind of cells that go wrong in Parkinson's patients. Once purified, these cells are surgically introduced into the patients' brains. In essence, the patients become living prototypes. Now, that's a massive step—to put the cells of a fetal pig into a human being's brain.

Traditionalists need certainty more than many H³s do. That's no big surprise. But what is interesting is just how H³s evaluate risk.

"We have to overcome many problems with cross-transplantation," Termeer acknowledges. The uncertainty can seem quite frightening. "The societal problems of trying to come to grips with it are immense. But we are prepared to accept responsibility." Termeer has a vision of curing Parkinson's disease. He believes that the route his scientists are taking is extremely valuable—enough to overcome the enormous risks. He and his investors are willing to plow through the uncertainty.

This exploration has so far taken Genzyme five years. So far, researchers treated eighteen patients in a double-blind study. Nine underwent surgery in which holes were drilled in their heads, but they did not get the cells. What could this frightening, invasive procedure possibly be worth to those patients?

Termeer knows that he will constantly be playing with fire. "The consent is very complex," Termeer warns. The patients have to agree to a pretty awesome uncertainty in order to participate. These eighteen people evaluated their options under the most uncertain of circumstances, but for them the potential for a cure was worth the risk. Not everyone sees the situation that way. "This is a very unattractive way, if you are in a more traditional pharmaceutical firm, to attack a problem," says Termeer. His own company is hardly a small-time gadfly. With over $1 billion in revenues and more than $10 billion in market capitalization, Genzyme Corporation is the fourth largest biotech company in the world.[4] The big pharmaceuticals can't afford to take such risks, not because of their size, but because of their approach.

At first blush it would seem as though the financial giant Capital One defies most of the points made in this chapter—the ones that give accolades to uncertainty, soft assets, long time-horizons, and all the rest of the mushy stuff. This company demands quantitative measurements of everything, from its product offerings to its customer propensities to employee nuances. Every year Capital One conducts tens of thousands of systematic experiments, refining its statistical models and building an unsurpassed database so that it can, with amazing precision, predict and optimize every aspect of its business. This is a company that revels in numbers—hard numbers. This is a company that prides itself on its ability to capture data, measure it, and optimally leverage it to achieve unparalleled success, with an average annual growth rate of 40 percent and a stock increase of more than 1,000 percent since its IPO in 1994.

My friend Carol became very annoyed when Gevalia, a mail-order coffee purveyor, with a wicked negative-option policy, kept sending her coffee and billing her charge card $28 a month for two pounds of coffee. She had signed up for a trial because she was intrigued, but decided that the coffee wasn't worth $14 a pound and gave notice that she was canceling her subscription. The coffee kept coming, despite efforts to inform the company. She didn't use that much coffee each month anyway, so it began to pile up in her kitchen cabinets. Carol put a call into the customer service department of Capital One, to get some help in reversing the charges and stopping the subscription. She barely finished pressing the last digit of Capital One's phone number, and her call was racing on its way, zipping through the company's extraordinary database so that it ended up connecting to just the right customer service associate for her specific set of circumstances. Carol charged a lot of online merchandise. It was easier than going shopping. The Capital One associate offered to help and then offered her a special web-based credit card, with advantages for online shoppers as well as for Capital One.

When you look more closely, you see that the information-based strategy goes far beyond typical marketing and financial measurements. The company is a successful innovation factory because of what's behind the numbers. Capital One closely measures the transaction behavior of customers and potential customers, correlates behavior with risk profile, and evaluates the potential profitability of each one of its hundreds of thousands of customers. Although most would claim that the banking and credit card industry is all about the numbers, Richard Fairbank, CEO, and Nigel Morris, president, get to the core of their alternate view. "Credit cards are not banking—they're information." If a customer calls to cancel her card, for example, Capital One knows almost instantly whether it can call that customer's bluff or win her back with a compromise or whether it wants to keep her as a customer at all. The company knows because it has conducted more than 45,000 tests (as of 2000) to measure behavior, correlate demographics, and find patterns of efficiency. Its competitors are looking at a much more superficial, limited set of demographic numbers.

NEW VALUES NEED NEW METRICS

> Life is not measured by the breaths we take . . . but by the moments that take our breath away.
>
> —*Unknown*

Filmmakers have Oscars and Golden Globes. Sundance values those out on the edge. Musicians have the Grammys. Writers have the Pulitzers. Sales figure into the evaluation, but these awards are also measures of creativity and talent. New ideas and the resources that are behind generating, developing, launching, and managing them need their own Richter scales.

Innovation assets are considered as "soft" assets and new ideas are considered "fuzzy." There's a whole lot of uncertainty involved, definitions are ethereal, substance is conceptual, and people can't wrap their arms around many of the things they need to consider when evaluating their worth.

We continue to base valuations on historical performance, even though, as every prospectus warns, the past is not necessarily an indicator of future performance. Hard numbers won't tell you if you are about to be trumped or rendered irrelevant. If there are faint stirrings of something newer, better, or cheaper, an idea is worth only the premium return it can yield between now and the new new thing.

You need to look at the numbers behind the numbers, the risks behind the risks, and a new set of innovation measures involving creativity, experience, brand, aesthetics, and a host of other factors.

The Creative Factor

> We should do something when people say it's crazy. If people say something is "good," it means someone else is already doing it.
>
> —*Fujio Mitarai, president and CEO, Canon Corporation*

Henri Termeer chooses not to work on incremental innovations. Genzyme measures opportunities by how much they can change the world, as we know it. "Everything gets measured in terms of creativity," explains Termeer. "Because it takes hundreds of millions of dollars to accomplish a real breakthrough, the ultimate investment decision is always based on the question of whether we can change the standards of medical care. Do we get a completely different outcome?"

Creativity is an expression of risk, and evaluation is, in large part, an assessment of risk. Most people screen out the more creative ideas and innovative concepts because they believe they'll be safer if they stay the more conservative, low-risk course. What they fail to see is the risk of not innovating.

The value of new ideas is often measured by the popularity these ideas attain on the streets of New York, London, or Paris. Malcolm Gladwell devotes much of his attention in *The Tipping Point* to the gestation of such trends and fads.[5] But degree of popularity can be a misleading indicator. Instead, a new idea can be measured by degree of creativity and newness as opposed to its current level of acceptance. We have been conditioned to consider the most popular as the best. But creativity, inherently, stays ahead of popularity, and that is where the leverage points are for future value. By the time lots of people like it, it's too late—it is no longer a new idea.

How do you measure the power of creativity? Beyond blips of excitement on the Richter scale, revenues from new products relative to existing products can indicate the strength of a company's creative and strategic ability to generate new ideas. When you evaluate Capital One as an innovator, you discover that in 1999, over half of its $732 million marketing budget was spent on products that didn't exist six months before, 80 percent on those younger than one year, and 95 percent on those younger than two years. You then realize that Capital One has innovated every piece of its business.

To get a handle on the creative factor, you can, for example, measure the number of new ideas proposed internally to indicate creative energy, freedom, and spirit. You can take a look at compensation systems to assess how well they reward creativity. You can value creative governance. The California Public Employees' Retirement System (CALPERS) can quantify the impact of an "enlightened" board of directors and creative workplace practices on a company's performance, as it assesses its portfolio of over 1,700 stocks worth more than $100 billion. That is one correlation between the evidence of creativity and the evidence of success.[7]

The Experience Factor

> Any sufficiently advanced technology is indistinguishable from magic.
>
> —*Authur C. Clarke*

When you sit inside a new car and sink into the plush leather seats, and the seat remembers the exact temperature and position you like best, and your eyes scan a beautifully designed dashboard, inlaid with burled walnut, and an awesome sound drifts out of the stereo, and you reach over to place your cup in the ergonomically positioned cup holder, and the tinted glass soothes your eyes from the glare of the midday sun, that experience can help justify the sticker price for some but not for others.

Experience is a value barometer. We don't understand or appreciate value until we experience what the idea produces.

Now that quality and low price have become more commoditized, it is often your experience with a product or service that makes the biggest difference. Complaints and accolades are traditional indicators, but they mainly show the extremes. You can rate experience relative to needs, expectations, and competition. For example, a Dell computer might be as good as a Gateway and they may cost the same. Your experience in dealing with sales and customer service at each company, or your aesthetic preference for cow motifs become the more deciding factors.

The Relationship Factor

Experiences help define relationships, and each has a relative value.

Ed Koch, the former mayor of New York, used to ask, "How'm I doin'?" His question is simply another way of asking, "How much am I worth?" Rating and review services on the Internet—for example, OpenRatings, BizRate, and epinions.com—enable customers to substantially increase due diligence. People can and do check out the companies they consider doing business with, so these ratings matter. Consequently, some companies look for ways to manage their reputations. It's one form of damage control, but, unlike putting a PR spin out there, these companies review complaints regularly and make appropriate adjustments. The Internet gives instant feedback, both positive and negative, to our questions about valuation.

Beyond profitability, the quality and extent of relationships are useful guides to evaluation, whether of a company to acquire, a potential business partner, a spouse, a set of friends, or a circle of creative associates. This is more than a mere accounting for goodwill. It is an attempt at forecasting potential problems and opportunities down the road.

The relationships prospective customers have with competitors can help you determine how much you need to do to woo them to your new products and services. If you are evaluating a potential spouse, looking at his or her relationships with the community, family members, friends, and business associates can tell you a lot about the future of your marriage—a lesson some of us learn way too late.

Similarly, the relationships that artists form with each other often affect the value of their creations. Philip Glass, Robert Wilson, Laurie Anderson, Twyla Tharp, and Robert Rauschenburg all interact with each other, sometimes in collaboration. Each one contributes to the value of the other's work. Basquiat commanded high prices for his paintings in large part because he hung out with Andy Warhol.

Networked relationships have great value, and the right partners and connections can strengthen any enterprise. They bring the advantages of scale, reciprocal back-scratching, and credibility. These relationships have a direct effect on an organization's ability to operate more efficiently, increase sales, and command higher prices. But there's a downside to this: As in nature, incestuousness can breed weakness and leave the group vulnerable to disease and catastrophe. The networks formed by technology and Net-based firms increased their power, but looking more closely, we see that the webs are fragile structures. In many, the companies are each other's best customers or suppliers. If one company in the group falters, it can bring them all down. So, the value of a network depends on the constituents' ability to perform on the high wire without the safety of the network. It may depend on their ability to network with other networks that are not vulnerable to the same kinds of threats.

The Brand Factor

The value of brand equity is not a new discovery, but it is more than the value of notoriety. The relationship that people have with a brand is a determinant of worth. In 2001, a record number of "household name" brands, including Xerox, Polaroid, Trans World Airlines, Chiquita, and Fruit of the Loom, failed to maintain a valuable relationship with people, some to the point of company bankruptcy. On the other hand, some innovators such as eBay are successful despite the fact that they have hardly any assets other than their brands. That is a new phenomenon.

Museums never branded themselves until Tom Krens came along to brand the Guggenheim. With museums in New York—the main museum at Fifth Avenue and East Eighty-ninth Street and one in SoHo—plus museums in Bilbao, Venice, and Berlin, one in cyberspace, and two in Las Vegas, and still others planned for New York's riverfront and Brazil—the Guggenheim is the brand for the latest and the greatest in contemporary art and design. Although Krens has had to withstand some brutal criticism, he has built the brand's value up further by bringing in exhibits such as "The Art of the Motorcycle" and "Giorgio Armani," extending the relationship of the brand further into the community.

The Aesthetic Factor

The value of innovative aesthetics has been dramatically demonstrated by the iMac. No one can dispute that the sleek, candy-colored design is what made it a hit. Similarly, Gehry's architectural design for the Guggenheim Museum in Bilbao sparked a revival in that city. Since the museum opened in 1997, it has attracted millions of visitors (and their spending) to this once-quiet town. They come not just to see the art inside the museum, but to experience the amazing structure that Gehry created, unlike anything seen before. The new Guggenheim Museum planned for lower Manhattan is also expected to draw millions of visitors, more than any other museum in the world.

The Flexibility Factor

"Keep your options open" is advice we hear frequently. In financial markets, options have a price tag, and their value can be quite high. As the world speeds up, we need to be able to flex, redirect, and move. If you can do so, you are more valuable. You have a greater ability to create and sustain new value. H³s consider both themselves and their projects to be working, flexible prototypes, a strategy that enables them to explore opportunities for innovation with less risk. This concept is explored further in Chapter 4, "Going Live."

The "World Citizen" Factor

Some H³s are creating stakeholder value by changing the definition of their bottom lines. They are reflecting the changing values of their employees and customers. Corporations such as Philips Electronics, Stonyfield Farm, and Acirca have begun tracking the "triple bottom line"—concerned not just with financial profits, but with social and environmental profits as well.

David Cole, former president of Internet Services at AOL, talks about the values of Acirca, a venture opportunity, which he shares with other investors and managers. Organics, he believes, are better for human consumption and for the ecology of the entire planet. "The company reflects our core beliefs and values about the world," Cole is proud to say. "We have several real advantages: Fast Cook, a recently developed food-processing technology, captures more flavor and nutrients. And, we can now say that we have nearly 100 percent organic ingredients—even the herbs and spices are organic, and no one else does that; in addition, we use distinctive glass packaging, based on new packaging techniques developed in Europe, that enables us to show off our soups, salsas, and sauces." Ultimately, he argues, valuation needs to encompass much more than direct revenues and costs. "We need to change our definition of capital to include things like air, health, and lifestyle." This is not to say that he is not extremely focused on profits. He is. But he wants to earn them and do something meaningful at the same time. As he puts it, "We need to invent a profitable enterprise that can mine a deep consumer need."

To Cole, the value of a brand, a product, a company, and an individual can only be enhanced by their ability to make a positive difference in the world. "The best brands have soul," Cole says. "Our brand's soul includes aligning with non-profits. We measure not only by financial performance, but also by social impact. For example, we take into consideration the improved business health of farmers and suppliers in addition to the health of our customers." The point is that Acirca is valued more highly because it seeks to help people live better, healthier lives.

Are you worth more because you help others? More and more people are beginning to think so.

The Model Factor

Business models used to be fairly straightforward, and there wasn't much variety among them. With the new economy, models became a focus of innovation. Unfortunately, many of them had at least one big missing component: a path to profitability. Priceline.com, Webvan, Urban Fetch, and scores of others rode high on the wave of stratospheric valuations because their models were novel—they were counterintuitive, they seemed too good to be true and, of course, they were.

There are others, such as eBay, whose models are the key to their worth. The online auction house's model of reaping revenues without ever producing anything, never holding inventory, never being burdened with the costly overhead of real estate and equipment, and not even being subject to litigation, is brilliant. Its value lies in the fact that eBay provides a basic service without ever touching anything—never getting its hands dirty.

The value of AOL's business model is practically priceless. In its mission to bring the Internet to the masses, it moved quickly to secure a large paying customer base, leveraged that to extract high fees from advertisers and partners, expanded to play in all the fields of media, and used its unmatchable clout to create one of the biggest and most important mergers of our time with Time-Warner.

The delivery component of the model holds great value. Until the Internet Age, we were used to waiting for things. The time from placing our order to getting what we ordered could take days, weeks, months, sometimes even years. But then, new companies began to promise a lot in hardly any time at all. And we liked it, of course.

Fulfillment systems are often the largest capital outlays for online businesses. They are worth a lot. If they are good, there will be lots of happy customers and streaming revenues. If they are flawed, customers will defect, cash conversion cycles will lag, working capital will erode, and profit margins will shrink.

Fulfillment is actually a revenue-generating piece of the business. The things we promise to deliver and how we deliver on our promises have always been a measure of our worth to colleagues, friends, and families. It is a measure we internalize, and it belongs in the valuation equation for every endeavor.

RECKONING BRAINPOWER

Absence of evidence is not evidence of absence.

—*Carl Sagan*

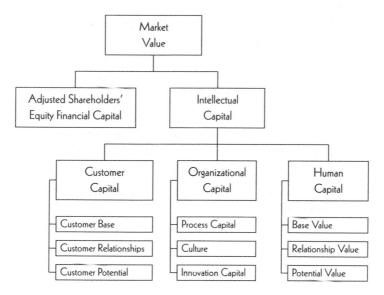

FIGURE 3.1   Skandia's Elements of Intellectual Capital[5]

The soft assets we've been discussing, such as people, knowledge, patents, brands, software, customer bases, and strategy, are key values to get a grip on. For example, the money that companies spend to create these intangible assets could potentially be measured as a capital investment as opposed to an expense.

A number of companies are leading the way in developing metrics and reporting models for intangibles, including Dow Chemical, Avery Dennison, and Hewlett-Packard. Skandia, an insurance company in Stockholm, Sweden (134 billion SEK in Sweden, $10.2 billion in U.S. sales in 1999), reports on groups of what it terms "Intellectual Capital" (IC) (see Figure 3.1)

Skandia uses such innovative measures as an employee empowerment index, which evaluates its people in terms of motivation, support, and awareness. It also uses a knowledge-flow index, which looks at measures of corporate IT literacy. In all, it uses an impressive array of 164 indicators in assessing its intellectual capital.[8]

Attitudes towards soft assets are slowly beginning to change. The American Institute of Certified Public Accountants (AICPA), the International Federation of Accountants (IFAC), and the Securities Exchange Commission (SEC), for example, now encourage companies to provide more "forward-looking" information and discuss non-financial performance factors that create longer-term value. But the struggle continues on how to do so. There is no standard.

Like their more solid counterparts, these soft assets add up to value for the enterprise. The return on innovation assets (ROIA) may not always fit into neat formulae, but if you look at all of the assets and factors that enable you to innovate better than everyone else, you can determine how much better or worse you do when you increase or decrease investments in those assets.

FUZZY RISK FACTORS

People are assets. They are also risks. If employees are restless, if the brightest and most talented are fleeing, or if cultures are clashing, the company is worth less than one with a happy family. Employee turnover is a hard number that can shed some light on this risk, but it won't tell the whole story. It won't tell you if the smartest talents are plotting to bolt to another company or to their own venture. Buying new talent is difficult and expensive—and without it, innovation prospects, the lifeblood of an enterprise, drain quickly and leave you cold. The value management places on its talent has a direct impact on its risks. How are they treated, compensated, incentivized, nurtured, and empowered? Are these values all in alignment with the company's innovation goals?

Even so-called hard assets can be full of fuzzy risk. Intellectual property such as patents or proprietary software programs are listed as "real" assets. But do they really belong to the company in question? They might possibly belong to individuals inside or even outside the company. They may be minor adaptations or extensions of nonproprietary programs. A company with legal protections against future claims is worth more than a company without them. Development agreements and rights assignments can be even more valuable than the intellectual property itself.

THE ULTIMATE WINNER

Our brains are growing bigger. Our minds are expanding. They hold more knowledge. They are caches of a growing diversity of data. We are moving along an evolutionary path, although some might argue that we are devolving. The more we take in, the more we must decipher, prioritize, and edit.

It was midnight. Henri Termeer's glazed leather chair creaked as he leaned back in it. His best friend's child had just been diagnosed with cystic fibrosis, an extremely debilitating genetic disease that cause great damage to the respiratory system and dramatically shortens the average life expectancy of its victims. Almost immediately upon hearing this news, Termeer began to scroll quickly through hundreds of fragments of ideas about how he could help save his friend's child. Little blips of light would shoot past his consciousness, some leaving trails of possibility in their wake. And he continued to search, as he witnessed the frequent heartbreaking episodes of hard pounding on the child's back to help loosen the thick mucus that was constantly building up and choking off breath.

Termeer's personal commitments and desire to help people in need fire his determination to find cures. It began when Termeer served as general manager of Deerfield, Illinois-based medical device company Baxter International, Inc., and led the charge against hemophilia. It continues as Termeer leads a genius group of scientists who are pushing through the fog to discover and develop cures for catastrophic diseases and resolutions to seemingly intractable healthcare problems. They tackled a portfolio of big and nasty enemies of the human body, including Parkinson's and Gaucher's disease, kidney disease, severe burns, and cardiothoracic diseases, pioneering an impressive array of diagnostics and solutions. Now, Termeer wanted to plunge into molecular oncology, an entirely new path for the company.

Genzyme's directors were heavily against taking on an area in which no one else had been able to make significant progress in the past ten years. They didn't want to spread the firm too thinly across a broad a range of mountains. Oncology was so different from the other medical troubles in their viewfinder that the directors questioned Genzyme's ability to stray so far off course and win. They did not believe the idea was worth the effort needed.

The scientists in Genzyme's radical laboratories know tons about biotechnology. They fool with genes and enzymes. They tinker with engineered organic and synthetic pieces that will actually become parts of people. They focus on compromised tissues, bones, and organs. They solve living problems with living cells, biomaterials, and helpful organic hardware.

Alternatively, oncology researchers have been mainly focused on inorganic chemistry. It's a whole other world, with another set of rules and tools. Most have been out to cure cancer with toxic chemicals and rays. They played with ideas for new molecules and new ways to work with killer electrons.

It's not that these two worlds were mutually exclusive, but there was a dividing line that few had crossed. Termeer kept seeing reasons to cross it. He thought that a marriage of oncology scientists and biotech scientists would have a chance of producing a strong prodigy.

For Termeer, going outside into a bigger universe is more exciting than scary. The departure didn't unnerve him. As he began to talk about the idea, his peers gave him even more flack. But Termeer has an opportunistic way of dealing with negative pressure. He says: "When I get three calls from really well-recognized people that have read something about what we're doing, and they say, 'Henri, you're on the wrong road. That's not going to work. I warn you, our chief scientists have said this, and I say this as a friend to you,' I know just what to do. I double my original efforts. I do the same if the dissent comes internally—and of course in 99 percent of the cases it's true that indeed they're right.

"Real breakthroughs don't happen in 99 percent of the cases. They would have happened if they were obvious! Breakthroughs happen in places where we couldn't quite see the possibilities. And if you're looking and you have knowledge of where to look better, the cost of stopping to look is so high—to society and to the program."

Genzyme Molecular Oncology has created important breakthroughs in antigens, vaccines, and pathway regulators that enhance the immune system's cancer-fighting abilities, starve tumors by cutting off their blood supply, correct cancer cell defects, and selectively attack tumors.

Intuition helps you to make choices that are not always obvious to everyone else—or even to yourself. After all, you don't need to tap intuition if things are neat and clear. Intuition is more powerful than what you think you know. "I don't take it that I know anything, because I am not even a scientist. So I trust my own intuitive sense," Termeer says.

Intuition is an internal, personal, intimate assessment process. It is a way of filtering out the noise. It provides an escape from external stimuli. Everyone else's voice quiets for a while, everyone else's position fades back so that your own inner voice and your own position can come through. And then you "know" what the answer is. You "know" whether it's right for you.

Termeer pushed back against his board and key stakeholders. "Why do you think you can win now when everyone else has failed for the past ten years?" they asked. "My intuition let me see that the moment was right," he says emphatically. "It felt right. I get a sense —and then I get the feeling that 'Yes, I can get there!'" He compares it to other momentous decisions. "It's a bit like when Kennedy said, 'Let's go to the moon!' It seemed like an arrogant comment to make, but it was very appropriate because all the things were there for us, in that moment. We just needed to get it done, to pull the right things together. And that's the same sense that I developed."

H³s tend to be an intuitive bunch. It is an interesting trait to have in common. These deeper levels of consciousness and thought tend to produce more advancement. Creative people tend to tap, trust, and value their intuition more. They believe that ethereal intuition is grounded in a hard reality. It is not a fantasy. It is of a real moment.

Satjiv Chahil, chief marketing officer of Palm, values himself. "Intuition is a result of a collection of all of my real-world experiences," Chahil explains. "It comes from the gut. And the gut is faster. Like a computer, the brain stores many data points. I trust my intuition because I know it is based on knowledge and experience."

"Sometimes intuition leads me to something really radical that stands in the face of popular opinion," says Chahil. "But I go for it because I know that's how I get to new ideas. Popular opinion never produces innovation."

Before joining Palm, Chahil founded the multimedia division at Apple. He describes an example of how intuition drove him to make a bold marketing decision. He had the idea that he could promote Apple's multimedia supremacy in Japan. This was an extraordinarily ambitious task, considering that Japan was home to the world's largest consumer brands, such as Sony and Panasonic. To distinguish Apple, he partnered with Janet Jackson to promote her "Rhythm Nation" tour in Japan to demonstrate the benefits of Apple's multimedia technology. This promotion included special events for the physically impaired segment of the population. In the late 1980s in Japan, African Americans, especially females, were not considered to be valuable spokespeople. Furthermore, in Japan, the disabled were kept hidden from view. This promotion idea was radical. It contradicted a whole country's values and culture. But it worked. Apple achieved its objective to become the most preferred brand in Japan, way ahead of major competition in less than four years—it became a cultural phenomenon. Chahil credits his intuition for guiding him, for helping him evaluate his odds, and giving him strength to stick by this decision.

Chahil encourages his staff to test their own intuition and not get bogged down by analysis paralysis. "I give them the opportunity to go for it, and empower them to achieve success." He believes that success breeds confidence, so staff members are more likely to trust their intuition again and again until it becomes a powerful resource.

INNOVATION PORTFOLIOS

Most of us are familiar with the portfolio strategy to investment advocated by financial managers, chancing better returns while reducing risk. With all of the uncertainty and fluidity surrounding innovation projects, you can follow suit with an innovation portfolio, to include a mix of short-term and long-term, safer and edgier initiatives. H^3s tend to have a significant percentage on the edge.

Genzyme Corporation helped pioneer the concept of tracking stocks to allow the company to maintain a portfolio of risk/reward ratios while allowing stockholders to opt for the one that matches their own personal investment profiles. The high-risk, high-reward investors could invest in the most leading-edge part of the company, while the more risk-averse could invest in the most conservative part of the company. There are three divisions: Genzyme General (GENZ), Genzyme Molecular Oncology (GZMO), and Genzyme Biosurgery (GZBX), each valued differently and each traded on the NASDAQ. Each division is owned by a group of shareholders who own one class of Genzyme stock, and together these three classes own the company. Other companies have recently begun to follow suit, particularly in tracking e-business separately from core business. AT&T, for example, did it for its wireless business.

"We have simultaneously very advanced research going on in cardiovascular, heart disease, in cancer, in genetic disease, and in a number of other broad-based areas like MS, and so on," explains Termeer. "We keep them separate financially so they don't hamper each other. But the science and other resources are very shared and each division pays for what it uses." Termeer also points out, "That's another big advantage of doing it this way."

Likewise, artists have portfolios of their work. Typically, they don't maintain a widely diverse set of projects at the same time—although some certainly do work parallel paths. Instead, they tend to explore one pathway for a while until they get another inspiration. The significant diversity of their portfolio is laid out across a lifetime. Picasso went through his Cubist period, his Blue period, his Rose period, and others. David Bowie has a pinnacle portfolio of artistic periods across his lifetime, from Ziggy Stardust to Aladdin Sane to The Thin White Duke, from artist, to musician, to producer, to financier—floating Bowie Bonds. For artists, the portfolio is not just a risk management device, it is a vehicle for creative transformation and freedom.

PORTFOLIOS OF PERSPECTIVES

"I have a certain view about how things come about," admits Henri Termeer, acknowledging the limitations of his own view-shed. "That means that I have to allow many other different activities to survive." He even supports visions and ideas that he strongly disagrees with. It is a biodiversity concept. The more variety of interpretation, the more chance there is that something will succeed in a changing world. The ones that meet the tough criteria, the ones that make the cut, the fittest ones move the world forward—and they are worth the most.

"In biotech, everything is pretty unclear," says Termeer. "You don't know what you have until you do a Phase 3 clinical trial, prob-

ably six, seven, or eight years later. So everything gets interpreted."
With different perspectives, you get different interpretations. Termeer wants the benefit of a range of value interpretations. "We set
up outside relationships to help us figure things out," he says. Genzyme invites a wide range of people from other institutions, large
and small, established and start-up, to broaden his perspective and
to diversify his project portfolio, such as Genzyme's new HIV anti-
gen initiative with Massachusetts General Hospital. In a similar
vein, as we have learned in working with our Leading Edge Expert
Networks[sm] at SPWI, exposing clients and ourselves to very diverse,
multiple points of view always increases the chances for innovative
ideas, insights, and new sparks. The purpose is to be measured by
our clients' scales and rules as well as our own.

Corning's Roger Ackerman also advocates leveraging diverse perspectives internally. "There are audits every year across the company. A lot of that is just information sharing. One plant does particularly well in one thing and you compare it to another plant in a
totally different business." Corning's approach is a variation on the
concept of "internal benchmarking." In a creatively handicapped
culture, people throughout an organization tend to nix each other's
ideas—they don't see the value—they see all the reasons why their
ideas won't work. In a new-idea culture, people in different parts of
an organization look for ways to support and leverage the value
other people's new ideas.

DANCING TO THE MOON

Ten people can observe a focus group through the same one-way
glass window and at the end of the session, each of the ten will have a
different accounting of what took place and a different interpretation of what was said. They will also propose different reasons for
why the participants said what they said and reach completely differ-

ent conclusions. Part of these differences depends on what questions are asked and how they are asked.

It is a kind of dance contest. Your idea is your partner. You move with your idea, back and forth, round and round, trading the lead, as you head for the door and shoot for the moon. All along the way, you are sensitive to your partner's rhythm and pace, stamina and flexibility, and you adjust to keep it moving toward the prize. The process informs the decision.

How do our own beliefs influence our customer preferences? We need to make sure that the concepts we present to our customers in testing and evaluation are not only the ones we believe in. It is necessary to explore foreign, even contrary beliefs. In most cases, winning innovations did not meet the original valuation criteria and were not supported by qualitative and quantitative research. In fact, they often met with strong objections. From penicillin to Viagra, from nylon to Teflon, from the PDA to the Internet, if they were all held to their original quests and criteria, the world would be a very different place today.

Even if you don't have a tidy set of sharp rulers and standard calibrations, you can still consider innovation to be part of the valuation equation. Even if your numbers are fuzzy, even if you can't come to agreement, you can still ask the questions and make allowances for the value of creativity and all that goes into producing it. Might you make mistakes? Might you overestimate or underestimate? Of course, that's true of any assessment—even of hard assets like real estate or jewelry. But as high quality and low cost become the norm, as creativity is more and more required to compete, as the demand for innovation grows stronger, as hard assets are shed, the value of creative talent, knowledge base, R&D, brand, culture, relationships, societal impact, and other intangibles grows and needs to be accounted for.

The hot, hip, and happening are what they are because of the high value they place on creativity and innovation along with the resources and systems that promote these values. What enables H³s to keep their edge is the investment they make in innovation assets and the energy they devote to maintaining and increasing these assets.

Innovation competencies are increasingly worth more for organizations and individuals. That worth needs to be reflected. There are no scales to measure love, but somehow we manage to approximate its worth to us. Somehow, we realize that it is an asset to our lives. Somehow, we gauge the amount we are willing to invest in getting, keeping, and growing it. We need to become more aware of how creativity adds value to every aspect of who we are and what we do and to realize that it makes us, and our ideas, more valuable.

In many H³s, evaluation is a continually iterative process. They take today's hypothesis, twirl it around, get it out, and test it quickly. As more information comes, the hypothesis changes, they morph the model in play, and they quickly test that. Sometimes, they throw out the hypothesis and look for a new one. They keep changing and testing until, ultimately, they have enough to make it all hang together. Typically, these iterations happen with searing speed. Often, they happen as the products are already out in the marketplace.

Valuation, as in innovation itself, needs to be a more holistic endeavor. Neither the old metrics and ratios nor the new dalliances are, by themselves, enough. Views of worth need to deepen and widen. Many innovators consider the evaluation process to be a learning process. Evaluation is not about excising, it is about building, adding to the knowledge base, finding ways to make more out of less—to add value.

In the next chapter, "Going Live," we explore the ways H³s realize the value in the process of moving from idea to reality.

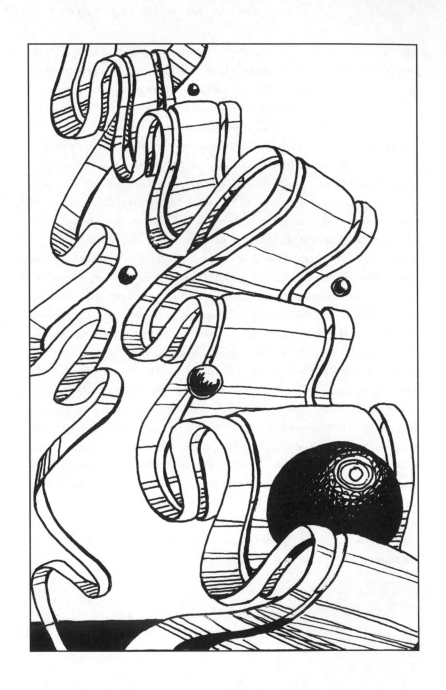

. 4 .

GOING LIVE

Bringing New Ideas to Life

Every blade of grass has its Angel that bends over it and whispers, "Grow, grow."

—*The Talmud*

In a major retrospective of Frank Gehry's work, twenty truckloads of his architectural models went on display at the Guggenheim Museum in New York. Although these models represent only about a third of all those Gehry had completed, the exhibit was vast and comprehensive. The models ranged from his earliest works to a proposal for Peter Lewis's dream home to Gehry's designs for a fabulous new art museum in lower Manhattan. Each is, in its own right, a work of art.

Before the show opened to the public in 2001, I walked up and around the Guggenheim's corkscrew slope, accompanied by museum director Tom Krens, Peter Lewis, and Gehry himself, viewing

the stages of an architectural career that has spanned over four decades. I admired how Gehry's creative process unfurled.

Images of undulating shapes had lingered in Gehry's mind—since childhood. Decades later, as he contemplated the direction he wanted to take with his building designs, he could still "see" the silvery fish in the bathtub, as they swirled and stretched, curved and coiled. They shaped his vision of curves, waves, and forms never before used in architectural designs, yet his early works, while conceptually novel, were still extremely linear structures, with straight forms and right angles. He was compelled to push beyond typical hard-edged barriers, to search for ways to replicate the beauty he saw in the magnificent movement of those silver fish.

An epiphany came in 1989, when Peter Lewis hired Gehry to design and build his dream house. With carte blanche from an enthusiastic patron, Gehry began experimenting with new shapes. He developed an interesting vocabulary with strange new phrases such as "metal cocoons." He explains, "I started playing with movements, making shapes that are dynamic and have a quality of movement to them." Twelve years and $6 million in design costs later, with an $80 million cost-to-build, ground still had not been broken, and the dream house remained a dream. But that doesn't bother Peter Lewis in the least. He knows full well the enormous impact that work had on Gehry's artistic development. Lewis considers Gehry's design and construction of the Guggenheim Museum in Bilbao,

Spain, to be the manifestation of his dream house. Anyone who sees the two models can immediately see that Lewis is right. He even refers fondly to the museum as "his house."

The Lewis house model sat atop a pedestal near the beginning in the museum exhibit, so you can see Gehry's evolution as you walk up the spiral ramp. You can see how that house virtually *became* the landmark Bilbao Museum for which Gehry is so justly famous.[1]

Gehry's sketches reveal the transition from idea to reality. The ghosts of those curves and shapes flutter across all sorts of surfaces: sketchpads, envelopes, scraps of paper, and wood. Turning them into habitable structures was a challenge Gehry explored in three dimensions, with ribbons of cut paper, crumpled aluminum foil, cotton balls, and fashioned toilet paper. He played with molten plastic and glass. He draped velvet, infused with wax. He looked at ways to carve up space with curving shingles of glass, reminiscent of fish scales.

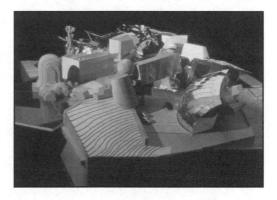

Gehry's models reveal a flowing frivolity: casual cuts and dribbles of glue, accidental and intentional tears repaired with Scotch tape, and pieces held together with straight pins. Who knows, but there might be wads of chewing gum serving as the adhesive du jour. Architects frequently use what's called a "massing model"—a three-dimensional way for exploring shape, structure, and context, which we will discuss further later in the chapter. The massing models that Gehry created for the new Guggenheim, in its crown-jewel-of-Manhattan setting, reveal his gift for sculptural context. The progression from sketches to massing models, to process-design models, to site models, provides a wonderful map of Gehry's journey, as he makes his ideas come alive.

Going "live" with a concept or product is often harder than striking the right spark in the first place. The enormous divide between vision and reality—between knowing what you want and actually doing something to make it happen—is populated by many demons, stoking fear of failure and trying to trip you up. Once you have an idea that you feel good about, bringing it to life is, in large part, the process of working through fears. Each step forward brings more confidence—as well as a new set of fears to face. It is no coincidence that the push toward innovation, entrepreneurship, and a new era in business has been happening right alongside trends in extreme sports and adventure travel. These people, in many ways, have a check on fear.

Advances in technology have dramatically reduced development cycle time—the time it takes to get from idea to execution. Development costs have been significantly reduced as well. A new crop of courageous creative leaders are willing to experiment and move forward without as much preliminary validation—without as many steps in between—as traditional counterparts. H^3s tend to incur more risk, of course, but they find ways to both embrace and reduce uncertainty more rapidly. They feel more comfortable with mystery. By innovating the process of development itself, they shorten the distance to "live" success.

Some H^3s work with an end-to-end view—from spark to market. Through various iterations, they focus and release focus; they fantasize and get real. They innovate the process between knowing and doing.

THE PROCESS IS THE PRODUCT

How do you build real buildings in irregular curves and waves? This was Gehry's biggest challenge. "My first attempts had been based on the descriptive geometry I learned in college," he recalls. "They were odd and unfeasible. I couldn't describe them, and the builders couldn't build them."

He might never have gone live with one of these designs were it not for the fortuitous convergence of several new technologies—namely, computer-aided design (CAD), computer-aided manufacturing (CAM), and computer-aided engineering (CAE), together with titanium and steel micromilling. Gehry and his team began to see some similarities between the curving metal of airplane bodies and his fanciful designs. As Gehry tells the story, "One of my guys met an aircraft engineer and convinced him to come play with us."

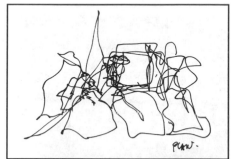

Together they experimented with aircraft design software, adapting it to architectural design. This technology allowed Gehry to finally communicate, within seven decimal points of accuracy, to the construction contractors, showing how the specific

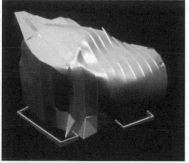

materials and shapes would work together. The program could even predetermine project costs.

Finally, Gehry was on his way to building what previously he could only dream about. The floodgates opened. Gehry produced hun-

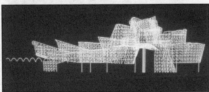

dreds of variations for his projects, pushing and stretching the structural convolutions to thrilling extremes, experimenting with blackened copper, chemical washes, mesh, and chain link. He reinvented materials, worked out the construction challenges, and formed new processes as his work progressed.

There is no such thing as an ideal solution. While most of us look at a handful of possibilities, Gehry scrutinizes hundreds. He selects the best, only to throw them out and start again. Many of his projects are never built; others were started years ago and are still being designed or are under construction. By 2001, Gehry had produced dozens of landmark buildings far and wide, including the Disney Concert Hall in Los Angeles, DG Bank Building in Berlin, Millennium Park in Chicago, and Paul Allen's EMP rock-and-roll museum in Seattle. These buildings have rocked the world, in their own spectacular way.

Some complain that Gehry's latest Guggenheim designs for lower Manhattan and the Weath-

erhead School of Management
building at Case Western Reserve
University in Cleveland, Ohio,
are merely copies of his Bilbao
success. You can definitely see
similarities in the billowing
shapes and metal cladding. But

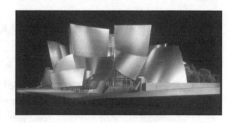

Gehry claims that his buildings are all part of one continuous
process. "You can't invent a new language for every building," he
argues. "Designs need a long incubation period. They need to
evolve." In fact, Gehry wants to always keep an unfinished aesthetic
to his buildings as a signal to himself and everyone else that the
process is the product.

As the Gehry retrospective suggests, everything is R&D to an
artist. In an endless, tireless tango with time and space, with fantasy
and reality, with customers and suppliers, H³s operate on a development continuum. They may start out, as Corning did, in one
business, but end up in something entirely different, just as the
Lewis house became the Guggenheim Bilbao.

EVERYTHING IS R&D TO AN ARTIST

If the process is the product, and the
product is an innovation, the process is
bound to be filled with innovation too.
One example of this principle at work is
illustrated in Richard Serra's process.
Serra, one of the world's foremost sculptors, creates enormous pieces of art out
of steel plate weighing many tons and
stretching hundreds of feet in a process
that is opposite of most artists. Whether it

RICHARD SERRA GOING LIVE

Most sculptors start with an image, which becomes a sketch, which directs the models, which guide the finished sculpture. Richard Serra does just the opposite. Considered by many to be one of the greatest living sculptors, Serra is known for his enormous-scale works. "I never work from drawings." he explains. "I make drawings only after a sculpture is done, and sometimes, not even then."

Serra, who grew up around shipyards and worked in steel mills, became drawn to steel plate as a material. His creative process often begins with an exploration of the land where he will install his sculpture. He might splatter molten lead or manipulate wooden blocks until an idea moves him. Rolled, bent, and forged, his pieces emerge like tankers, some as high as sixty-five feet and weighing as much as twenty tons.

But the process is not done when the sculpture rolls out of the shipyard. It continues: Serra uses Cor-ten, a special steel that can take up to eight years to oxidize. Part of the going live process is delivering the piece, and that is not easy. For his exhibition at the Geffen Center at the Museum of Contemporary Art in Los Angeles, Serra's pieces had to be shipped through the Panama Canal due to their extreme size and weight. The installation part of the process involved cutting a huge hole in the rear wall of the museum so that Serra's delivery trucks could drive through. Serra's installations are difficult, often dangerous work—moving giant steel plates with cranes and a rigger crew, placing, shimming, and balancing.

Serra's process continues when people see his art. His sculptures *involve* spectators. The pieces are experienced as people walk around, outside, inside, and through them, interacting with the space, sensing the art "physically rather than optically," as Serra puts it.

Part of the process is the controversy that is stirred. In one breakthrough series, entitled "Torqued Ellipses," Serra's sculptures invite people to experience shapes never before seen in art, architecture, or nature. Part of the process is the disorientation one feels in the center of such a space. Space and experience are as much Serra's materials as steel is.

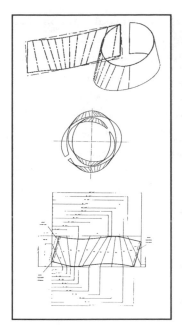

is the serial leap innovation products of Corning, Enron's creation of totally new markets, Capital One's profusion of newly segmented financial products and services, or Genzyme's remarkable biotech discoveries, H³'s processes distinguish them. They are simultaneously loose and tight, fantastic and real.

PLASTIC FANTASTIC

When I was a kid, my siblings affectionately nicknamed me "Preparation H"—not something I was thrilled about to be sure—referring to my obsession with preparing the "perfect" dining experience. (I preferred my other nickname, "Doodlebug," which spoke to my other, looser, artistic nature.) They teased me because when I sat down to a meal, I made sure that everything on my plate was just so—

prepared in the perfect state of readiness before I could take one lit-tle bite. Even as a kid, my sense of taste, texture, aroma, and visual aesthetics drove me to make sure my plate was set up perfectly—that the broiled chicken breast sat discreetly next to, but did not touch, the mashed potatoes; the broccoli nestled next to the potatoes, be-tween the carrots and applesauce. They formed a perfectly coordi-nated circle of color, texture, and flavor. Bread and salad kept their distance on side plates. The butter, salt, pepper, sauce, dressing, Bac-Os bits, chopped parsley, and lemon wedges all were passed to me, in sequence, for expert application—by that time, the rest of the family was practically ready for dessert.

When I volunteered to cook dinner for family and later for friends, I prepared complicated dishes—French cassoulet, salmon koulibiac, rhubarb strudel—in contrast to my mother's simple recipes. I might consult a dozen cookbooks, open fourteen spice bottles, prep twenty-two fresh ingredients, and use practically every pot, pan, and utensil in the kitchen. I needed to present choreo-graphed courses, perfectly balanced across the food groups and taste sensations, offering the perfect seasonal ingredients, the perfect level of sophistication, and the perfect aesthetic experience.

Behind the scenes, it was sometimes not so perfect: I might scorch the mirepoix while trying to perfect the Hollandaise sauce on an-other burner. Soup got too cold while it waited for me to filet the salmon. Fishbones were missed and accidentally left as booby traps. Once I almost sliced through my thumb at the palm because I was hurrying to get my perfect meal ready at the perfect time to serve at my perfect dinner party. Obsessed with perfection, I was chained to the recipes. If I didn't have every exact ingredient, I would fret un-less I could somehow get it—unable or unwilling to substitute regu-lar thyme for lemon thyme. I was a good chef at the time, but not yet a creative one. Taking so much time to painstakingly perfect each as-pect of my efforts, I was too exhausted to enjoy being with my guests. Fortunately, I eventually learned better.

Our desire for perfection wraps us in paradoxes. On the one hand, we are taught to strive for the best—the ideal. We view perfection as an ultimate. It keeps us moving forward, with hopes of reaching Nirvana. On the other hand, perfection implies no room for improvement or change: It stops further development and, in fact, it often holds us back.

The truth is that perfectionists always fail. Recognizing that truth, many H³s ask, "How perfect does it have to be for now?" Most would rather be "messy" than flawless. They jump into the game early, before they even try to perfect their moves. "Research, analysis, and the pursuit of perfection don't ensure the creation of killer apps, and no one can predict what they will be," says Satjiv Chahil, Palm's chief marketing officer. Palm went live with its first PDA as soon as researchers figured out how to solve the handwriting readability problem that had plagued the Apple Newton. Apple designers had tried repeatedly to perfect the Newton's ability to recognize cursive handwriting. At Palm, engineers focused elsewhere. They believed that perfect handwriting recognition was less important than fast, accurate graphic communication. They went live with the Palm Pilot as soon as they hit upon the "graffiti" solution. It wasn't perfect, but it was perfect enough to start with. Palm could gain some traction while designers worked to make the next models better and better.

Microsoft was a pioneer of the rough-start strategy as it launched its far-from-perfect "Version 1.0s" into the marketplace. Although consumers didn't realize it when they bought the software, Microsoft used them as free beta testers. Typically, product testing is an extremely expensive and time-consuming phase of development. But Microsoft managed to get its customers to accept significant design flaws and limitations. The company got customers, in essence, to fund its R&D. Learning from user frustrations, as bugs were discovered and complaints were made, programmers worked to solve the problems in the next versions.

You can go through the perfection process without getting to perfect. Or you can keep trying to get better and better, knowing that you'll never reach absolute perfection. You can also choose to go live with a work-in-process. You can choose to stay loose and malleable, more focused on the exploration than on the journey's end.

LIFE AS AN EXPERIMENT

> You don't want to start out with a perfect thing. That shuts you down.
>
> —*Leonard Dobbs*

David Cole left his job as president of AOL Internet Services to create Acirca and Sunnyside Farms, where he could pursue a longtime interest in organic foods and sustainable development. For Cole, life is an experiment. "I'm shy about market risk," he says, "but I embrace execution risk." He experiments most in the execution of ideas once he feels fairly confident that there is a market in which he wants to play. "It doesn't mean it has to be large or readily discernible by others. It just means that I've satisfied myself that a fundamental need is there."

In the organic food business, he recognized that many consumers were increasingly concerned yet thoroughly confused about food products and health. Without knowing exactly *how* he wanted to play, Cole bought a 500-acre farm seventy miles west of Washington, D.C., and began converting it to organic. Next, he bought the company behind America's original organic brand, Walnut Acres, and began to sketch out a vision of building an international family of organic brands—the organic equivalent of Kraft.

Cole is loose, open, always seeing new patterns before others do, and extremely successful at building new businesses. To avoid getting hamstrung by "perfection," he schedules life transformations.

He goes live with a new business venture every three years, pulling together resources in powerful new and interesting configurations. Cole generates new sparks, nourishes, and protects them until they scale up, gather strength, and get up to a promising speed. Then he steps aside like a wise parent, intentionally deflating his involvement with those projects as he prepares to go live with the next ideas. He never gets to absolute perfection; instead, he makes it perfect enough.

THE MUD POINT

One minute it is a vibrant set of imagery, expertly painted on a canvas that I am working. I like it. I've been watching it develop since I started with the blank surface many hours ago. I have been looking, painting, studying, blotting, redrawing, adding, and refining, getting it better and better. Just one more thought, one more brushstroke, a tiny touch more of paint . . . and in an instant it's all mud. The colors have merged into overworked forms of dingy grays, dank browns, and generally unpleasant darkness.

In every creation, there is a point at which just one more step can foul it up. A symphony can become a drone. A design can become a tangle. A recipe can fall flat. A plan can stop making sense. You make it better to a point, and then you make it worse—in a lot less time than it took to make it better.

In fact, many innovators intentionally leave some things undone—leaving a window open to the future. There is always a better way to find and a new skill to hone. But there is also a point where something is "done" just right for the time being, given the current circumstances. It is "Optimal Done." And it is ready to go live.

Gail Maderis, president of Genzyme Molecular Oncology (GZMO), agrees. "One of the critical questions in cancer research is 'How far do we go in understanding how something works before we move it forward?' It's a challenge. You can test things to the nth degree and spend two decades in the lab without ever moving out into the clinic. At the other end of the spectrum, we can say, 'I have an idea, let's try it in people because the mouse models aren't predictive anyhow.' There's no absolute, right-or-wrong answer. I think there needs to be a balance: On some issues we just declare victory and say, 'I'm going to move forward without testing this, even in the face of uncertainty'; on others we have to test thoroughly because it's critical for safety or performance."

How well and how fast you can move is often a function of whether you've over-engineered, reduced your work to mud, or stopped short of what is needed.

A MODEL LIFE

To this day, whenever I face a new canvas, I choke up a little bit. It is often a big, scary leap from idea to paint. It used to be worse when I was a young art student and canvasses were a serious budget strain. Even now, they aren't cheap, and it takes a lot of work to stretch and gesso them. I can't go through them like paper. Economic issues aside, there is an emotional transition, crossing over from blank to commitment.

Sometimes I jump directly from an ethereal vision to a splash of color. It's a real rush to do that. The immediacy, spontaneity, and freshness often result in an innovation: Sometimes it is a big leap, sometimes it is small.

Often, I sketch out the idea first in my mind, then on countless pieces of paper, then maybe do a couple of watercolor or pastel thumbnails. By the time I meet the canvas, I've already explored and "painted" the painting over and over, changing it each time. If I'm working in oils, I can push through changes on the canvas itself, manipulating and moving the wet paint around as I go for quite a while before it eventually dries. All the while, I'm bringing the idea to life. The process informs my decisions.

ALWAYS PLAYING AROUND

Some of the best learning comes through play. Play is a form of modeling—testing new limits, trying out new behaviors, creating new shapes. My son plays with Legos; I play with paints and words.

At Enron, CEO Jeff Skilling played with markets. Genzyme's Henri Termeer plays with capital structures. In his book *Serious Play*, Michael Schrage discusses playing with prototypes to improve innovation success.[2] To play is to test—whether it's the limits of how high a ball can bounce, how many wheelies you can pop, or how you can stretch the parameters of a system. Of course, you can always fall and scrape your knee. But going live without playing is even more dangerous, especially when the stakes are high. That's why automakers and architects create models first. In fact, there is often a direct correlation between the level of risk and the number of iterations using demos, samples, mock-ups, scale models, layouts, storyboards, and proofs of concept.

TO A CREATIVE MIND, EVERYTHING IS A PROTOTYPE

Schrage believes that the quality and quantity of personal interactions and play during modeling have a great impact on the quality of an innovation outcome. He goes so far as to say that you can't have an innovation culture without a significant amount of modeling. Digital imaging, mega-processing power, and the Web have unleashed new prototyping and simulation capabilities that can greatly help the way people interact, share, dare, and create.[3]

A CONVERSATION PIECE

My friend Carol's parents kept an odd box in the center of a coffee table. Decorated in mosaics, it may have come from another country or another time. Its imagery was symbolic, but no one really knew what it meant. Carol's parents were a bit uptight, or maybe they were just shy, but they didn't talk to us very much. Once, however, when I asked her mom why she kept this box on the table, she replied, "It's a conversation piece." She needed help interacting with her guests.

Many companies that use intranets today for internal communications, such as messages or limited interaction, have significantly increased the amount of conversation among their employees, but they have not figured out how to improve the level and quality of the conversation. They need conversation pieces to help them interact better. Some H³s have found new ways to stimulate ideas through "conversation pieces."

Devising a model to test the cultural impact of collaboration, IBM, for example, invited all of its 320,000 employees to a giant brain-share. This was not just random musings. Challenging employees with ten business problems, IBM turned them loose to work for three days, communicating by means of electronic bulletin boards, moderated chat rooms, instant messages, and online surveys. Within the first three days, over 52,000 employees joined in the creative mêlée, logging over 6,000 proposals. Everyone had access to see and comment on the ideas proposed. Web pages were created and embedded with "thinklets"—bits of creative provocation designed to stimulate new thoughts in all who read them. The experiment, called WorldJam, proved a major leap in collaboration capability. Although IBM does not claim that WorldJam adds real value to the innovation process, the bets are that it does. After adding a bulletin board feature, the website counted over 25,000 visits in its first twenty-four hours of going live.[4]

WorldJam monitors site traffic flow, recording the number of visitors to various areas of a site, which system options they used most, how they were used, and what results occurred. IBM is exploring how this program can become a routine tool, used by its own employees and packaged for its customers.

IBM seems to be developing a penchant for exploring with over-the-top models. Its RS/6000 computer, the unbeatable champion chess computer nicknamed Deep Blue, for instance, is a prototype that allowed engineers and programmers to play with the applications of artificial intelligence. More than just a toy or a headline, Deep Blue spawned many new ideas that IBM commercialized, yielding a major return on its investment. The Blue Gene Initiative, IBM's latest giant conversation piece, is an experiment in bioinformatics. Combining the power of over one million processors, able to perform more than a quadrillion operations per second, Blue Gene works on real-life problems, specifically how proteins are shaped to accomplish certain biological functions. It is expected to yield solutions that will go live in fewer than five years.[5]

LIBERATION

If life is an experiment, everything is a model.

H[3]s often find that new modeling technologies set them free to think and design rather than worry about feasibility. These technologies enhance an innovation manager's ability to explore options, predict costs, and estimate time to completion. They enable both a reach to further fantasy and a guide to closer reality.

"We are at the edge of understanding what we can do," says Nathan Myhrvold, in reference to the new genome projects. The human genome occupies about one gigabyte of information. Amazingly, our individual differences account for only 0.25 percent—an amount that can fit comfortably on a floppy disk. Billions upon billions of pieces of knowledge can now be captured and accessed, according to Myhrvold. The genomic information of the six billion human beings that constitute today's population worldwide amounts to a mere 3.7 terabytes. If you add in the rest of the animal kingdom, the information could fill the Web. New technology can liberate us, allowing us to conduct countless experiments by modeling innumerable combinations, configurations, and permutations.

Every part of Capital One's business is a model. From new product ideas to new management ideas, virtually everything is continually tested, re-adjusted, and re-tried. The company finds opportunities to play with thousands of new ideas. In 2000, for instance, the company performed 45,000 experiments—testing to evaluate new product concepts, advertising approaches, markets, and business models. "We test everything," says Marge Connelly, executive vice president for operations. "That's liberating, because our employees know that if they have a new idea about something, they can test it whenever they want. They don't have to prioritize or budget for it. Every nook or cranny of the company's operations is a potential site for innovation. People experiment more, talk more, and go live more quickly. Our model-oriented culture has given birth to the over 6,000 credit products currently being marketed."

If you make it easy for people to experiment and encourage them to contribute, you give them the freedom and support they need to succeed at innovation initiatives. Making it easier is not just about removing bureaucracy and pledging resources. It also becomes easier to experiment when knowledge and experience barriers are lowered. For example, surgeons have to learn an incredible amount, submitting to years of schooling, internship, and residency before they can take a scalpel to a live patient. The load is so heavy, there is little time and energy for creative thinking, and there are a limited number of people who will even try.

But what if young people who have yet to start the journey toward becoming a surgeon, or people who have no intention of practicing surgery, could experiment with no-risk models such as virtual pa-tients? What if it didn't matter whether someone knew a lot about the circulatory system before she can to contribute to the innova-tion process? What if people could play with ideas in a simulation? A lot of those experiments wouldn't pan out because they would clash with reality from the outset—a more knowledgeable experi-menter would not have tried them. But no harm done—no dead pa-tients. And chances are that those naïve experiments would yield a number of successful innovative solutions as well.

As mentioned in Chapter 1, naïveté can be an asset. New ap-proaches to modeling and simulating can allow naïveté to operate more effectively. If you look at the way technological advances in the music industry have made composing, performing, and producing music so easy and so accessible, it is easy to see the drivers behind new music trends. "I think a lot of people go straight to producing music because they have the easy-to-use equipment, without having the ability to think about creative issues or work them through. It is whatever comes out," says Tod Machover, co-director of the MIT Media Lab. Machover spends a lot of his time developing smart en-vironments and smart instruments that deliver exceptional sound quality and flexibility in an extremely user-friendly format—allow-ing people who don't have a lot of technical musical skills to engage in the musical creative process. But he balances that concept very carefully. He cautions, "You don't want to make it extremely easy to make mediocre things."

If we treat our life as a working model, we are free to think as artists in whatever we do.

SPEED ZONES

Jack Welch was fond of saying that it's better to act too quickly than to wait too long. The logic sequence is all too familiar: The faster you go, the more ground you can cover. The less time you take to get to market, the more you reduce your costs and the sooner you can start making money. The faster you go, the sooner you edge out your competition. The sooner you learn what to do better next time, the better you can adapt to a quickly changing world.

Time is a key factor in "going live" decisions. Development cycle time, or how long it takes to get from idea to market, can be critical to success. Sometimes it is the most important factor; sometimes it is not.

In the latter half of the 1990s, the love affair with speed became almost an obsession. The race to be first to market was never run so hard by so many. Technologies came together that enabled companies to gather information, design, develop, manufacture, and deliver faster and faster. *Fast Company* became the bible for the speed religion, and fast companies in every industry presented themselves as the new heroes. Everyone wanted to reduce product development cycle time and manage supply chains on a just-in-time basis to reduce costs. In general, product development, business development, and strategy development times have been getting shorter and shorter, most dramatically in the past decade—some with positive outcomes and some not.

Winds Variable

Fast companies and people need to slow down in some areas if they want to create successful new ideas. If they go too fast, they can fall flat, compromise quality, miss opportunities, and short-circuit the creative process. They can also burn out fast. Where and when to be fast or slow depends on the development stage, conditions, and circumstance (competition, technology, regulation, and so on). Software companies such as Microsoft stand at one end of the spectrum, given the extremely short development and life cycles of their products. Biotechs and pharmaceuticals stand at the other end, taking years or decades to develop products, thanks to complex science, painstaking protocols, and mountains of regulatory red tape.

Venture capitalists and incubators have tried to turbocharge start-ups, getting from zero to up-and-running within months or even weeks. The faster these companies scaled up, the faster they could stake out a territory. Unfortunately, this line of thinking propelled many so-called New Economy businesses to act first and plan second, only to implode on a flimsy model.

When Is Fast Good?

Researchers at the McKinsey consulting firm found that speed helped only 10 percent of the eighty Internet companies examined—and then only under certain specific circumstances.[6] Being first to market was an advantage only when a company had direct control over key business drivers, could quickly build strong sustainable barriers to entry as well as barriers to customer switching, and aimed for large multibillion-dollar markets.

Being first was key, for example, when David Cole and his executive management team put AOL's pedal to the metal before the company had enough server capacity, and the company was flooded with a rush of new customers. AOL did not wait for perfect conditions. It raced into an inconceivably huge, wide-open, new market area, continually innovating along the way, staying fantastically far ahead of emerging competition.

Part of innovation strategy is deciding where it is most important to be first. Many biotech leaders, for example, have little concern about being first into clinical trials. For them, it's much more important to be first out of the clinic.

Beyond speed to market, some things are generally better fast than slow. It is usually better to get information sooner versus later, for instance, so that you have more time to think, experiment, act, and develop competitive strength. The faster you can conduct experiments, the more ground you can cover and the more hypotheses you can try. The quicker you can get through basic analyses, the sooner you can get to basic decisions, and the sooner you can get to new levels of exploration. For the most part, the less you absolutely need to know, the faster you can move.

Some H³s have found new ways to reduce the level of complexity, so it is easier to move faster. New standardizing processes and components can also increase speed. In these cases, there are fewer decisions to make and fewer actions to take, so time is stripped away. Putting more resources against a problem or initiative can sometimes yield faster results, but after a point, it can slow things down.

When Is Slow Good?

As David Cole says, "I like to move slow on scoping out market opportunity. I need to have a high level of confidence that the market that I'm going after is real. And it doesn't mean it has to be large or readily discernible by others, it just means that I've satisfied myself that the need is fundamentally there. For example, people kept telling me that we should move quickly into Pen Computing, but I just couldn't see the market for it."

When competition is more lax, it can be better to enter a market slowly, to test the waters—to test your own hypotheses and capabilities. Sometimes it makes sense to move more slowly in order to amass better resources. Slow can also be helpful when observing and absorbing new information, incubating ideas, appreciating nuance and aesthetics, and savoring experiences.

In either case, fast or slow, relative quality is a key issue. The first questions are, "How good does it have to be?" and "What kind of experience is desired?" Then you make decisions about speed to match your quality criteria. In many cases, the faster you can accomplish something without compromising your quality objectives, the better. But it can also be a good idea to keep a slow approach happening in the background or on the side even when you want to move fast, to challenge your assumptions and explore possibilities you may have overlooked.

H³ A-TO-Z

H³s adopt different attitudes about gestation time—from idea spark to finished execution. They use time as an innovation tool rather than a resource constraint. They have developed new ideas on managing the speed of the development process. Among the most useful are the following:

Marination and solo time: Innovators stress the need for time to poke around, tinker, putter, and explore. They need time to actively explore, and they need time to sit, observe, and absorb. For them, this time is scheduled into the development process—either formally or informally. I carve out time to be alone as well as time to work with colleagues. When I need to ponder, I need a private time and space where I don't have to interact with anyone but myself. Ideas need time to percolate or incubate.

Spreading creative responsibility: Spreading idea development around means that there are more people thinking critically about the business from more angles. As a result, more ideas come through.

Accelerating: Incubators and accelerators get fledgling businesses up and running faster than usual. A typical example is idealab!, an incubator founded in 1996 by Bill Gross, which houses baby companies in its parental facilities, supporting its progeny with significantly cheaper rents and other resources as it amortizes the parent's total costs across all of the offspring. Parental clout is leveraged in securing advantageous deals and relationships, raising capital, and recruiting talent. And the babies get access to the parent's hotshot board of directors, the caliber of which they could never access on their own. While many idealab! companies, such as e-Toys, have failed, the failure was not due to flaws in the incubator model but rather to unsustainable business models with no clear path to profitability or competitive advantage.

Enron, for example, started a new division, called Enron Net Works, whose sole purpose was to develop new businesses to exploit the Web-based Enron Online commodity trading platform. As a result, Enron's business model tested itself in completely unrelated markets well beyond energy. ClickPaper.com shot from zero to trading 1 million tons of paper, pulp, and wood through Enron Online. EnronCredit.com, EnronMetals.com, Commodity Logic (a management aid in improving internal logistics), and DealBench.com (collaborative web-based project management) are now following suit. While this idea could be highly successful if properly managed, Enron's specific management choices have come into question.

Automating: Usually considered an efficiency tool, a way to get more done for less money, automation can also be used as an innovation tool. It frees up many resources, including mindspace, to allow more room and energy for the creative process. The less you have to think about accomplishing mundane, repetitive, and mechanical tasks, the more you can think about new ideas.

One of the last major areas yet to be automated is the new product development process, a complex and typically unwieldy bundle of activities. As with most things, once complex things get reduced to practice, they seem simple. Once you automate existing processes, such as pricing, you can move on to new territory and develop new innovation capabilities, such as real-time pricing. One major technology advance, networked IT, makes this kind of automation possible. For example, IDe, a technology platform conceived by Michael McGrath, managing partner of PRTM, automates development guidance and decision paths. It allows real-time innovation management based on dynamic merits as opposed to a predetermined budget.

Rapid ideation: Sometimes H³s push for quantity rather than quality of ideas. This is a way of quickly scouring the mind, first to flush out the obvious points so they don't take up mental space, clearing the way for less obvious ideas—the fuzzy, sticky, or hidden imaginings—before we have a chance to self-edit them. Robert Wilson, the renowned visual artist and director, recalls, "When I was in school, studying architecture at the Pratt Institute, in one of my first assignments, I was given three minutes to design a city." Such stretch goals are a useful technique: "Let's go for 300 ideas in ten minutes." Chess masters use a similar training methodology known as "speed chess," in which players must make moves within seconds of each other, never taking time to deliberate, forcing their minds to fly fast through the battlefields.

Rapid prototyping: This tool packs a lot of modeling iterations into a short period of time. It asks players to make as many experiments, discoveries, mistakes, and improvements as fast as possible. As John Sherriff, CEO of Enron Europe, points out, one obvious advantage is that these kinds of mistakes, made early, are usually cheaper and easier to fix. "We like to make lots of mistakes early on, fast and cheap," he says. "We try more new business ideas than anyone else I know." Of course, some mistakes are more regrettable than others.

Parallel processing: This is a form of rapid prototyping, in which tens of thousands of trials are conducted at the same time. For example, chemists at Symyx Technologies can test 25,000 variations of a new material, all at one time. They imagine, define, and create any number of new materials for the company's many partners, including Agfa, BASF, Bayer, Celanese, Dow Chemical, and Unilever. The trick comes in the technology, which allows scientists to compile a set of thousands of possible combinations of chemical elements. This set, or "library" as it's called, is miniaturized, reducing the sample size to save time and money. Detectors scan the new material's properties and enter all the information into a huge database. Scientists can identify those products that most nearly match the desired characteristics of a new polymer for DNA analysis, a new phosphor for use in mammography, or a new type of plastic for the film industry.

A traditional team of one chemist and one technician might, in one year, complete 500 such experiments at about $1,000 each. At Symyx, however, that same kind of team can conduct up to 50,000 experiments a year, at an average cost of only ten dollars each.[7]

Obviously not all processes are amenable to parallel processing. One woman needs about forty weeks, give or take a few, to make a baby. But ten women on the team can't make a baby in four weeks. Some ideas have a schedule all their own. Light always travels at the speed of light.

REAL TIME

When the time it takes to get from point A to point Z is virtually nil, you're dealing in the popular H^3 timeframe of "real time." When you buy something online and as soon as you click the "buy now" button the item is removed from the seller's inventory, that is a real-time transaction. Instant messages approach real time for e-mail. Receiving or transmitting information in real time enables real-time decisionmaking, development, and pricing. The Internet, of course, has been the "killer app" in this area, and IT software now gives users unprecedented power to determine the status of projects, orders, and the like. Dynamic pricing becomes collaborative commerce in real-time transaction. Using secure IT connections, customers and suppliers can all see the same work in progress and adjust their steps accordingly.

With its online technology, Enron engaged in real-time pricing. It could price commodity trades thirty times in one minute, as opposed to the typical thirty times a day. In addition to the standard protocol, the company added a proprietary suite of object-oriented control software, similar to one originally designed for NASA. Using software design intended for real-time systems control, Enron aimed for "unreal" time transactions—the speed at which they operated was faster than anyone else ever imagined. According to John Sherriff, "You can buy bandwidth through Enron and be up and running in fifteen minutes." Having taken the twists and turns out of the hose between buyers and sellers, Enron exponentially increased the number of real-time transactions, topping one million in May 2001, making Enron Online the largest web-based platform for trading commodities in the world.[8]

IDe takes the concept of real time further by enabling everybody associated with a project to get the same information at the same time. Executives know where all projects stand at any given moment. At the project level, cross-functional communications use web-based centers where team members and managers gather and distribute information—all now integrated in one database. IDe allows networked real-time resource management to optimize new developments. Whenever anything changes—a new finding, a change in a customer's order, a breakdown, a new opportunity—you can know in minutes or even seconds. A dashboard for project drivers, such as IDe, gives managers and teams a real-time, holistic view as they drive development on both the project and enterprise level.

CHOREOGRAPHY

There are many possible strategies to employ in setting the pace for innovation development. Some strategies maintain an even pace, whereas others change speeds according to different needs in different development periods. Some creative leaders like to start fast and stay fast. Some like to sprint, then slow down. Some like to spend

more time up front making sure they build a good foundation to
support future hyperspeed.

Tempo

Consider, for example, the case of Enron, where Sherriff came up
with the idea of commoditizing things you wouldn't normally think
of, such as transactions, bandwidth, credit, airport runway
space—they have even commodified negotiations. Enron reduced
complexity to create new markets. Instead of the usual slow drag to
work out the terms in utilities transactions, Enron Online invested
almost two years, with heavy resources up front, to establish common ground among buyers and sellers. As Sherriff explains, "We
got industry consensus on what we were actually buying and selling
so that we didn't have to negotiate with small groups on each transaction." With everyone on the same page, speaking the same "language," in a transparent pricing environment, Enron was able to go
live quickly. On November 29, 1999, the company introduced its
new market prototype, building it up from zero to over 1,500 commodity wholesale products worth notationally over $590 billion in
one year—an unparalleled rate of growth.[9] Transactions could now
take place in seconds instead of months or years.

A top Enron Online trader could execute about $1 billion per day
in trades. As is true with many commodities, weather and soil conditions, political and economic conditions, along with many other
factors, affect supply and demand. Zipping into an Enron Online
trader's consciousness is a real-time stream of these diverse information bits that might affect the company's amazingly swift buy-
and-sell decisions. On the back end, all trades are analyzed and
processed by a proprietary risk management system and transmitted
to a global network of computers. An indisputable sign of success
was that, according to Sherriff, over 60 percent of the world's natural gas was traded on Enron Online, just one year after launch.

AOL's heated landgrab is an example of starting fast, scaling fast, and then slowing down to focus on quality and features. Obviously the strategy has worked extremely well for the company. Conversely, many of the New Economy upstarts tried to stay fast for too long, never slowing down enough to think through their paths to profitability.

Troupe

In any organization, projects operate on different timetables; each occurs at a pace all its own, based on complexity of development, needs, and expectations. Many H³s maintain innovation portfolios of projects requiring a mix of paces. Long used as a way of managing risk in investments, portfolio management is a new idea in directing creativity and innovation. Among forward-looking H³ organizations, we find a number of portfolios, including multiple projects, systems, and experience levels.

Going live with a new idea is largely dependent upon the other ideas already in the pipeline. Some H³s go for volume, pushing dozens, hundreds, or even thousands of new ideas. Enron, for example, derived 80 percent of its income from businesses that were less than ten years old. Many H³s make sure they go live with some far-out, risky, long-shot ventures in addition to their safer portfolio mates.

Tod Machover of MIT's Media Lab speaks of the benefits in having numerous projects on different time tracks to completion: "I think it's interesting to simultaneously set up problems that have different time scales," he says. This may sound familiar—short-term/long-term investment balance. But timeframe also affects the way people see, think, and behave with respect to innovation. We all think differently about a one-year project than we do about a ten-year project. "Once a week, or once every other week, it's a good practice, for example, to give people things to think about that are very difficult and don't necessarily have really concrete answers," Machover advises.

Other H³s such as Macromedia keep a portfolio of experience levels, knowing that people at different levels of experience and expertise do not think and create in the same way at the same rate. They recognize the "experience paradox": People who do the same thing for long periods of time can grow too comfortable in the patterns and find it hard to think of something new. A neophyte, in contrast, can naïvely raise a question that turns into the next new vision.

GETTING REAL

Turning a jet nose down and diving toward the earth at better than the speed of sound, you would experience several negative G forces, enough to send your blood to your head and cause the blood vessels in your eyes to burst, resulting in "red eye" and blurred vision. That's why fighter pilots and would-be astronauts train first in simulators, where the experience seems real enough but is less likely to do real damage. It's better to make mistakes in the rough stages, when they are cheaper and less harmful.

Massing Models

Sometimes the first question is "Where do we want to play?" rather than "What do we want to play with?" That's the question that motivated Bill Hewlett and David Packard, who knew they wanted to do something cutting-edge in electronics, but were unsure what they wanted to manufacture when they started Hewlett-Packard in 1937. They delayed that decision until the right pieces fell into place. Henri Termeer knew he wanted to be an early player in biotech, but was not sure of how to play it. So, he and his partners developed Genzyme, based on sketchy ideas and rough models, before they even had a technology or path in mind. David Cole knew he wanted to be in organic foods. He went ahead and bought a major plot of farm land, before knowing exactly what he was going to do with it.

Like a painter who roughs out a composition or a sculptor who masses out a form, these H[3] leaders began their new businesses with grand dreams and approximations—with massing models.

Often made of plasticine clay or blocks of wood, massing models are a dimensional way to explore shape and structure. Most designers, whether they are developing cars or toasters or buildings, like to work with such models because they can be built up, carved out, stretched, and reshaped easily. There is no detail, just enough reality, in rough lumps and blocks, to deliver visual impact of the shape and size of the concept as it stands alone and as it relates to the world that immediately surrounds it. Frank Gehry, for example, moves from thought to sketch to massing models to design process models to site models, as most architects do. With each level, the idea becomes more possible, often changing shape along the way. For months as he thought about designing the Palm Pilot, Jeffrey Hawkins lived with a block of wood, carrying it around in his shirt pocket, pretending it was a PDA. During the course of his day, he would pull it out, enter a name in his imaginary address book, check on an appointment, or play a game of chess. All the while, he went through the motions of pushing imaginary buttons or using a make-believe stylus. At the end of the exercise, he would turn off his block of wood and return it to his pocket.[10]

Massing models help innovators to focus on the core concept—the essence. Some H[3]s choose to bring the core piece to market first, adding more refinements, bells, and whistles later. Michael Mc-Grath, for example, saw the crude shape of his company years before he actually created it. "I anticipated that Information Technology would transform product development, but didn't know exactly how," explains McGrath. "I knew enough to know that we needed to invest in creating a software company." He realized that it would take many years and millions of dollars to create the software before he could make the transformation real. In fact, it took five years to set the stage. "You have put things in place that give you the options to build on," he says. "It's not exactly a plan. Rather it's like investing in the technology because you think that technology is going to be necessary for a next generation product. You may not know exactly, and sometimes you're wrong, but if you think far enough ahead, you can begin to put in place the investments in technologies, company action plans, skills, and capabilities you think you'll need in the future."

The process can work in reverse as well. "De-massing"—stripping down to bare essentials, or "reverse engineering"—occurs when complex projects or processes are reduced to simple models.

As John Sherriff knew from experience, the utilities market system was too complex, slow, and relatively unproductive. As he thought about how to improve it, he began to envision it as a group of simple and powerful information processors, gathering supply and demand data, and maintaining a pricing equilibrium between the two. "We are just merchants, buying and selling," says Sherriff, "although we come about it with an entirely different mindset than others do." Most people aim for the highest possible profit margins, using an opaque pricing strategy, where customers do not know true costs. While the SEC began investigations into Enron's "opaque" financial statements, Enron thrived in a transparent pricing environment, in which products are standardized and transactions are commoditized. "'Commodity' tends to be a dirty word," says Sherriff, "but at Enron we tend to move in toward

> Inferior minds seek convoluted scenarios; it takes a brilliant one to achieve simplicity.
> —Unknown

those opportunities because everybody is going in the opposite direction." By reducing as much as possible to commodity, you take mass out of the system. Fewer people and other resources are needed because there is less to be done in the development process.

Virtual Reality

Because physical prototyping and its modifications can be physically challenging, time-consuming, and expensive, some designers work with virtual models. In some areas—notably medical and pharmaceutical research—virtual designs can be "more perfect" than real-life models. In fact, they can be so perfect that designers sometimes have to add flaws so the virtual model can be even closer to reality.

Simulators and IT technology allow us to try practically anything by mimicking a real experience, in real time. As with most things, however, "real" is a relative term, not an absolute. The level of "real" that you need depends on how expensive or dangerous the development initiative is. It is the difference between what a brain surgeon in training and what an interior decorator might call for.

In becoming more "real," computer simulations are much more than risk-management tools, allowing for mistakes when stakes are low. They also expand our vision, allowing us to see opportunities we could never see before. Sophisticated versions of computer simulation games—for example, SimCity, Civilization: Call to Power, and Railroad Tycoon—give the user the experience of creating new worlds and watching them flourish or founder each time a choice is made.[11]

It is tempting to dive into virtual reality and start designing and creating. But that cuts out an important part of the creative thinking process—starting rough and organic, "feeling" an idea, developing a design first on paper or with clay. If you don't understand sculpture in the real world, for example, you can't sculpt on the computer.

Live Models

In the days before pencils and erasers, if you were a composer, you'd sit down with pen and ink, and you'd write your composition out on a sheet of paper. If you were Beethoven, you would then plop it down in front of an orchestra ten minutes before the concert—and lo and behold, you'd have the Ninth Symphony—which then wouldn't need any corrections.

For Beethoven, his model was his finished piece.

For those of us who are not exceptional geniuses, there are usually some corrections to make on our first attempts. We need to feel our way through our thoughts, going through at least a few drafts or models. When we play with models, we play with a dramatization of reality—not with reality itself. The working prototype is not a new phenomenon, but putting it out on the market for customers to buy and use *is*.

Satjiv Chahil launched the world's first webcast, a concept he developed and a term he coined, during a New Year's Eve celebration in San Francisco on December 31, 1996, without really knowing what its immediate impact could be. In this webcast, Carlos Santana's live performance was viewable around the world via the Internet using Apple's multimedia technology. Immediately the telephone lines were jammed with calls from people the world over wanting to experience this Web event. Chahil knew that night that the company had a hot new market to serve and started to form content partnerships right away. Within two months, webcasting was officially launched on the world stage at the Grammy Awards in February 1997. Sting and several other artists went live on webchats with their fans from around the world. Apple engineers perfected the technology so no lines would be dropped and high-quality video could be streamed in, all in keeping with the excellence of the Grammy event itself.

Real people in the real world are the ultimate arbiters of innovation success. No matter how fancy, no matter how fast, no matter how realistic virtual technology can get, it can go only so far in allowing you to see the feasibility and potential of ideas. Ultimately, the rubber has to meet the road—you have to see a concept come alive before you can appraise its worth.

Some H³s go live by sharing their designs with their customers, and together they develop the product. Corning, for example, co-develops products with some of its largest customers, such as Nortel. Both organizations invest and commit resources to the project and to each other, collaboratively determining what is needed and what is possible.

Traditionally, companies have relied on surveys to discover the public's reaction to new ideas. Many conduct focus groups to test their concepts on live audiences, dutifully recording the thumbs up or thumbs down, and hoping to screen out the chatter that surrounds each pronouncement. These processes have relatively limited usefulness.

Alternatively, SPWI works with "testers" to co-develop concepts with its clients. At the front end of the development process, our Concept Development Groups℠ bring customers, influencers, and other stakeholders in on the concept design in an iterative series of proprietary creative workshops. Instead of just responding to questions about your ideas, customers become part of the strategic creative process early, weaving their perspectives together with yours.

Some H³s put their ideas directly into the market in the form of real products to see how real people react in real time. On a whim in late 1999, Ducati, the hot Italian motorcycle company, decided to test out an idea with the biking community. As the New Year approached, the company thought its top-dog customers might be in the mood for a brand-new bike, so it put its new mega-bike, the MH900E, up for exclusive sale over the Internet at precisely one minute after midnight on January 1, 2000. Within thirty-one minutes, Ducati's entire first year's production—500 of the 2,000 limited-edition motorcycles—had proud new owners. Within three weeks, the remaining 1,500 sold out. The cost of going live was next to nothing. Given the success of that marketing venture, Ducati tried it again with another new creampuff, the 996R model. Within one day, customers had purchased $9.1 million worth of bikes. From that point, the live model process has become part of Ducati's product strategy—a major contributor to Ducati's success and cachet.[12]

As Gary Hamel, management consultant and author, has been known to say, the Web "is the cheapest laboratory around." It has exponentially increased our potential for connecting with real people, in real time, to get feedback on products under development. John Sherriff at Enron would agree. While some people argue that they must first sign up customers before posting prices on the Web, he responds with the opposite argument: "No, you have to get your prices out there, and then the customers will start wanting to trade with you." The dotcom fiasco may be over—but the Internet is still a child prodigy that has barely begun to reach its full potential in facilitating live models and real-time discussion.

CUSTOMIZING LIVE

Prototyping live begets customizing live. Both seek to optimize a product for a customer through iterative alterations, but customizing optimizes a product for an individual customer based on his or her needs and desires. While real-time feedback from customers can help new products and services fit the market better, many companies are getting from idea spark to revenue stream by giving customers the ultimate power to have it their way. Customization has been on the radar screen for several years, offering everything from custom-fit jeans to just-for-you vitamins. According to a study by Jupiter Research, almost 80 percent of all online services enable customers to personalize what they buy.[13] It's no longer a question of selling an average or an aggregate. It's about the seller asking the customer, "How can I make us both happy?"

Reflect.com, the online cosmetics and personal care business developed by Procter & Gamble, offers site visitors a questionnaire about skin type, fashion sensibilities, color preferences, and other beauty-related subjects. Customers' answers enable reflect.com to custom-design as many as 50,000 versions of cosmetics and fragrances, including customized packaging. The site has gone live with a strategy that is the opposite of that of Enron Online. Rather than commoditization and live pricing, reflect.com operates a live customization model.

Capital One leverages its "monster" information systems to elicit a lot of real-time input from customers on the design of products and services. Beyond customized functionality, Capital One can further its one-to-one marketing efforts by individualizing its image with an innovative approach to branding—customizing brands.

INVENTING HELP

Sometimes, the fastest way to go live is to let somebody else do it, especially if that somebody can leverage your ideas better than you can.

Traditional organizations tend to be rather stoic in that they'd rather do everything themselves, with as little help from outsiders as possible. H³s, however, usually don't hesitate to ask for help when they go live with a product or new venture. Seeking outside help is actually part of their launch and growth strategies. Rather than depending on their ability to deploy people and hard assets such as factories, delivery systems, and storefronts—they focus on managing information and creative talent while getting help with the rest. For some, when they can't get help, they invent it themselves. Here the

Figure 4.1   Traditional and Innovation-Based Relationship Models

Biotech Companies	Big Pharmaceutical Companies
High Risk	Low Risk
Low Resources ⇐ ⇐ ⇐ ⇐ ⇐ ⇐ ⇐ ⇐ ⇐ High Resources	
Science ⇒ ⇒ ⇒ ⇒ ⇒ ⇒ ⇒ ⇒ ⇒ ⇒ ⇒ Marketing/Sales	
Value ⇒ ⇒ ⇒ ⇒ ⇒ ⇒ ⇒ ⇒ ⇒ ⇒ ⇒ Profits	

message is clear: If you need to move fast because your window is closing, build the core competency and find someone with whom to partner, who can help on the rest of the going-live process.

The biotech industry provides an interesting example of how these relationships come together (see Figure 4.1). Large pharmaceutical companies, dubbed Big Pharmas (BPs) by the biotech crowd, tend to have huge stockpiles of money but few innovations in their pipelines. Conversely, the smaller biotech firms have relatively little cash, but they have built up pipelines that are engorged with innovation. Together, the big fish and the little fish have formed a food chain. The biotech firms do most of the research, discovery, and development, taking on most of the risk. To get much-needed cash and sales infrastructure, they typically license their new products to the BPs. Then the BPs do all of the marketing, selling, and distribution, taking on most of the reward.

But market dynamics are radically changing the flow, thanks to genomics, bioinformatics, and the Internet, which are all lowering barriers to entry and giving smaller biotechs more of an advantage. Relationships will change. The need for help will change. Personalized medicine will soon change pharmaceutical marketing. Random blockbuster success is giving way to the development of targeted applications and indications franchises. Blockbuster drugs will be giving way to individualized treatments. Customized products will require more bundled services. Focus on physicians will give way to

Figure 4.2   Contrast of Old and New Pharmaceutical Marketing Models

Old Model	New Model
Mega monolithic sales force	Multi-channel relationships
Large size and resources	Leveraged partnerships
Random blockbuster success	Targeted applications and indication franchises
Physician-focused	Integrated with patient
Product	Product and service bundles
Generic message	Patient-specific message

focus on patients. As a result, deployment of behemoth sales forces will give way to multi-channel relationships. Generic marketing messages will give way to patient-specific messages. Doctors already have less and less time to spend with BP sales reps. The Internet is leveling the playing field for biotechs by offering easier, cheaper, and more convenient access to doctors—and an Internet-based marketing relationship system is scalable without adding a lot more employee and technology overhead. In addition, this system gives biotechs the ability to capture data at every interaction point, which it can use to better manage development, production, and inventory (see Figure 4.2).

Some biotech companies have already begun to get wiser. Rather than paving the way for lots of BP payoffs, they have devised strategies to capture the value and keep the rewards of their hard work for themselves.

One alternative approach, developed over the past decade, is the use of contract sales organizations (CSOs), which is tantamount to "Rent-a-Rep," turning the typically fixed sales overhead into a variable cost with pay-as-you-go or pay-by-use plans.

Sam Waksal was a biotech pioneer in finding a way to hold onto the profits from ImClone's flagship products, such as C225, rather than have them siphoned off by a BP. As described earlier, he did what no other biotech ever dared to do: he refused to license out rights. Rather than take money from a BP just to support R&D, he raised enough on his own to fund sales and manufacturing infrastructure development.

With these trends under way, we will see more and more biotechs developing their own resources and building strengths to rival or even outdo big pharmaceutical companies. Conceivably, a biotech such as Millennium could buy a BP such as Merck by 2006. Sounds hard to believe, you say? In 2000, Quest, a then five-year-old communications upstart, bought the giant USWest. AOL bought Time Warner. It could happen. The Top Ten companies in pharma today are thirty years old or more. In ten years, Nathan Myhrvold predicts nine of them will be new companies.

GETTING IT THERE

Logistics have become so streamlined by the Web that some innovators are coming up with new, more efficient ways to move products out through the marketplace. Enron Online, for example, could move gas, electricity, and forest products to wherever these commodities are needed. The company actually took delivery of products it trades, a unique approach—unheard of in regular trading communities where traders act more as matchmakers. This way, it was the only trading company that could guarantee delivery of the goods.

Progressive Insurance sells and delivers more auto insurance policies over the Internet than all its rivals put together. And, thanks to the Internet, some smaller companies in remote locations now compete with the big boys, by reaching and developing relationships with a broad base of customers, efficiently managing sales, inventory, and distribution.

Innovation strategies are experiments. The strategy you go live with today has a limited lifecycle, just like the products you launch. In many industries, these lifecycles are getting shorter and shorter.

If your strategy is a good one, you become a target. You need to be a moving target.

For many H³s, innovation strategy is like a prototype: It is designed to be re-designed, with loose ends and holes intentionally left to keep some things open. That includes marketing strategy, creative strategy, development strategy, and portfolio management strategy.

As the leaders and innovators I talked to agree, the decisions in going live are weighted with the questions that inform a company's attitudes toward perfection, risk, customers, influencers, competitors and market forces, for example:

- How perfect does the product or service have to be before launch?
- How much information do you really need at each phase of development?
- How fast must you get the product to market?
- How and where can you make changes even as the product is in the process of being marketed?
- Is it better to first ask *where* do you want to play or *what* do you want to play with?
- What will you do with money you save or extra profits you earn? Will you plow it back into R&D, distribute it to employees and shareholders, or reward yourself with a vacation in the south of France?
- Is it a good idea to co-develop with customers or suppliers?
- Are you prepared to fail and keep trying?

Whatever innovation strategy you construct for bringing a new idea to life, it will be essential to determine just how integrated your systems, processes, communication lines, and people are or need to be. As we will see in the next chapter, "Integrated Circuitry," many H³s make it an art form—part business, part science, and part aesthetics.

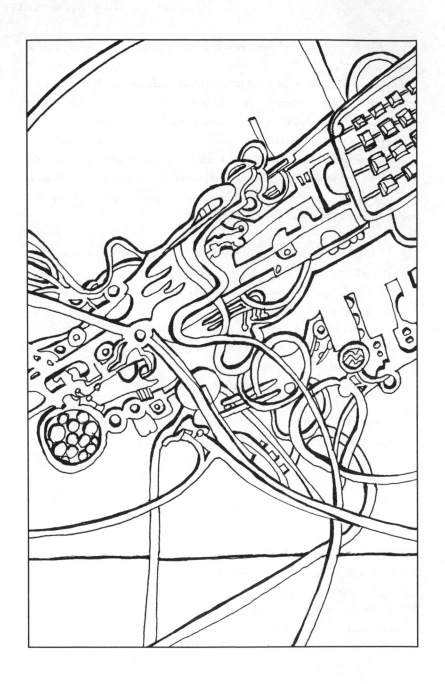

. 5 .

INTEGRATED CIRCUITRY

Mechanisms of Innovation Action

It began in an unpredictable way. The force of the Italian government converged with the power of art when Peggy Guggenheim, patron to avant-garde artists and a world-famous collector, died in 1979. For years, Guggenheim had tried to figure out what to do with her vast collection of paintings, manuscripts, and sculpture that she kept in her Venetian palazzo. Once she thought about giving it to the Tate Gallery, but when she went to London to work out a deal, government officials would not let her bring in her prized Dachshunds because of strict quarantine laws. That was not acceptable to her. Instead, Tom Messer, then director of the Guggenheim Museum in New York, convinced her to hand over not only her art collection but also the Venetian palazzo itself.

Messer's idea was to bring the art to New York where it would join the Solomon R. Guggenheim Collection, named for Peggy Guggenheim's uncle. But that vision was never realized due to a Venetian "roadblock." Contemplating a potentially huge loss, the

Italian government declared Peggy Guggenheim's collection a national treasure and forbade anyone from taking the art out of Venice. With that stroke, the Guggenheim Foundation became a de facto landlord. That became the seed for a new constellation—a new integrated museum system, unlike anything the art world has ever seen. The first of its kind to expand beyond the confines of one building, the Guggenheim has forced us all to rethink what an art museum is and does, thanks to the vision of Tom Krens.

When Tom Krens succeeded Messer as director of the Guggenheim in 1988, he decided to change the museum economy. He asked, "How can we make this the greatest museum in the entire world?" That was a gutsy question considering the fact that the museum was only drawing 350,000 visitors a year. Krens faced another key challenge: Great museums need great collections. But today, you can't collect as you could in the nineteenth century—there are no more kings and princes around handing over that kind of enormous wealth to commission artists or to build art collections.[1] So, Krens began to solve the problem in an innovative way. He set out to build a circuit of museums around the world, programming them with a sophisticated, elegant, and ambitious roll of exhibitions, including works from the Guggenheim's own collections, new assemblages, works of artists local to each outpost, and works from new alliance partners—great museums such as the Hermitage in St. Petersburg and the Kunsthistorisches Museum in Vienna. Krens expanded the framework of the museum, and a new model, which he calls a constellation, began to take shape.

"I see the Guggenheim as one institution that, by matter of geography and circumstance, happens to be disconnected or discontinuous gallery spaces in different parts of the world," Krens says. He sees the constellation as innovating both the concept of the art museum and the city in which each Guggenheim resides. As of 2001, there were seven Guggenheim Museums: two in New York City (Fifth Avenue and Soho), Venice, Bilbao, Berlin, and two in Las

Vegas. The original Guggenheim Museum on Fifth Avenue is a piece of "destination" architecture, a building to which visitors are attracted by the thousands simply for its own sake, like the Sydney Opera House, the Empire State Building, and the Tower of London. Designed by Frank Lloyd Wright in 1959, the Guggenheim on Fifth Avenue still looks sharply fresh—a radical spiral of white cement, curling upwards, like a corkscrew, through the grid of cubic, ornate pre-war and plain post-war buildings that surround it. With the addition of the new Guggenheim Museum, designed by Rem Koolhaas, which opened in Las Vegas in October 2001, and with plans under way for other museums with equal tourist appeal, including Frank Gehry's design for Manhattan's southern tip and one due to open in Las Vegas in the fall of 2001, the constellation is growing rapidly.

THE BILBAO EFFECT

In 1991, officials of Bilbao, Spain, and representatives of the Guggenheim Foundation held an international competition to determine the winning design for their own piece of destination architecture. The government wanted to transform the city from a sleepy, declining maritime town on the northern Basque coast to a modern metropolis and cultural center. "The Basques wanted to change their own economy," explains Frank Gehry, who created the brilliant design for the Guggenheim Museum Bilbao. "They decided, one day, that there was no reason in the world why they couldn't compete with the great cities of Barcelona and Madrid," Gehry explained. Setting their sights on tourists, they figured that they had better upgrade their local art museum.

Gehry's construction instantly and profoundly changed the economy of the entire region. Within a few months of the museum's opening, the government fully recouped its entire investment. After one year, the museum tripled original attendance projections and generated over $198 million in revenues. New profit streams poured in for the local owners of restaurants, hotels, and shops. Flights to the new airport carry over 1 million visitors who otherwise would never have come to Bilbao. A new subway system transports them to the museum. This phenomenon—the "Bilbao Effect"—became the flashpoint for the stellar Guggenheim constellation.

Suddenly representatives of other cities—from Los Angeles to Geelong, from Buenos Aires to Bendigo—started asking, "Why can't we have a Bilbao?" Gehry has been flooded with calls, while Krens has received over one hundred invitations from cities around the world to bring the Bilbao magic to their soil. One of the museums slated is planned to be built in New York City—a $1.5 billion, 570,000-square-foot complex supplemented by 279,000 square feet of public parks and gardens. Financed in part by private donors, in part by the city of New York, the structure is to be built on new land—a man-made extension of Manhattan into the East River. Plans call for thirty-six galleries, a 1,200-seat theater, a sculpture garden on its own adjacent island with its own ferry, an ice skating rink, a mammoth light-filled atrium, a center for arts education, and a trove of executive offices. The project is expected to create over 2,500 jobs, attract millions of visitors, and generate $280 million annually in economic activity, plus another $14 million in tax revenues for the city. The new Guggenheim could be a major contribution to the rebuilding of lower Manhattan after the attacks of September 11, 2001, creating a "Bilbao Effect" even in one of the most developed and "over-museumed" cities in the world.

Today the Guggenheim constellation is bringing in an enviable heap of revenue. Beyond the cash brought in by admission tickets, gift shop and food sales, companies such as BMW, Hugo Boss, Enron, Target, and Nokia have been eager to supply major sponsorships and advertising dollars. Bilbao has paid over $20 million in "franchise" fees, and other cities have committed even more.

Beyond achieving great economic benefits, Krens began to solve one of the biggest problems all museums face: Large or small, museums have enough wall space to display only about 3 percent of their collections. They keep the remainder in their basements or storage facilities an extremely inefficient way of handling inventory. With 250,000 square feet of wall space in Bilbao and hundreds of thousands more in the other Guggenheims, the constellation has succeeded beyond Krens's wildest dreams, reaching an untold number of people with an unprecedented number of the Guggenheim's treasures. Artworks from each collection rotate through the other museum locations. By leveraging each collection, millions of people, not all of whom are lucky enough to be in Venice, for example, can see paintings they might otherwise not be able to see. With each of these strategic moves, Krens has substantially built up both the collection and the Guggenheim brand.

Critics call it "McGuggenheim." In their view, the Guggenheim is becoming less and less about "real" art. Museums, critics say, are not hamburger joints and were never meant to be franchised and branded. As they trounce recent exhibits presenting the Art of the Motorcycle or the Giorgio Armani retrospective, detractors say that Krens has sold out, that he is becoming too commercial.

The critics' cynicism doesn't faze Krens. The Guggenheim brand brings great art to the masses without dumbing it down. Although his views may shock some art critics and connoisseurs, Krens sees no difference between the art of an ancient Greek vase and that of a motorcycle, and none between the art of an Egyptian mummy wrapped in strips of linen and that of an Armani ensemble. He sniffs at the derogatory connotations some attribute to the word "brand." His brand is not about the efficiency of uniformity, but about a connected power of stellar contemporary art museums. "I think the metaphor of the constellation is appropriate," he says, "because each one of the stars has a particular character. The idea is not so much to create new branches of the same museum, but to pull together new stars, each with an independent unique vision. Some are small. Some are large. But when one connects the dots between the five points, that forms another identity."

If one measure of a museum's success is the size of its audience, Krens's constellation is far ahead of the competition. With the Las Vegas museums completed, the Guggenheim audience is expected to reach as many as 6 million people a year. "That would put us Number One in the United States," Krens says. To put that figure into perspective, consider that the British Museum—albeit a single institution, but one with over 7 million items in its collection—had only 5.5 million visitors in 2000.[2] Ever expanding the circuits, Krens has created a virtual museum on the Internet at guggenheim.com, a private company established in May 2000 as a partnership with GE Capital, the Tokyo-based holding company, Softbank, and Pequot Capital Management. He has transformed an also-ran museum into a major cultural phenomenon, a white-hot, integrated circuit—a system where information, ideas, art works, and creative energy flow constantly and freely through various interconnected channels, generating the power to change economies and move hundreds of millions of people simply, yet grandly, by showing them art. Sponsored by his host cities, Krens has done it all without spending a penny of the museum's own cash.

Nothing is created in a vacuum. Innovation comes from connectivity, intersection, and the integration of ideas. We all draw on our own experiences, feelings, emotions, and perceptions. As we connect with others, these come together to form new patterns. Ideas merge to form new ideas. Generally, the more diverse and numerous those data points are, and the better they are interconnected, the more creative the entire system becomes.

The power of integrated circuits is illustrated further in new ideas about managing and mining valuable innovation assets such as knowledge and ideas. In the last decade, information technology has been advancing exponentially. We can now store, organize, and access immense quantities of data. For example, information science and biology have teamed up to create a new circuit called bioinformatics, giving us an explosive capability to create new drugs, find new cures, and perhaps eventually modify human DNA to avoid certain diseases or conditions.

But it's not just information that is flowing through these circuits. Marketing and funding also form a part of the current. Buyers can be instantly connected to sellers and enablers in ways that light fires for innovation. In fact, entire innovation ecosystems and creative economies are forming as companies such as Palm win with new concepts in relationship management, targeting, and system metrics.

CREATIVE ECONOMIES

Creative people and organizations form creative configurations—an "ecosystem" in which new forces interact in nontraditional ways. Beyond the Internet and intranets, these systems capture, organize, harness, and enable a healthy flow of information and ideas. Integrated circuits carry the power of customers, suppliers, colleagues, friends, and outside experts. Some form clusters, loosely analogous to the Japanese keiretsus. Some are fed by angels or incubators, who inject financial fuel or provide strategic support. One-to-one or many-to-many, they are protean and constantly adapting.

An *economy* can be defined as a marketplace, an integrated circuit of buyers, sellers, traders, suppliers, regulators, distributors, merchants, and investors. While each group has its own circuits, the trading of goods and services relies on the degree of integration among them. Economies that are more creative tend to have a greater diversity of players and more of them. Their roles are changing, both in context and dynamics. The interrelationships among the various players are more permeable and flexible than they normally are with traditional organizations and relationships. The give-and-take goes beyond typical market transactions to include ideas, expertise, and support.

The Palm Economy

Palm has over 150,000 smart, motivated creative people working for it, while fewer than 2,000 of them are on its payroll. The symbiotic relationship works: This talented pool generated more than $1.5 billion in sales in 2000, a one-year growth rate of approximately 50 percent.[3]

Satjiv Chahil, chief marketing officer, calls it the "Palm Economy," but essentially it is an innovation network. As he explains, "We expand virtually into the world. Much innovation and development comes from people outside our company, from developers, service providers, consultants, even communities. We encourage people to share our vision and join in the opportunity."

At SPWI, we help our clients build such innovation networks, including both internal and external, core, and fringe domains. This network includes customers, suppliers, competitors, regulators, and a group selected from our Leading-Edge Expert Network[sm] (LEEN), some of whom are considered as "core" participants, whereas others in the same categories may be seen as more peripheral. A true innovation network seeks to establish clear lines of communication among participants.

Ecology of Services

The number of services that touch our personal lives is astounding. They include everything from utilities to lawn mowing, legal advice to manicures. John Seely Brown calls their aggregate an "ecology" of services: They support us, we support them, and we all somehow coexist in the same general space. The busier our lives, the more services we use in our own microcosms. If you consider all the time and energy spent on managing these services—assessing needs, searching and hiring, informing, billing, organizing, scheduling, troubleshooting, dealing with problems, negotiating, managing paperwork, monitoring—there are many tasks that may not need our particular expertise, not to mention tasks we'd rather not do.

One person's personal services bundle, for example, could easily include the following:

Utilities	Media	Childcare
Housekeeping	Landscaping	Financial services
Mail delivery	Dry cleaning and laundry	Hair care
Nail care	Skin care	Repair services
Insurances	Car maintenance	Shopping services
Pet care	Health care	Security services
Design services	Subscription services	Home maintenance
Transportation services	Spiritual services	Government services
Employment services	Education services	Pest control
Information services	Catering services	Personal trainer
Piano tuning	Real estate services	Counseling services
Entertainment services	Photography services	Answering services
Prescription services	Meal management services	Ski sharpening
Bike tune-up	Delivery services	Wake-up services
Eldercare	Legal services	Tax and accounting services
Travel services	Dating services	Communications services

And this is only a *partial* list!

I often think about what life would be like if I had one smart, capable mega-service that could integrate and manage all of these service relationships for me. All I would have to do is manage one service relationship. Even an ace personal assistant can't manage all of that alone. Just thinking about the possibility momentarily lifts about 5,000 pounds off my shoulders. I fantasize about the zillions of things I could do with all that "free" time.

Building an ecology of services around the workplace frees up many resources for more productive, pleasurable activities such as innovating. The more services to manage, the more we need aggregation. John Seely Brown and his colleagues at 12 Entrepreneuring, a new-business incubator specializing in developing new-business ecologies, have started two companies based on this concept: Grand Central, which integrates business processes and delivers shared services among customers, vendors, and partners via the Internet; and iBuilding, which manages renters, contractors, subcontractors, and all building services for large commercial buildings.

While most companies concentrate on their own organizations, Brown and his colleagues are focusing on the "white spaces" between companies within ecological systems or industries. Brown is intent on actually getting these companies to work together productively. That's where he thinks most of the opportunity is now—in the spaces between knowledge pools, the spaces between disciplines. Creating innovative networks in those spaces relies on a fully integrated circuitry among the participants. In some cases, achieving that integration will require reengineering entire industries, but it can create tremendous new value.

Consider the healthcare industry, for instance. Some have estimated that over a third of all healthcare spending is wasted because of duplication and inefficient record-keeping and because companies operate on different systems. With different vocabularies and different ways of viewing the world, they cannot communicate with each other effectively. We visit a doctor, who sends our blood samples to a testing lab. From there the information returns to the physician, perhaps taking a detour to an insurance company—shuttling from department to department there and finally back to us. The headache or danger of a breakdown is unfortunately something many of us can understand from personal experience. A network

with fully integrated circuits reduces the possibility of such an occurrence, or at least lessens its severity. An integrated network can
also reduce cost, reduce cycle time, and increase innovation.

The Cancer Economy

Other major economies have grown up around diseases, particularly cancer, and include many circuits: doctors, nurses, patients,
pharmaceutical companies, advertising agencies, the media, the
FDA and other regulatory agencies, hospitals and their employees,
medical schools, insurance providers, R&D labs, universities, medical device and diagnostics device companies, diagnostic laboratories, social workers, prosthesis manufacturers, medical supply companies, pharmacists, physical therapists, home-health aides,
medical journals and other publications, fund raisers, associations,
lobbyists, cadavers, religious and political organizations, rehabilita-
tion centers, hospices, support groups, medical waste companies,
clergy, lawyers, investors, donors, volunteers, and lab mice. For
better or worse, all of these are integrated to form the cancer economy, which itself intersects with other economies, some focused on
the living and others on the death economy.

As pointed out, innovation occurs when two or more different
circuits connect. This principle is illustrated in the work that Dr.
Sujuan Ba, director of the National Foundation for Cancer Research, and Dr. Graham Richards, of Oxford University, are doing
in cancer research. They have found a new way to integrate, giving
them computing power and capacity never before achieved. Ba and
Richards realized that every time a computer sits idle, its brainpower
is rendered useless. Imagine what could be done if the power of all
idle computers could be linked together and used in conducting research and analyzing the billions of pieces of data about proteins involved in cancer research.

Ba and Richards teamed up with Intel, United Devices, and the

American Cancer Society to create a means of harnessing that power, which the owner of any idle computer can "donate" voluntarily. Running on supercharged tracks, THINK software enables researchers to analyze data in order to determine whether a specific molecule will bind to a protein and become a prospective cancer killer. The faster researchers can perform the analysis, the faster a cure might be found.

If you decide to donate your idle computer's brainpower, THINK works in the background much like a screen-saver. It kicks into gear whenever your computer meets certain criteria for "idle." Joined with thousands, perhaps millions, of other computers through a live link on the Internet, it crunches away at the data, screening the molecular possibilities. Receiving data in real time, the research team estimates that it can access about fifty teraflops of computer power, the equivalent of 6 million researchers working at the same time on the same project. The team already has 250 million molecules ready to screen, yielding as many as 10,000 prospects for a cure.[4] Although Oxford University will own the data, it promises to give free access to other researchers, thus expanding potential development even more. Of course, what we call "cancer" is actually over 400 different diseases, for which it is unlikely there is a single "cure." The potential breakthroughs as a result of high-tech investigations with microarrays and other innovations continuing to inspire the researchers and promote new discoveries.

Whoever makes the best use of the data wins. If a cure is found, we all win.

POWER GRIDS

The approximately 275 million people in the United States are connected in one giant grid, one of the biggest "machines" on earth. Every time we plug an appliance into an electrical socket or turn on the lights, our electricity comes through a network of wires stretching thousands of miles in all directions. Wattage can be generated anywhere and added to the reservoir. Someone in Tacoma turns on a lamp and accesses the same electrical reservoir as someone in Miami using a blow dryer. Electricity from one wire flows into the next, following the path of least resistance until a substation or a router determines that California needs more power or the air conditioners are running overtime in Atlanta. An excess of electricity flowing in or out can cause a short, leaving people into the dark. The Grid is balanced across 150 control stations across the country, monitored and adjusted at each, to match supply with demand as it changes constantly.

An innovation power grid operates in much the same way. Too much input or output, and the grid becomes overloaded and unproductive; too much bureaucracy or management, and people in the organization may develop a resistance to the system. According to John Seely Brown, 80 percent of designing knowledge management (KM) systems involves adapting to the social dynamics of the workplace, and only 20 percent involves technology as an enabling mechanism. Social flows and technologic flows share similar dynamics.

People operate from different power bases with different systems and practices. When the grid lines don't match up with each other, huge costs are gobbled up because there is no flow between entities.

But imagine if there were . . .

CONFLUENT FLOWS

In fiery ribbons of traffic, like the vibrating garlands of headlights along the autobahn at night, the impulses race at blinding speed. Billions of bits of information, ideas, questions, answers, experiments, and sales zip among more than 20,000 employees of Capital One Financial Services, through its clusters of integrated call centers. Responses to all customer calls come within an average of thirty seconds at Capital One, which is one of the top three credit card issuers in the world (the other two are Citibank and MBNA). Like flooring a Maserati, it's fun to work there. That's part of what makes ideas fly through the bank's proprietary information-based strategy (IBS). Capital One has information in its systems on tens of millions of households in the United States. Marge Connelly, executive vice president of operations, describes the entrepreneurial culture and collaborative setting, in which employees continually create, share, and develop innovate ideas. Much of the IT buzz you hear today from other H³s about concepts such as customer relationship management programs (CRM), data mining, and smart call-routing was born out of Capital One's management innovations.

Linking operations to customer service, and process to infrastructure, Connelly heads up both card operations and IT infrastructure. She is the executive board member who "owns" customer service, sales, credit processing, back-office operations (for example, payment processing, and statement rendering), and IT systems, including network management, data centers, and the Internet.

Most organizations don't combine these domains under one governor. That Connelly oversees it all says a lot about Capital One's integrating its idea and resource flows. "We're not constrained to think of one place as central," she says. The customer is touched by every part of the organization, and everyone in the company is responsible for the customer experience. There are agents, such as language and niche product specialists, who specialize in certain types of customer calls. Requests for applications, credit line and payment inquiries, balance verifications, complaints, and on-line assistance come in droves. Amazingly, within a split second of a customer's punching the final digit of Capital One's phone number, the system identifies who is calling, predicts why he or she is calling and what else that customer might be interested in, then decides which agent receives the call, based on expertise and availability.

Capital One's integrated circuits handle a load of $35.3 billion in managed loans and over 38.1 million accounts (as of July 17, 2001). That base expands daily with some 25,000 new customers. Capital One answers over 1 million phone calls a week, catching patterns when they are still wisps, pushing forth streams of new ideas and turning them into gold. The financial giant, for instance, pioneered the introductory-rate credit card; cross-promotions through strategic partnerships with non-credit card businesses, which now account for over half of annual sales; and mass-customization. Capital One has thousands of distinct product offerings, 80 percent of which are less than two years old.

PUSHING ELECTRONS

Idea flow is the movement of possibilities—the way in which thoughts move from randomness to pattern, from observation to recognition, from insight to design and execution. Data is transformed into knowledge and knowledge is transformed into ideas. The central problem is movement. It is defined by what is held, what is used, what stays, what gets stuck, and what leaks out. It is the way resources move through innovation circuits, around impediments, responding to friction and gaps, losing ground or gaining traction.

How do you know when it's better to speed up or better to slow down?

Speed was the mantra of the New Economy. Purportedly, the faster one moved, the faster one could grow, the faster one could reach success. The problem was that for many, their speed was reckless. They floored the accelerator without thinking about the consequences of their choices. They moved on scanty information, flimsy business models, and products that weren't ready for Prime Time. They forgot about profitability. They defied the laws of economics and succumbed to the law of gravity, crashing hard.

While in many cases speed is an advantage, many of the most innovative people are more concerned about increasing the quality,

---

EMC² AND THE SERVICE PIECE
OF THE CIRCUIT

EMC² products were failing miserably and the company was on the verge of bankruptcy when Mike Ruettgers took over as executive vice president of operations and customer service in 1988. Since the company specialized in data storage systems central to large institutions' operations, such as a bank's transaction data system or a retailer's running sales and inventory data system, one mistake could shut down everything in an instant. And, back then, the circuits were often breaking down.

To turn things around, Ruettgers offered to replace a client's storage system products, for free, with either a new EMC² system or a new one from his toughest competitor, IBM. It was a brazen move, to be sure. EMC² paid for its mistakes by shipping more IBM systems in 1989 than it did its own.

But Ruettgers's approach to customer service lifted the company up from near death, with a net loss of almost $8 million on sales of $123 million, to almost $9 billion in annual sales and a stock market valuation of about $70 billion, within a mere ten years. Now, EMC² claims its customer retention rate is 99 percent.

EMC² manages to keep these integrated circuits healthy by "mirroring," a protocol in which large client systems are cloned and set up in EMC²'s $1 billion simulation facility. Engineers can work with the same equipment, configurations, and networks that they have installed at a client's facility. They see the exact same problem that their client

---

integrity, and power of the flow of resources and communications. They build organizational systems in which speed is a function of efficiency, alignment with stakeholders, and relationship strength.

COMMUNAL LINES AND
BOUNDARY OBJECTS

One of the reasons why innovation is so hard to achieve is the lack of flow between individuals and between what John Seely Brown calls

is seeing and can work on the mirror image of the set-up immediately, to trouble-shoot the problem and construct a solution—all within hours.

EMC² also has an internal circuit in which customer problems are centrally dispatched and managed to make sure everyone is in the loop. The process can begin with a customer's machine sensing a problem during one of its routine self-diagnostic scans and sending an SOS signal to an EMC² machine. EMC² fields about 3,500 of such calls each day. If the problem cannot be automatically solved, it goes to customer service engineers. If they can't solve it in four hours, it gets kicked upstairs to tech support. If the problem is still around after six hours, the senior vice president of global customer services is called in. At eight hours, Ruettgers, now executive chairman, knows that his phone will ring.

Besides offering customers other companies' products, if that's what it takes to make them happy, EMC² also routinely fixes problems caused by competitors' equipment. EMC² doesn't charge a dime or register a complaint. This part of the operation is not about profit. It is about keeping the customer up and running, regardless of the cost to EMC². Ruettgers believes profit and service motives conflict. The system he designed intentionally keeps them apart. "It is service at all costs," Ruettgers explains.

Ruettgers helped to design this customer service strategy, not only to keep his customers happy, but also to integrate the feedback into EMC²'s product development process. His design places service technicians and engineers in the same workspace, unlike other companies where they reside separately. The customer's problem is the engineer's problem, immediately.

"communities of practice," such as engineering or research and development. As he explains:

Within the community of practice that creates innovation, there is such a fine-grained reading of each other that you really have to know how to trust each other, what to trust each other with, who to trust, and so forth. You work in this magnificent way. It's like a basketball team where you are constantly improvising, compensating for each other. You can have a powerful, positive collision of crafts or a creative abrasion, such as what happens when material science, optics, communications, and computer guys bump up against each other. One might say, "If that's too hard for you, if you are trying get the physics to do too much for you, let me compensate by bringing in some information control technology." Or, "If that algorithm is too complicated, let me try to get the physics to do more work for you." There are very subtle, incredibly interesting handoffs to get the right balance.

For example, if I have an idea for a vertical cavity laser, a whole series of very tricky crafts have to come together. I ship it off to engineering and say, "Here is the concept, you have to make it work. This is really bulletproof stuff. This is *technology-ready*"— which is *the* magic word—and the chief engineer looks at me and says, "Sure, John, what the hell do you know about manufacturing? You researchers think *anything* is ready to be manufactured. You don't have *any* idea what it means to make this!"

The worldview of manufacturing is distinct from that of research; the shared practices of one are different from those of the other. In an ideal world, there is flow between crafts: Everybody talks to each

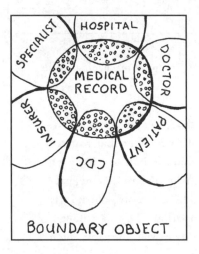

BOUNDARY OBJECT

other along the development way. With an artifact or prototype, the manufacturer might say, "You know, if you could make this change to the arm, it would make things a lot better for me." And you might say, "Not really, because if you manufacture it this way, it will cause other problems for me." This prototype becomes what Brown calls a "boundary object," which facilitates innovation development flow. It is a focal point of cooperation and interactive communication for everyone in the innovation process—across organizational and cultural boundaries.

A medical record, for example, is a boundary object among hospitals, nurses, doctors, insurance providers, and others in the healthcare economy. When improvisation happens, these providers, acting together, figure out new solutions. That same system, however, can become a political barrier, as when a manufacturer says, "I won't even check on that thing until you do what I say." And then the innovation process comes to a standstill. The boundary process in that culture is not enabling. It actually restricts improvisations. In a creative culture, however, boundary objects can facilitate a creative dance that results in delighting the marketplace.

VECTORS

Beyond improving internal innovation flows, many H³s have found new vectors for boosting the flow of ideas into the marketplace. They often start with *lead users*, the first kids on your block to get a scooter, or the first of your friends to eat goat cheese, the first to try Echinacea or get a PDA. Their current needs are the future trends for the rest of us. Lead users can help an idea gain traction before potential competitors even feel the vibrations. They know how to get the most out of a product: They push it to its limits and beyond, they provide early design input and feedback, and they are happy to share their opinions, advise the followers, and spread the buzz. This has the power to speed up the traditional adoption cycle from early users to mass markets, by spreading the word fast, exemplifying the "law of the few," which Malcolm Gladwell contends is behind a hot new idea's popularity: It begins to spread through the "efforts of a handful of exceptional people."[5]

Buzz is contagious communication that infiltrates communities, like an extensive rumor mill. On a mammoth scale, it underlies such phenomena as the *Blair Witch Project* and Napster. Providing the perfect conditions for the rapid, exponential replication of messages, the Internet more than any other medium reaches the most receptive people. An idea can begin with one person and conceivably infect a whole population within minutes.

A kind of buzz was stoked in the Naples heat in the spring of 2001. Hundreds of copies of Lou Reed's face looked out onto the ancient Italian city from the walls and billboards, on which his portraits were pasted, announcing the opening of photographer Timothy Green-

field-Sanders's twenty-year retrospective exhibition. Everyone wanted to see Greenfield-Sanders's extraordinary portraits of Reed, David Bowie, Orson Welles, Willem de Kooning, Yves St. Laurent, Nicole Kidman, Tom Hanks, and scores of other celebrities. Unfortunately, buzz also fueled the greed of some star-struck bandits who hijacked the truck carrying the entire collection of the photographs to the site. No photos, no show. The buzz grew even louder—more and more people were gaining more and more interest in seeing the show. A ransom was paid, and the show went on. "For me it was a happy ending," Greenfield-Sanders says. "A thousand people came to the opening night—many more than ever before for one of my exhibitions."

Steve Jurvetson, managing director of the venture capital firm Draper Fisher Jurvetson, coined the phrase "viral marketing" in 1997, to describe Hotmail's strategy: piggybacking a promotion for its services onto each e-mail sent through its system.[6] Predating this event, evolutionist Richard Dawkins originated the concept of the *meme,* an idea that replicates itself like a living organism, growing and evolving as it passes from one person to another.[7] Hotmail's self-replicating promotion created an epidemic, bringing the company from zero to 12 million customers in just eighteen months—with zero marketing budget.

According to Seth Godin in *Unleashing the Ideavirus* and Emanuel Rosen in *The Anatomy of Buzz*, the marketer releases a relatively minute new "thought-virus" into the carrier/host environment—the Internet.[8] On the Internet, these thought-viruses spread through e-mail, instant messages, bulletin boards, and chat rooms, behaving much like destructive viruses, except that they spread mostly to those who *really* want them, not to those who don't. The Internet is the perfect breeding ground, spurring rapid, exponential replication, as the thought-virus tears through the world from lead users to last followers. It's fast. It's pandemic. And it's free.

Given the exponential size of the potential audience, the idea can grow into a major cultural movement or become simply a fad. Fads, of course, are not new phenomena. What is new is the viral strategy and tactics deployed to exploit this aspect of consumer psychology and new technology—to engage in "hyper word-of-mouth."

For buzz to lead to significant profits, companies need a multi-channel strategy. Palm, for example, connects with customers at hundreds of thousands of contact points through dozens of vectors, including the web, telephone, retail stores, events, trade shows, and educational seminars. The company also monitors websites such as epinions.com and planetfeedback.com to find out what people are saying about its products and services—to make sure the buzz out there is good.

"Free" has always been a good buzzword, especially for fueling and driving new offerings. Microsoft gave away 450,000 copies of Windows 95 before selling it on the market. Dwarfing all Internet service provider competition, AOL blanketed the landscape with free floppies and free hours to build up its base of customers, a market-ing tactic that the company continues to use frequently. Many other new companies, however, have found the "free" tactic disastrous be-cause they failed to figure out where their profits would come from.

INFLOWS

Some H³s turn the tide. In addition to putting their products and messages out into the world, they become the "perfect host," devel-oping a coffee klatch among interested users. Instead of crumbcake or jelly doughnuts, the new breed offers Web fare such as commu-nity portals and bulletin boards. Without spending much on mar-keting or sales, these H³s find they can attract customers at practi-cally no cost. Sales efforts shift to customers who help to sell themselves and each other. Leveraging inflows becomes a key inno-vation strategy.

Imagine: The phone rings, interrupting your dinner. You do what millions of other people do: You answer it, then you get an-noyed by some telemarketer wanting to make a sale, not caring that you were in the middle of sipping your soup. Telemarketers are not your friends or your family. They shouldn't be invading your home and bothering you. No one but a telemarketer really loves a tele-marketing company.

Capital One found a better way: by leveraging inflow—that is, in-coming calls—as a way to generate sales. Why call people when they don't want to be bothered? Why not use all of the information al-ready harvested, align it with incoming calls, and sell to customers when *they* call in? The cost of sales on an incoming call is negligible as opposed to the expense of telemarketing, and it's much easier to score a hit when the target comes to you. While telemarketing may work at some level to make sales or acquire new customers, it is an expensive and often not cost-effective way of doing business. Capital One has found that leveraging its incoming calls avoids many of the drawbacks to telemarketing while it builds stronger relationships with customers. Capital One developed the means to glean more information about customer preferences and attitudes and used it to predict what else the customer might want to buy now or in the future. By 2001, Capital One had turned this innovation—inbound selling—into a completely new revenue stream. Although some companies such as American Express have engaged in "upselling" and "cross-selling" for many years, what Capital One is going is quite different: It is selling new products, including many outside the financial services industry, to existing customers who call in with questions about their credit cards.

Another form of inflow is backflow. After centuries of conducting business designed to enhance the well-being and convenience of the corporation, after pushing products and technologies based on R&D and marketing departments' inclinations, it finally dawned on managers that getting feedback from customers would be a good idea. As this approach proved successful, new techniques sprang up to help bring the Voice of the Customer (VOC) to the company. The Internet became a "killer app" for VOC, making it exponentially easier, faster, cheaper, and more measurable to research VOC. And companies could tailor responses to customers' voices. One-to-one marketing enabled an even closer, tighter Voice-Response relationship. NBC's *Today* show now invites viewers to vote for their favorites among everything from wedding ring design to dress to cake and honeymoon destination in order to determine the arrangements for a real couple's actual wedding—which appears on the *Today* show, sponsored, of course, by the jewelers, dressmakers, travel services, and so forth. This is more than mere polling. In this case the television audience is designing the wedding from start to finish, using someone else's money, namely NBC's. It's a new form of marketing with a democratic twist.

Warning: Listening *too closely* to your customers is as dangerous as listening too closely to yourself. Most customers will only tell you about ideas that are a slight modification of what you already have.

They form wish lists for improvements based on their own experiences with an existing product: Make it bigger, cheaper, faster, easier, safer, or prettier. They are not likely to give you the next equivalent to the light bulb, the telephone, or the drug to cure cancer.

We search for those future *eurekas,* combing through industry trends. But discovery is probably going to involve trends outside of a given industry. Integrating with parallel or peripheral industries can yield undiscovered patterns that can lift you to a new edge. They can create new neural pathways, extending beyond our self-editing brains and nervous systems, allowing us to think of a new idea that will shape the future—the way it happened when Corning invented fiber optics, when Transmeta melded hardware/software solutions in the Crusoe Chip, and when Robert Wilson merged the worlds of opera, choreography, and architectural design.

NEW TOUCHPOINTS

In research programs discussed earlier, increasing the number and diversity of inputs greatly increases creative capacity, flow, and likelihood for success. Including people with different experiences and knowledge bases helps expand perspectives, opening up new opportunities and new solutions to old or new problems. Beyond connecting in specific studies, some H³s integrate various touchpoints into their innovation systems. For example, Xerox PARC integrates young people and artists-in-residence into its research programs. The London Business School's i:Lab and the MIT Media Lab are regular crash pads for assorted cutting-edge musicians, artists, designers, filmmakers, and game developers. Students and crashers give each other feedback, experiment together, and meld minds. They trade business ideas, technical ideas, and ideas about art. They expand the circuit by more broadly defining the "stakeholder."

The traditional definition of *stakeholder* includes shareholders, employees, and customers. "That's too narrow a view," says David Cole.

"If those are the only constituencies that you are paying attention to, you're failing to live up to the leadership potential that's in you. You need to understand and strengthen the communities in which you operate. Strong, healthy communities result in healthy employees, healthy consumers, and, in fact, healthy shareholders." A broader definition of what a stakeholder is helps to sensitize leaders to the impact of their decisions. It also puts them on a different learning curve. "It informs your decision making in new ways," says Cole.

Cole's point is well illustrated in the food industry. Most innovations in food production and processing have centered on reducing cost, increasing yield, and extending shelf life. These benefits can touch both producers, who widen profit margins, and consumers, who get cheaper, more abundant food. They can also result in problems at every level of the ecosystem. All things being equal, wouldn't you rather eat an apple that is naturally produced rather than one genetically modified, aided by herbicides, pesticides, and chemical fertilizers? While comparisons at present are typically un-equal—organic foods still are more expensive than traditionally grown items—the costs are coming down dramatically, making them accessible to more and more people.

Instead of looking for natural solutions to cost, yield, and spoilage problems, the food industry has typically pursued chemical innovations, without making long-range health and environmental impacts the highest priority. The industry seems out of touch with new demographic and psychographic trends, showing organic food to be the fastest growing specialty foods category in the United States. With an average annual growth rate of 24 percent through-out the last decade, American retail sales of organic food are esti-mated to grow from $8 billion in 2000 to nearly $20 billion in 2005.[9] Although that is still a small piece of the $400 billion food industry in the United States, there is a lot of reason to believe that organic food will keep gaining ground at a steep rate. A survey con-ducted by the Hartman Group found that 10 million Americans bought organic food in 1999 and another 60 percent were ready to try it. Their reasons: Organic foods are safer, healthier, and more environmentally friendly than other foods.[10] Sales of packaged organic food (as distinguished from organic fruits and vegetables), already at $3.5 billion in 2001, were expected to expand even faster, enjoying growth rates of 30 percent annually over the next four years.[11]

Cole broadens his view of stakeholders to include communities associated with agricultural production, health care, and future generations. All are members of the stakeholder group he needs to touch—well beyond the consumer who buys a can of soup or box of cereal. Accordingly, Acirca is plugged into the larger network of circuits, helping Cole to build an international family of organic brands under the umbrella brand of Walnut Acres. In this regard, Acirca is poised to become as wide-reaching as Kraft or Frito-Lay.

Where there is a strong brand, there is a strong set of touchpoints. People are compelled to connect with that company's branded products. Welch's, for example, keeps this at the core of all of its innovation initiatives. "No one else can come out with a white grape baby juice," explains Welch's CEO, Dan Dillon. "No one else has the brand name for that. If there is going to be a baby juice and it's going to be grape juice, it's going to be Welch's. No one else can do it better than we can—not Tropicana, not Dole, not even Gerber." Of course, that doesn't prevent any of these companies from deciding to compete in that market, but no one has seriously done so. Welch's strong brand name has so far kept the competitors at bay.

One of the big factors in the dotcom bombs was the lack of established brands. Despite the new focus on customer relationship management (CRM) and one-to-one attention, many dotbombs fell because they had little basis for a relationship in the first place: Most people never heard of their new brands, did not know enough about them to trust them, and had an uneasy feeling about what might or might not be behind the curtain. These new companies had to spend a fatally disproportionate amount of cash on marketing just to get their brand names out, and all of their hip names and cool logos never really touched anyone meaningfully. Instead they passed through our consciousness like a breeze through a screen door. There were lots of "hits" but few connections.

Many of these young companies underestimated the value of brand equity as well as the resources required to build up an unknown brand. The dotcoms played in a market space—the Internet—where it is easier to find and switch to a cheaper brand or a more novel brand and it is easier to get any brand regardless of geography. In other words, they played in a market that discourages customer brand loyalty.

Amazon.com and Yahoo are two relatively young Net-based companies that are exceptional in that they were able to establish phenomenal brands with worldwide recognition, and they are still alive and kicking, yet they are still far from being profitable. Even many long-standing, traditional companies missed the mark. They didn't realize how valuable and how important their established brands were. Despite understanding the benefits of brand leverage, they didn't "get" how the Internet worked. Many made the same mistakes that dotbombs did, trying to establish new and separate brands, which were not in touch with their customers, as K-mart did with bluefly.com. In contrast, Capital One attracted millions of customers by leveraging its brand, tailoring and presenting itself a little differently to hundreds of extremely narrow niches. Tom Krens figured out how to build the Guggenheim brand by developing an integrated circuit of museums in the "unbrandable" world of art. And now, most brick-and-mortar companies that have a Net-presence do leverage their established brands, using the Internet as simply another channel of distribution for their existing branded products and services. For example, walmart.com is just another Wal-Mart.

In a number of research projects, MIT Media Lab investigates the flows and interplays between a range of touchpoints within a variety of contexts. Joe Paradiso leads investigations into responsive environments, looking at different kinds of sensing modalities and technologies to create smart spaces. The Lab's work in responsive intelligence can be applied to everything from interactive media and art to smart highways and climate control. Tod Machover's group focuses on inventing musical instruments that are so in touch and integrated that they "understand" the intentions of the performer.

"I need to dialogue with an audience," says Philip Glass. "There are constant transactions. It really feeds into the music." Arguably the most renowned contemporary living composer today, Glass has built up a body of work that spans five decades and was created largely through myriad touchpoints and collaborations. Ranging through work with African, Brazilian, Native American, East Indian, and Portuguese cultures, Glass touches many sources to create his compositions. "My dream in life was to reach a point where I could collaborate with anyone I wanted," says Glass. His original collaboration with Robert Wilson in *Einstein on the Beach* is widely considered to be the flashpoint for both artists' success.

New networks such as these enable a multidirectional flow of creative energy through a vast collection of touchpoints. They elevate the level of access, communications, sharing, co-development, customization, and distribution. At the same time, they can expose new vulnerabilities.

TRICKY SWITCHES

Most systems hit snags somewhere along the way. The more complex the systems are, the greater the chance of hitting them. Sharing is great for innovation, but it can also cross the line into negative territory. Access to information and resources helps more people get involved with the creative process, but it can also backfire and become a gift to competition. People want more convenience and efficiency in their lives, but what if personal privacy is compromised?

Openness

Each culture chooses its own level of comfort with exposure. Although fashion might favor midriffs and miniskirts, string bikinis and cleavage helpers, the norm in the business world has pretty much been to play close to the vest, fully clothed. H^{3}s, however, tend to prefer greater transparency. They figure if they don't open their kimonos, they can't get thrilled. It goes beyond team spirit. At MIT's Media Lab, people believe they will get more ideas—and far better ones—by jumping together into the pool . . . naked.

Open-source system design such as Linux originated because people believed there would be more development and innovation if every designer in the world were able to tinker with this operating system and use it as a launch pad. Peer-2-peer network technologies such as Napster and Gnutella pushed us to new levels of openness where people could replicate and share the latest Destiny's Child and 'N Sync releases for free. Freedom, openness, transparency, and sharing are all wonderful things until they start to rob us of important rights, level everything to the point of homogeneity, and strip us of all ability to compete.

For all of the accolades given to sharing, Wal-Mart, the Number One U.S. retailer with over 2,500 stores, decided in May 2001 to stop sharing checkout scanner sales data. Previously, anyone from company employees to Wall Street to competitors had pored over the company's sales information for personal gain. No more. According to the *New York Times,* a spokesman for Wal-Mart said that the company had decided that it could better serve its own competitive

interests by ending the sharing practice.[12] Wal-Mart shares rose on the news. I believe that others will follow Wal-Mart's lead—that the pendulum has begun to swing back toward more discretion, but will likely settle at a point more open than, say, that of even a decade ago.

Rights

As employees, customers, competitors, or marketers, we all seem to be a nosy lot. With all the sharing and collaboration from open circuits, one asks, "Who owns what? What rights do we as individuals have?"

MIT's Media Lab encourages two opposites: sharing and proprietary ownership. It is a highly collaborative environment in which individuals can soar. "We want people to think out loud," says Tod Machover. "Everyone benefits when everyone else thinks about their ideas. We want people to be egoless in coming forth with their ideas, but at the same time we want them to have the right to run with their own vision." People at the Media Lab and their sponsors pour their ideas into one cauldron, as all ideas are shared with everyone at the lab. Each person has a spoon for stirring. Everyone contributes by challenging, expanding, or redirecting the ideas to help along the path to fruition. And each person has the right to scoop out anything of particular interest for subsequent use in his or her own projects. Later developments are not necessarily shared, but are owned by individual developers.

Similarly, Palm, Inc. invites the world to innovate with the company. The more the merrier. If some other company or individual wants to develop a new product related to Palm's products and operating system, Palm is delighted. If the companies want to reap their own profits from the sale of these new products and services, that's even better. Traditional companies, in contrast, create barriers to external ideas. I was shocked when Mattel told me it didn't even want to hear about my idea for a cool new toy. I had helped to develop an idea for a snowball-maker, which my partners and I named the Snowdragon. It seemed to me this was a perfect fit for Mattel's product line, so I boldly called the folks at Mattel to tell them how great we could be as partners. Their response: "We don't accept unsolicited ideas. We don't take in ideas from outside our company."

Many companies reject ideas from external sources out of fear they will cause havoc or will create legal problems. In contrast, Palm integrates outside developers' work through licensing, partnering, and careful time-stamping of all internal work and all externally generated submissions. The company invites outsiders to connect with its internal circuitry, giving them access to its information and cross-selling its products as a way of expanding its creative economy.

Privacy and Security

Accessibility, however, also raises many problems: How can you maintain competitive advantage if your competitors know everything about you? Who owns your medical records? Who has the right to use information about what you watch, what you read, and what you buy? Who has access to your credit records? Who has the right to know your Social Security number or your mother's maiden name?

Long before Congress passed the Graham-Leach-Bliley Act, requiring financial institutions to inform customers by July 1, 2001, how personal data is collected and shared, Capital One saw the privacy issue as an opportunity for differentiation. "We respect customers' privacy more than other credit card companies do," says Marge Connelly. "We have always given customers a chance to opt out of providing nonessential personal information at any point in the information-gathering process." Connelly believes customers feel safer with Capital One and therefore remain more loyal.

Security concerns are on the rise because of Internet hackers, who are adding an element of darkness to the ideal of fully integrated circuits. The Internet, some say, can become a medium for war and destruction. In the 2001 collision involving a Chinese fighter pilot and twenty-four U.S. military personnel aboard an $80 million spy plane, hackers in both the United States and China tried to sabotage certain key websites in the other country by disabling them or replacing existing content with political propaganda. Some suspect that the governments on both sides backed the hackers. The threat of cyber attack has been real for many years, not only from the inventors and spreaders of computer viruses, but also from rogue states and unfriendly political groups that recognize the destructive power they can wield simply by disrupting the flow of information.

A healthy system has a healthy balance between openness and protection, as well as between sophistication and simplicity.

CONVOLUTION EVOLUTION

In the past few years, many companies have created knowledge management systems to leverage the collective know-how of their employees and to increase the flow of ideas. Replete with IT glitter, such as expert databases and intranet sites, these systems sound great until people realize how much work is involved in using them. The technology tends to be user-unfriendly, the process is complicated, and the incentives are often unclear. The simpler the system, the less work involved in adding to and accessing it, the less training needed, the less bureaucracy, the lower the level of maintenance required, the better the flow.

Complexity

As data proliferates and technology advances, creating more circuits, systems naturally become more complex, requiring higher levels of expertise. We all know the complications of complexity—systems crash, people back away, and potential benefits are lost. As systems themselves become more widely used, their complexity is often reduced to practice. Miniscule microprocessors today are a lot more complex than what used to take up a whole room, but hundreds of millions of people use them every day without really thinking much about them. It becomes simply second nature—until the next wave of advances rolls in.

A classic way of managing complexity is to create standards, reducing the number of variables, ensuring a minimum level of quality and performance, and enabling increased access or usability. UL ratings, the DOS standard, VHS are all examples of this. There are also process standards such as Stage Gate in product development, which lays out a template and milestones for new product development initiatives. Standards tend to increase the efficiency of systems. But the question needs to be raised, "Do standards curtail creativity?" If you have to do things a certain way, does that stop you from looking for a different way? It might be a good idea to keep a hedge portfolio of projects that challenge standards; for example, new formats or reporting systems can be explored, new molds can be tried, or novel materials can be tested.

Another way to tame complexity is to automate processes to free up time and other resources. IBM is pushing further by creating flexible self-adapting, self-healing circuitry. IBM sees a growing gap between the amount of technology that needs to be managed and the number of skilled workers available to do the job. The company predicts that its customers will have ten to twenty times more technology to manage over the next five years. As environments become more unpredictable, computers have to be more adaptable and able to withstand stress. IBM created subsystems that monitor traffic and electronic behavior—sensing troubled patterns and responding automatically. Likened to the human immune system, the subsystems are able to identify and nullify threatening bodies.

As organizations, systems, and processes become more complex, the biggest problem is lack of integration. The ultimate goal is to integrate information as it comes in or changes in real time at every decision-point along the way—reducing the process to practice. "In most companies, project budgets reside on individual computer desktops and are inconsistent across projects," observes Michael McGrath, managing partner of the Waltham, Massachusetts-based consulting firm Pittiglio Rabin Todd and McGrath (PRTM). Long-range plans are rarely in alignment with short-term projects. Islands of information are created, without bridges or tunnels connecting them. Fragmented systems yield fragmented information and efforts. Success is more subject to chance.

Visibility and Dashboards

Many of us feel as if we're bundles of projects-in-process, and our circuits are overloaded. McGrath, who has more simultaneously active creative projects than just about anyone I know, created the first product-development management platform. It is called PACE, and it is still the envy of his rivals. In addition to running and aggressively growing his company, which has managed over 5,000 major projects with over 1,100 technology companies in the past eighteen months, McGrath has designed and overseen the construction of his new 15,000-square-foot, high-tech house on the coast of southern Maine. At the same time, he is nurturing a fine arts business, developing a grand plan for election reform, keeping a heavy speaking schedule, and aiming to save the world. "I have ambitious goals to try to transform society," he says, referring to his plans for eliminating poverty in our lifetime, tackling violence, and reforming education. "I'm working on a plan," he says, "and you'll see it in three or four years."

McGrath thinks about how to integrate diverse data streams to create bigger and better success. "I am gathering lots of information all the time on things that I'm interested in," he says. For example, he just finished reading thirty books on the electoral process, along with hundreds of related articles. He's in the process of reading every major biography of every U.S. president. In the past eighteen months, he has read the entire *Harry Potter* series, the *Narnia Chronicles*, and the *Little House on the Prairie* series to his four-year-old daughter. In addition to being an avid golfer, he manages to integrate vacations and sabbaticals. In his spare time, he designed a new enterprise-level software program, secured millions in financing, and built a new company called IDe around it.

Separate from PRTM, IDe grew out of an intense need McGrath faced: how to better connect and coordinate hundreds of key activities. Working with clients over the years, he saw how badly they needed it too. The central problem he identified is poor visibility: If we could know exactly where everything is at all times, we could navigate flawlessly. To provide managers with such capability and extended vision, McGrath developed a software system called IDweb. Using it, an executive can see—at any point and in real time—where all projects and project portfolios stand. It becomes much easier to make the right calls in resource deployment, as companies such as W. R. Grace, Nortel, and Hasbro can testify. Each uses the software across a variety of divisions. The system, which McGrath calls development chain management (DCM), integrates the functions of portfolio, resource, and project management within the context of each company's development process.

Whether IDe will rival SAP or Seibel Systems is anyone's guess, but many expect the new company to do quite well, largely because it is able to fully integrate all project circuits. Like some Web-based team centers, which manage portfolios and cross-functional activities, for example, IDe maintains one integrated database and broadcasts the same updates to all participants simultaneously. Each active project appears on the same "dashboard" with its dedicated meter readings.

Context

Information doesn't get used much when you have to expend a lot of energy going after it. But if information is well integrated in a specific context, it becomes more accessible and powerful.

Imagine: You are the marketing person on a project team responsible for determining pricing. The context-based IDe system knows that *you* are going to work on pricing, and it knows everything about pricing. On Monday the system says, "Today, you're going to work on pricing. Here are the company's guidelines on pricing, along with the Microsoft workplan for navigating the tasks. Here are the current rates for international currency and the financial model recommended to use in your analysis." The system automatically plots the pricing curve. "Here are the last five similar projects in which pricing decisions were made. Finally, here are eight articles to read about pricing, as well as an amazon.com link to three books about new pricing concepts. By the way, here is an AMA course you may also want to take."

Pricing is one task within hundreds of development tasks. You can try to keep track of revenue history and make forecasts for every product, but that's a composite of millions of pieces of data, requiring the integration of various databases. A context-based system such as IDe enables us for the first time to look at all revenue forecasts for all projects, consolidating them onto one dashboard where we can see where and how efficiently you are progressing as a whole.

It is better to adjust plans based on when resources become available than to allocate resources based on a planned formula. An integrated picture on the dashboard, in context, gives the information you need to stay loose and adjust your plans efficiently.

Electric Aesthetic

> The arts are an even better barometer of what is happening in our world than the stock market or the debates in congress.
>
> —*Hendrik Willem Van Loon*, The Arts

The aesthetic aspect of circuitry is often ignored or sacrificed in most companies. It is far behind functionality, efficiency, expediency, and practicality on most priority lists, yet aesthetics can significantly motivate people to adopt new ideas. Although the question of beauty is not a part of most inventions and discoveries, it has played an important role in innovation success.

As mentioned earlier, city leaders recognized the value of an art museum in attracting a tourist economy to Bilbao, for example, but it was Gehry who wanted to integrate people, the environment, and the art. With sinuous titanium curves, orthogonal limestone blocks, glass curtain walls across a mammoth space, he integrated technology and art, industrial metropolis and ancient landscape, creating a transformative experience for all who view from afar and all who enter, including the artists who exhibit there. While many museums are nondescript houses for art, Gehry's *is* art.

Art and science have danced together throughout history, sometimes art taking the lead, sometimes following. The first ceramics, for example, were figurines, not vessels. Metals were fashioned into necklace beads and ornaments long before they were used to make tools and weapons. Glass and the basis for optical devices were first discovered in ancient jewelry-making processes. Rolled metal was first developed as channeling for stained glass art. Innovative companies such as Corning and Xerox PARC employ artists who stretch concepts, materials, and physics, in hopes discovering a new commercial success. Corning, for example, developed its powdered glass business based on an artist's use of the material. Durable and resistant to UV rays, high temperatures, and electrical conductivity, the product is used as an abrasive, a packaging agent, and a lubricant.

From the Grecian urn to the suit of armor to the parasol to the postage stamp, aesthetic design has been integral. In the 1800s and first half of the 1900s, even a package of soap or a can of peaches was an artistic study in typeface, color, composition, and imagery. Somehow, along the way our priorities changed. Practical concerns held sway: how a product works and what it cost became the only concerns, not how it looks. Most of today's products are more pragmatic than delightful to behold.

> I want to make things that are beautiful and moving. I want to make art; they want to make things that are fast and useful, practical.
>
> —Laurie Anderson

Many H³s, however, hope to boost the appeal of their new products with compelling designs and aesthetic experience. While art had nothing to do with the invention of the computer, it had a lot to do with the turnaround at Apple. The iMac would never have made people take a second look had it not been graced with a sleek, postmodern, candy-colored design. The PDA was first developed as a breakthrough in mobile technology, and art seemed irrelevant. As developers built each successive model, they got deeper into what Satjiv Chahil calls "the Zen of Palm": award-winning designs that are unconventional, simple, elegant, and powerful solutions.

"Many technology companies are frustrated because they don't have content for their form," says Laurie Anderson. "Tell that to any artist, and it's a laughable thing because, in my opinion, the form and content of art are inseparable: They talk to each other. It is a code, but a very complex one." Beauty becomes a key criterion, right alongside functionality, practicality, and profitability.

Target Corporation differentiated itself from its fellow low-price retail chains by making aesthetics a top priority. Combining high design and low price, Target created a new strategy and brand identity: Michael Graves teapots and its Andy Warholesque red-and-white bull's-eye logo. Target has recently introduced a new smart card as a point of competitive distinction. "What is most important to us is to keep our brand hip and hot and innovative," says Gerald Storch, Target's vice chairman.[13] Other examples come easily to mind: Sony's aesthetically pleasing Vaio computers, Nokia's cell phones, and Volkswagen's new Bug.

High-fashion boutiques have always paid attention to the design of their stores, fully aware that the environment affects shoppers' perceptions and propensity to buy. The aesthetics of the brand sends the strongest message to customers. Prada, an Italian designer with one of the hippest clothing labels, looped back into the art/technology tango by commissioning architect Rem Koolhaas to bring in his cutting-edge designs, which incorporate movement and changeability, both real and perceptual. His designs for Prada stores include floors that drop down to other levels, enabling customers to move from one room to another without walking. That is, they stand still while the shopping or entertainment environment moves and changes around them. He has turned clothing stores into theaters and back again as parts flip and glide from one function to another.

Sam Waksal believes that his own sensitivity to aesthetics has helped him enormously in how he has managed his maverick firm's ascent. Early in his career, Waksal was impressed by a story Francis Crick told him about the discovery of the DNA double helix, which earned him and James Watson a Nobel prize. A controversy raged at the time about whether the helix was right-handed or left-handed. After trying to prove his right-handed argument by using crystallography and biophysics, Crick imagined himself small enough to fit inside the helix. He "saw" that a left-handed helix just wasn't aesthetically pleasing to him. It was enough to confirm his contention for right-handedness. A major collector of contemporary paintings, Waksal believes: "When you study art, different things affect you: The ways in which you integrate aesthetics into your life affect how you think, how you build, and how you innovate."

In times of prosperity, art and R&D investments are both more abundant. It is tempting to cut them when times get tough. But think, as Corning has, how much further you could gain on your competitors if you raised your investment levels as they lowered theirs. If you believe in your own abilities to innovate, you will see that integrating art and pioneering is much more of an opportunity than a risk.

o   o   o

The nature of relationships determines how fast, how well, and how productively resources travel along the wires of a circuit. In your organization or on your team, how well do you listen to each other or to those on the "outside"? How much do you trust each other? How easy is it for you to contact each other? How much do you consult each other and share information? What kind of information do you share among yourselves or with those who are external to your team? How much and how well do you use what you get from each other? How much and how well do you support each other, both in good times and in tough times? Do you form a true community? How much and how well are you integrated? How do you build the social spaces, the physical spaces, and the informational spaces into alignment so that each one is mutually supportive of the other?

With all of the new tools and ideas about connecting, collaborating, archiving, and accessing, you would think that we would see an unprecedented rise in innovation success. But, for many of us, the hit rate and frustration levels remain the same. Billions of dollars are being spent on information technology and, while the money has helped to make things move faster and cheaper, it is not spitting out more or bigger breakthroughs. New product failures are still at about 90 percent. Communications gaps are still with us. We want more and more data before we act. Our creative geniuses are still the rare exceptions. Some of them use the new tools better. But everyone else is still mired in mediocrity. Some estimate that expensive new knowledge management systems, designed to capture and share the collective content of employees' brains, are being used only at an average of 10 percent of their capacity—curiously the same capacity utilization of the average human brain. What gives?

The answer lies in our collective heads and hearts—in our cultures. "I don't care how well you document software and applications," says John Seely Brown, "ultimately, everything is in the minds of the people who developed it." If R&D and engineering cultures design fancy systems and gadgets, and they haven't considered the cultures of the people who will be using them, there is little or no value. If the culture of a marketing department develops its own ideas and ways of doing things, its own interpretations of data, and even its own language, as do R&D, finance, operations, IT, HR, and other divisions, together they build an innovation Tower of Babel. It's the organizational equivalent of our personal "men-are-from-Mars,-women-are-from-Venus" conundrum. That is why many H³ leaders pay close attention to the integrated systems they create—the processes, cultures, structures, and environments where people have to work and communicate. As we will see in Chapter 6, the best way of integrating circuits is to design the organization right in the first place. It's not just putting together a business plan. This is rocket design.

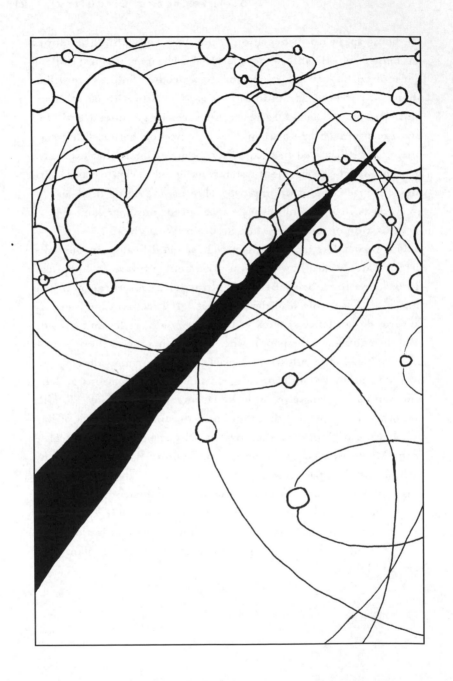

.6.

ROCKET DESIGN

Innovating the Organization

> Real corporations have. . . real problems. These are all opportunities for innovation.
>
> —*John Seely Brown*

Many of us grew up playing with Erector sets, building complex things out of little metal parts. One of the first things you learn is: Don't tighten anything down until you really have to. If you tighten too much, no matter how good your instructions are or how precise your equipment is, you'll have to take it all apart. As long as you keep the structure loose, more or less, you can jiggle things around, within a set of constraints, so everything fits right at the last moment. John Seely Brown believes the whole catch is: "How do you build loosely bound systems and then tighten things up at the last moment?" And how do you keep things open to future ideas? In a sense, you need a framework in which to improvise, one that can act as a resource to the organization.

H³s are loose-tight creative machines. This chapter looks at how H³ organizations are designed, constructed, and worked. Large or small, they have compelling ideas about order and disorder, managing talent, leadership, and working environments. They have built new structures and systems, all driven by their mission of innovation. This chapter explores the innovation strategies and creative tactics that keep the gears well oiled, the engines well fueled, and new ideas for growth and prosperity bubbling up.

CREATIVE LEADERSHIP

> The biggest challenge is always the status quo.
> —*Glenn Renwick*

No creative organization or innovative team is going to get off the ground if it doesn't have a creative, innovative leader. A common theme running through the observations made by the business leaders and artists interviewed for this book is *passion:* passion for life, for work, for discovery. It is not something they develop late in

life. While not all are child prodigies, they have from their earliest memories been adventurers, explorers, questioners, and seekers. Their quests have given them a unique perspective on the universe—whether it's the cosmos that Columbia University professor of physics Brian Greene sees, or the universe of a subject's face that photographer Timothy Greenfield-Sanders sees through his camera, or the universe of the DNA molecule that Sam Waksal sees through a microscope. All of these people possess characteristics that make them as H^3 as the organizations or groups they lead. They are the rockets that boost their organizations to ever-higher creative heights.

Solid Boosters

Curiosity, pain, and inspiration can fuel all kinds of reactions. In H^3s, they trigger creativity. Some start to experience their own creative forces at an early age. Others can have a much later epiphany. Either way, they find creative passion within themselves, a passion so strong that it fires them up and propels them past everyone else.

Launching Pads. "When I was a kid, I went to work, painting walls for a new TV station," recalls Jeff Skilling, CEO of Enron.[1] As he painted, he took special note of each shiny new piece of equipment that was delivered and assembled. "I was fascinated about how these pieces fit in with everything else, so I stuck around until the TV station finally opened. On that day, the chief production officer quit in frustration. Desperate to get on the air, the station manager broadcast a plea to the entire staff: 'Does *anyone* know how to operate this equipment?' I was the only one who could run everything in the station," Skilling says, "so *I* did it." He became chief production officer at age twelve and stayed on another five years before going off to college.

While musical prodigies are well known—Mozart composed incredible music for the clavier and harpsicord at age three; violin virtuoso Joshua Bell was discovered plucking out melodies on rubber bands he stretched to differing lengths across the pulls of dresser drawers when he was four—many creative thinkers in the arts, sciences, and in business also discovered their talents early.

Some had a tough start. It takes extra creativity and extra strength to rise up out of difficult circumstances and to land on the leading edge. A father at seventeen, David Cole used penury as a launching

pad. He put himself through graduate school by laying under-
ground track from II P.M. to 7 A.M. for the Washington, D.C.,
metro, while simultaneously engaging in the Antioch work-study
program at the law school because he could not afford to pay his tu-
ition and feed his three children otherwise. Cole wasn't stopped or
even slowed by the difficulties. Instead, Cole believes conventional
wisdom is one of the biggest and most ubiquitous obstacles. But that
hasn't stopped him either. Cole rocketed, becoming a great business
innovator and creative leader. He has served as CEO of Ashton-
Tate, marketers of dBase II and III; president of Ziff Corporation,
as well as director of the Nature Conservancy, the World Wildlife
Fund, and the American Farmland Trust. He was lead investor in
Shiva (later sold to Intel), in Tops (later sold to Sun Microsystems),
and in Macromedia. He was founder and president of Navisoft
(later sold to AOL), where he became president of Internet Services. He is currently the chairman of the board of Acirca, Inc.

When she was a young girl in the isolated Australian outback, Jill
Ker Conway began a similar ascent. At age ten, her father died and
Conway had to take over some of the hard work. "There were few
men around—all the able-bodied ones were drafted during the Second World War—so I had to figure out how to do a lot of tasks that
were for a person much bigger and stronger than I. That meant I
had to redefine the problem, because I could never do it the way the
adults did it. We had no extra parts, no access to professional expertise. If an engine broke down, you took it apart to see how it fit

together, then you tried to fix it," she recalls. The practical education Conway received served her well, and she has been leading charges ever since. As a graduate student at Harvard, she worked to reconceptualize access to higher education for women in the United States. "I've been interested in changing the accepted script for a woman's life—from a romantic one to one that involves a mission, courage, risk-taking—a story that's not about needing the romantic hero," she says. After a successful teaching career, she became president of Smith College and now is chairman of the global real estate giant, Lend Lease Corporation.

Adversity and tragedy didn't stop or slow young Peter Lewis either. Instead, it immediately propelled him to become a creative leader. In the summer after Lewis's college freshman year, his brother was killed in a car crash. Two years later, his father died of cancer. "Things that I never knew I could think about started to descend on me," Lewis explains. Suddenly he assumed the head-of-household role, acting as "father" to an eight-year-old brother. In no time, Lewis became a young husband and father of three, while taking over the reins of his father's small insurance company. Nobody was around to tell him what to do or how to do it. Naïvely he asked questions such as "Why do we have to restrict our services to low-risk customers?" and "Why can't we tell a prospect that a competitor has lower rates?" Few others in the insurance industry bothered to raise such questions, and Lewis ended up building his father's business into the world's fourth largest auto insurance company. Ever since, Progressive has been a leader in changing the insurance industry landscape. "I know that I would not have accomplished nearly as much had my dad lived," says Lewis, "because I would have been his son. I got a running start because of what he started. But I had no idea what I was doing."

Leaders who come out of such experiences are often better able to inspire others to take similar risks, an essential characteristic of H[3] individuals and organizations. That quality translates itself into the organization's culture, as it has at Lend Lease and Progressive, where people are encouraged to take off on their own to work on innovative projects.

Lift. The best creative leaders use their own launching pads to help lift others up around them. H³ leaders get excited by new ideas, but often they also have a special ability to get everyone else excited too.

> An artist needs only three things: first, he needs encouragement; second, he needs encouragement; and third, he needs encouragement.
>
> —Unknown

That was not always the case for Jeff Skilling, who recalls his reaction upon learning that a new idea, an online gas trading system, was about to be launched. Initially he resisted the concept, resentful that he had not been informed earlier. John Sherriff, the CEO of Enron Europe, had come up with the idea, which he had handed over to Louise Kitchen, a thirty-one-year-old natural gas trader, to build and manage. She attracted 350 people within the company to form a new team. Together they worked on their own time for seven months to get the project ready, informing Skilling only two months before the $15 million project was scheduled to go live. Despite Skilling's misgivings, the idea lifted Enron to unimagined heights and redefined Enron's identity: that idea became a $36 billion business (as of August 2001). Enron became one of the fifteen largest companies in the world, growing at a rate of 400 percent within a three-year period, with over $100 billion in sales for 2000.[2]

"Now, if someone comes to me with a good idea," Skilling says, "I get visibly enthusiastic. People can see that it matters to me. If I asked, 'What are we going to do for quarterly earnings?' that response would kill off a lot of enthusiasm. I believe strongly in real options, which means I encourage people to do as many things as possible *as long as they do them cheaply.*" And, one hopes, people do them legally.

"Enron was structured so that every year we could make hundreds of cheap bets," says Skilling. "I prefer those that don't require a lot of analytical precision. I'd rather have lots of experimentation. I know ninety out of one hundred may fail, but we can get enormous paybacks on the ten winners."

Big ideas or small, Skilling encourages them all. "If someone can get a relatively small business going at very low cost, they should go for it," he says. "If they can get a larger business going at low cost, even better." This is very different from many traditional companies, which establish substantial hurdles for projected sales, and discourage "small" ideas. Most blockbuster ideas, however, start small. It is impossible to know ahead of time how big they might grow. The newer an idea is, the tougher it is to call. Often, if they are very new concepts, such as the first personal computer, they are rejected at first by the marketplace—only to be widely embraced after people get used to the ideas. If "small" ideas are discouraged, big ideas may also be repressed. If you consider all ideas, large or small, to be valuable, you boost creative morale.

Many creative leaders support even ideas they don't like if the proponents have a high level of passion for them. "I just get out of their way," says Roger Ackerman of Corning, because he has seen ideas win big despite his skepticism. He doubted the wisdom of moving Corning into biotech—it seemed like an odd choice for a glass company—but he let it fly. Now biotech is Corning's third largest business. Even if it had failed, Ackerman would have supported those who tried. Skilling has a similar attitude. "If the last group that went and created a new business all got fired because it did not work, I guarantee you innovation is *over* in that company," he says.

If, for some reason, your organization cannot see an idea through, it can be shared with another organization, or set free. Peter Lewis, for example, has helped a number of key employees to leave his company and build new successful businesses on their own. Twenty-five former employees of Progressive have become CEOs elsewhere.

One of the leadership skills David Cole is most proud of is his ability to lead his people further than they ever thought they could go with their ideas. "I systematically ratchet up expectations," says Cole. Similar to the software industry's law of increasing returns, Cole created the law of increasing potential, and he uses it to build breakthrough organizations.

The ability to encourage others to take new leaps comes from your own inner fire.

Heat

Creative heat is a core part of who H³ leaders are, often from as early as childhood, throughout their paths in life.

"In Holland, where I grew up," Genzyme's Henri Termeer of recounts, "I joined the Air Force and was put in charge of keeping track of materials required to keep the planes running. What could be more boring than dealing with thousands of airplane parts in a typically military way? But I had to do my two years, so I said, 'I'll have some fun with this.' There are always lots things one can do. But some people didn't want to have fun. They wanted only to sit out the next five years, then retire as military professionals. I asked them not to show up anymore. 'Stay home! You're not *doing* anything, and it's just not right. You need interest!' And they said, 'Who the hell are you?' And I said, 'I'm nobody, but we're in this together.'"

Termeer considers that experience pertinent to his view on leadership. "If you're running a company and you can't figure out how to be creative, you have to ask for a new job. You have to go to your board and say, 'I'm not the right person.' That's the test people should put themselves to: every leader should challenge themselves to make a creative difference . . . or leave." Termeer believes that his own passion for creativity runs through the veins of his company. "You can't organize heart into something," he says. "You have to transplant it."

Inner fire can begin at any time. "I was a prototypical buttoned-up guy until about twenty-five years ago," recalls Peter Lewis. Then he got divorced. His kids grew up. He stopped spending all his time in Cleveland, Ohio. And he discovered art. "I read an article about David Rockefeller's art collection at the Chase Manhattan Bank," recalls Lewis. "'How should we decorate *our* building?' I wondered. I didn't really like contemporary art. I thought it was a rip-off." Lewis now has one of the largest and finest collections of contemporary paintings in the world. He started down a path that has led to his bliss.

Lewis loves artists even more than he loves art. "I surround myself with art and artists," he explains, "and I travel a lot. I do it for myself and for my company. It's necessary for my life and for my happiness." When I asked him if he thought he would have been able to build his $8 billion insurance company without art and travel in his life, he responded, in a heartbeat, "I've never really *lived* without them, so I don't know."

Enthusiasm for pushing limits is contagious at H^3s. "People need to see that you step out a little bit and see that you are not judgmental, biased, or prejudiced in your approach to life," says Skilling. "They see me doing all sort of things—which have a little risk in them," he says devilishly, "like rock climbing and racing my motorcycle across Mexico." Skilling also goes on scavenger hunts in the Australian outback and has fun when he gets lost. "If something becomes routine," he says, "I am not interested in it." Creative passion affects how we think about our culture, structure, and environment. It affects how we see the world.

THE BLUE MARBLE

Sitting in front of a water fountain one day while working at Cadbury Schweppes, Mark Rodriguez wished that he had a way to take the water with him, as if it were a can of soda. Later, he pursued this idea when he became the CEO of the North American bottled water and specialty foods businesses of Danone Group, one of the largest food producers in France, maker of Evian water and Dannon yogurt, among many other products. By and large, Americans seemed to be consuming less alcohol, sugar, and caffeine, and Rodriguez wondered why small bottles of water couldn't be distributed as widely as soft drinks. Although many of his colleagues thought he was out of his mind to try to make money selling little bottles of water, he expanded distribution of Evian in small bottles to places never before considered as potential markets. He then pondered how to produce a global brand of bottled water focused on brand attributes rather than source attributes, much as Coca-Cola does. He wanted Danone to be the low-cost producer on every continent. Within the bottled water industry this strategy changed the fundamental dynamics of the business. Furthermore, he proposed selling the water, using the Dannon yogurt brand and thereby capitalizing on its naturally healthy image. Rodriguez saw forces coming together that no one else saw. His new view of the world and his pioneering leap into single-serve bottled water built an $800 million business for Danone, whose total worldwide sales topped $18.5 billion in 2000.

David Cole began to see the same accelerating drivers, which had resulted in the multi-billion dollar bottled-water industry, in place for organic food. "Natural" foods had already become big business, and health-conscious Baby Boomers were getting hungrier for more options. Organic food had just begun to get noticed for its steep climb in sales: It is currently the fastest-selling food category in the United States, Canada, Japan, and a large part of Western Europe; and Rodriguez predicts that by 2005, it will be a $20 billion industry.[3] Until recently, organic food was entirely a cottage industry, unable to scale up to meet growing demand. Cole wooed Rodriguez away from Danone and installed him as CEO of Acirca. Together, they combined their ideas and talents to achieve a killer distribution strategy and speed that would make a software company envious. They solved the industry's frustrating supply constraints by sourcing hard-to-find organic ingredients in other parts of the world, a tactic more typical of a computer manufacturer sourcing chips. The world is their playground in their attempt to build the first global organic brands.

Rodriguez, Cole, and other H³ leaders have a capacity for seeing complex things—systems, organizations, networks—in their wholeness. It's like what astronauts comment on when asked what the planet Earth looks like from outer space—they see the wholeness of that little blue marble as it spins along its path.

Brian Greene has a gift for presenting powerful holistic views. For example, he masterfully combined a string quartet, a beautifully animated film, and an artfully written narrative to illustrate his concepts in String Theory. As a result, many more people began to "get" this cutting-edge complex theoretical physics that only super-geeks "got" before. Greene's holistic view of the universe came through, as each art form illuminated the others, to explain the gestalt of String Theory. Also known as the "theory of everything," String Theory marries Einstein's general theory of relativity with quantum mechanics, answering a question that has stumped the scientific community for almost a century.[4] Greene's book, *The Elegant Universe,* was on the best-seller lists for much of 1999, an astounding feat for a physics book, leading us all to a new understanding of how the universe works.

Though Genzyme is considerably smaller than the pharmaceutical giants, Henri Termeer sees a much bigger universe than they do. He has a unique way of gathering all of the big obstacles together onto his canvas and painting a whole new picture of possibility. For example, he takes a holistic view of xeno-transplantation, a controversial practice of using the cells of other animals, such as pigs or monkeys, to cure human disease. Given the current system of approvals, no social or governmental agency is likely to support this experimentation. "So, you have to change everything," Termeer advises. "You have to change the way the FDA looks at xeno-transplantation. You have to encourage science within the company and outside, through peer reviews. You have to overcome the problem of doing

invasive placebo surgery on patients. Plus, you have to be able to finance it for ten or fifteen years, at a rate of $20 million a year."
Termeer believes Genzyme can accomplish all of this, not just to
treat, but to *cure* disease. That is the gestalt of Genzyme.

It helps to see the whole if you want to change the world, but especially in the past decade, fast change became the mantra. Managers became frantic to change things in their companies, reorgan-
izing and shifting people around, to out-compete rivals. Changing
too much too quickly, however, is like punching a hole in the bottom of your boat. As Cole puts it, "I think you weaken an organization with constant change. It's fine if you're small and you want to
stay small, but if you want to build significant institutional mass
against a market opportunity, you can't do it. People don't change
that way." Lend Lease allows people to move around and change
their jobs, but it doesn't go for major re-organization very often.
Voluntary job changes are part of its existing organizational strategy.

"The most powerful changes are ones that are completely supported by a very clear articulation of why we're here," says Cole.
"And, you can't do that all the time if you're always jiggering stuff.
That's list management versus gestalt management. There's a difference between fixing stuff and building to execute on a vision."

A fuller understanding of the universe includes a fuller understanding of self. We need to get a better understanding of our own
assumptions. But there is no final gestalt. There is always new data,
new experience, and new talent. If only we could convince NASA to
send a few artists on the next space shuttle mission, we might gain an
entirely new appreciation for the blue marble.

LIVING WITH WEIGHTLESSNESS

"You have to be brave," advises ImClone CEO Sam Waksal, "and say
to shareholders, 'You know what? For the next two quarters, we're
not going to hit our earnings projections—not because we couldn't,

but because we're doing something that's going to increase earnings in a year and a half. Now, if you don't believe us, sell your shares!'"

"I can't control shareholders' decisions," Waksal says. "But I can say to them, 'Hang tough during this period of stagnant earnings, and you'll be rewarded by a dramatic increase in earnings later.'" Realizing that this chutzpah won't go over well with everyone, Waksal has faith in his company's work and believes there are enough daring people who want to support the development of cancer cures, risks and all.

If you abandon your commitment to growth through innovation when the economy turns down or your industry is embattled, or because you are impatient, you miss important opportunities and expose yourself to a nasty risk. While others retreat to their bunkers, some H^{3}s step out and spend on R&D, talent, and innovation systems. Now, more than ever, is the time to aggressively seek new ideas. The competition is less of a threat, more talent is available, and mistakes are cheaper. Don't lose sight of profitability, and conserve where you can, of course, but don't stop taking chances.

In tough economic times, we can more carefully manage the resources that are applied to a new initiative early on in the process, before evidence of success. During these times, we can also focus more on businesses that are directly related to the core. But, we can still push heavily for innovation in those core areas as well as in business processes. It is important not to give up on innovation initiatives in times of crisis or distress. We need to continue to build new paths and we need to be ready when prosperity and opportunity returns.

If Wall Street won't let you take chances, you can hang tough, as Corning and Genzyme have. Their leaders would rather take their hits and suffer market cap cuts than get pulled off their innovation paths. Or, you can follow Seagate. When technology stocks got hammered, Seagate, the world's largest disk-drive maker, saw the price of its stock take a dive—so low that it was trading for less than the value of its hard assets. In other words, investors believed that the company was worth less than the value of its cash and securities holdings, factories, equipment, and revenue streams all added together. The same thing has happened, at various times, with Macromedia, Genzyme, and Corning. Imagine if your company recorded over $6 billion in sales and $18 billion in securities, but Wall Street analysts thought it was worth *negative* $5 billion. What would you do?

That is exactly the predicament Seagate faced.

Stephen Luczo, Seagate's CEO, didn't want to deal with that irrational behavior any more, so he told Wall Street investors to take a hike. He and a private equity group devised a unique and gutsy plan. In a $20 billion buyout, they took Seagate private—a highly unusual move for a company of its considerable size, particularly in a New Economy world where everybody else was clamoring to go public. Now Seagate can focus again on innovation and long-term growth without worrying so much about its short-term earnings.[5]

Constraints and tough conditions can actually push leaders to new realms of creativity. Artist/director Robert Wilson has seen this in extreme. "I spent a long time working as a therapist at the Goldwater Memorial Hospital, in a ward filled with people on iron lungs," recounts Wilson. "I was shocked to see people in a tank, in a box on legs, plugged into a wall. I became close with one of the patients who told me that he found a greater freedom being in this box." When resources are cut down and pressures mount, you get a different view of the world, and with that comes new ideas.

THROTTLE

Some leaders thrive on mach speeds.

A veteran of high-tech competition, David Cole considers high-speed decisionmaking a great asset to an organization. He believes that hyper-drive was a major key to his success in growing all of his businesses. He is now bringing all of his biases from high-tech to

Acirca, Inc. "We want folks here to have a pretty high clock speed," says Cole. He has established a rapid motivational rhythm for the company, "putting powder" behind his initiatives.[6]

It's not so much about speed as it is about a sense of urgency about the competition. If you do not have a sense of urgency and your competitor does, then you are out of business. That does not mean that everything you do you have to do fast. A sense of urgency means that the important things, the ones that differentiate you, get done quickly.

That said, there is room for "slow." For example, Cole loves the "slow-food" movement—the opposite of quick meals and bad take-out. It's a deeper aesthetic, a rebalancing and rethinking of one's relationship with the world. One of the benefits he derives from his ownership of Sunnyside Farms is that it sometimes forces him to live by the farm's rhythms, a very different pace than that of whirling around the country building his new company. "To the extent that people can slow down to ask basic questions about what they're eating, there will be enormous repercussions. To the extent that 'Slow' can increase conscious commerce, that's important," says Cole.

Speed by itself is a killer. We're not built for perpetual speed. We're supposed to do some slow things like sleep, love, and create art. There should be some tenderness in life.

ERECTOR SETS

Creative leaders' visions are sketches that constantly shift and morph. They see their organizational design as Erector set i-beams, spokes, nuts, bolts, and gears, which they loosen, adjust, and tighten, optimizing the company's relationship with the world. Every design has a platinum center: its creative talent. Everything about the organization—its culture, structure, and environment—hinges on creative talent.

Loose-Tight

> Consistency is the last resort of the unimaginative.
>
> —*Oscar Wilde*

Brian Greene fantasizes about what goes on inside hot high-tech companies. "I don't literally know how those corporations are set up," he says, "but I imagine that there are places where you've got a bunch of young people, with a big Coke machine—it's totally a mess—and they're allowed to just play. And from that play, all kinds of useful and powerful creations emerge."

He recalls one of his rare forays into corporate America. "During the summer months when I was in college, I worked at IBM on language translation, computer-aided design, and circuitry. They were very good to me, in that they let me do whatever I wanted—they even let me work on String Theory. I was surprised by it at the time," he admits, "you know, like *Wow!* they are *paying* me to do this! I thought that was great. That's the way it should be: Give people an environment that's safe for exploration."

"I think there's far less of that going on now," Greene laments. "It's much more directed toward product development, and there's much less freedom to let your imagination go where it takes you, regardless of what the marketplace says. That's unfortunate because I think the deepest creativity comes from undirected work."

John Loose and other H³ leaders agree. Corning has what it calls "loose-tight" management styles. Loose became the chairman and CEO of Corning in July 2001, as a successor to Ackerman—and Loose loves "loose."

"We say, 'Just get results,'" says Loose. "'You put it together any way you want.'" The most interesting thing is the way Ackerman established a commitment of faith and support: He would give somebody a $1 million-a-year business and ask that person to grow it to $50 million. His promise: "Whatever you need, you've got." Now,

Loose is the one pledging his faith and company resources to innovation initiatives and giving people the freedom and space to explore new paths.

"We are loosey-goosey on what people can do," says Loose, "but we do ask questions about things."

Corning keeps things loose so the company can pursue new opportunities to create and lead new industries. Ackerman liked his people to think like venture capitalists, with flexible natures and tight milestone controls, giving a certain amount of money at each milestone of an innovation project.

At Enron, Skilling designated four "tight" areas: sales commitments, contracts, money flow, and evaluation/compensation. Everything else was "loose." A business unit could pursue whatever strategy it chose. Employees could come in at 10 A.M. and leave at 3 P.M., so long as they got their work done. Training was available but not mandated. "You could do pretty much what you want as long as those four things are very tightly managed," explains Skilling.

Skilling credited Enron's incredible transformation to this loose-tight culture.[7] Enron's people saw how the big picture changes and how they could fit into it. "When we began, the whole objective was to build a wholesale natural gas business," he explains. "Two years into it, we started a wholesale electricity business; two years later we started our European and international business. Every two years there was a new wave of innovation. For me that's a lot of fun!"

In some H[3]s, the culture becomes looser or tighter depending on economic conditions. "An organization is like an accordion," says Peter Lewis. "When things are going well, I spread out the power and delegate a lot. When we're going through tough times, we pull it back into the center. We control it all centrally until the problems are fixed and times get better. The goal is to spread it out again when good times return, and keep growing."

Some H[3]s designate loose periods. For example, 3M is known for allowing people the opportunity to spend 15 percent of their time on their own personal projects. People at Corning like spending 10 percent of time on something "crazy." Maybe, we can follow the lead of one CEO of a major food-processing company: for one hour every Thursday afternoon, we would take the time to pursue something "ridiculous."

Creative spirits can't be tightly managed, but they can be suppressed and frustrated. That is why at companies such as Corning, it is part of everyone's job to be skeptical and challenge the system.

Talent-Centric

Many executives are not creative. Executives who are only into executing basically do what they're told. That is one reason why many H³s are more interested in bringing in talent than they are in bringing in executives. Many are talent-centric. Bell Labs and Xerox PARC were the first big talent magnets. Like these predecessors, innovative companies are primed for attracting the most talented people, who are passionate about the work, almost as if it were a religious experience.

H³s worship the cult of the innovator, not the cult of the manager.

Fire and Passion

When you have something that's big and is growing fast, you want to find great talent to help you get that done. You don't want them to be necessarily restricted to the business that is right before them—you want them to think beyond that.

The criteria for hires and promotions at most organizations never include creativity or passion, according to Geoff Smart, executive placement consultant of G. H. Smart and Company in Chicago. For H³s, however, creativity and passion are paramount. In fact, for many, creativity is the hottest priority in evaluating talent.

If potential employees' eyes light up and they've instantly got a dozen reasons as to why their mission is so cool, and they can do a mind-meld with customers, they are candidates. If they get clearly excited about the prospect in an unaffected way—as opposed to the five-year pro-forma analysis typical of an MBA—move them to the top of the list.

Macromedia also considers creative expression. "Our engineers are not like those at Texas Instruments," says CFO Betsey Nelson. "They are extremely creative. They have body-piercing in strange places," she says half-jokingly. "Many are musicians or artists. They have a huge life away from coding, but that informs what they bring to their products. And, I probably have one of the more unique finance teams around. Some write comic books; some are marathon runners, some are painters or sculptors, and we have a fabulous band!" Beyond all that, Nelson considers one attribute to be most important: a person really has to be committed to making a difference. "That's what I look for when I'm interviewing," she says.

If you are committed to innovation, you need to find leaders who encourage creativity and who are into being creative themselves.

H³s also have a passion for risk. "For people here at Corning, there is joy in being different," says John Loose. Risk is inherent in that joy. "I do an enormous amount of communicating and interacting with the people around me," says Loose's predecessor, Roger Ackerman. "I go around and try to pick people in important jobs that have the willingness to take risks. It's really a culture that encourages 'appropriate' risk, and I underline *appropriate* twenty times."

Frank Gehry was considered to be just an aspiring architect with wacky ideas twelve years ago because nobody had ever heard of him. Now he's *executed,* with major projects in Bilbao, New York, and elsewhere. Now many consider him to be the world's greatest living architect. The proof in the pudding is what defines innovation success for projects and it is what defines the level of talent of creative leaders and employees.

Getting it done is a real test of creativity. *"Everyone* in the top management of Enron built a business at one time in his or her career," says CEO Jeff Skilling. Besides inquiring about passion, knowledge, and experience, Dave Ditzel asks potential employees, "What have you *built?"* Some respond that they were on this or that team, but that simply indicates they were *there.* Others are quick to point out their accomplishments: "I worked on such-and-such a project, but I created this or that on my own." When he finds that person, Ditzel gets excited. "Aha! This person knows how to get something *done!"*

Natural Selection

To get something innovative done, in many cases, you need to know a lot of facts, you need technical depth, and you need intimacy with the history and latest developments in particular fields of study. As technology gets more complex and specialized, you often need an advanced degree, an intense concentration of study, and years of practice. In order to really exercise creativity in computer science, you may need twelve years of school or more. In medical science, you need to go through a grueling internship and residency. There are the punishing Bar, CPA, and MEDCAT exams to pass and many ladders to climb. A lot of creative people can't or don't want to go through all of that, so they opt out.

Rudy Burger of MIT's Media Lab describes a process that is all too typical, in which research grant applicants have to go through an intentionally difficult obstacle course because the grantors wanted to test their mettle—the underlying assumption being that only those individuals who had the stamina to endure this arduous process should be given any research money. "I look upon it in exactly the opposite way," says Burger. "Who wants to be bothered with all that hassle? In my hiring process, I would select out the people that had the stamina to stomach that sort of bureaucracy because they're the least likely to be the innovative people that I'd want in my lab."

Over the years, Burger has developed his own list for selecting and evaluating people at MIT. Among his criteria, potential employees or promotions have to be:

- Passionate about their work.
- Excited by interdisciplinary collaboration.
- Energized by taking risks.
- Able to handle ambiguity.
- Voracious in their learning.
- More likely to ask forgiveness than permission.
- Mentally agile.
- Abundant in energy and stamina.
- Culturally primed for new things.

Creative Echelons

As Dave Ditzel observes, "You don't just take ten people out of 10,000 employees in your cereal company and say, 'Here's some money. Come back with a new idea.' Talk to people throughout the company. They may tell you that over in that corner, Joe in manufacturing is coming up with a new idea for a new cereal every other day. That's the guy you're looking for!"

What's more, Joe will almost certainly attract and lead other talent.

It happened to Ditzel himself when he was at the most advanced research center of the era, Bell Labs. He was one of thirty-five people in the Computing Science Research Group, which was just one of the many divisions of Bell Labs. That team of creative anarchists, however, churned out one breakthrough idea after another—the UNIX operating system, RISC chips (which power Apple, Motorola, and Sun computers), the C programming language, and so on. "The people with the best ideas," says Ditzel, "constitute a small percentage. I used to go to each division, find the top performers, and put them together on one team."

In short, Ditzel presents a radical concept for the business world: *You need talent spotters, not talent trainers.* "It is far more productive and easier to generate leap innovation with the ten people in an organization who are already super-creative than it is with 10,000 creatively challenged employees who, at best, have been subjected to creativity training."

Creativity training is better than nothing. It makes people feel good for a while. But it gives them false comfort. "They need to hold a class on how to go find creative people," says Ditzel. "Trust me, you've got ten creative people in your company and you don't even know you have them. You have access to even more outside your company. The trick is finding them. You can train people to find those super-creative people, but you can't train them to *be* those people."

> Creative minds have always been known to survive any kind of bad training.
>
> —Anna Freud

If you're trying to educate someone at work, you're already twenty years behind. A person who has lacked creativity in the first twenty years of life is not likely to find it now in a seminar. In a well-established organization that has carefully built a culture around a collection of honored values that don't include creativity, it is excruciatingly difficult to turn over a new creative leaf. You could cast the net and offer everyone rewards for ideas to drum up new business that may yield incremental improvement. But for the really big things you need either some new people or some new perspective. "The best thing you can do is to join your top innovators together with new, creative hires," says Ditzel. He credits his own creative success to his start at the top of the top research centers at Bell Labs as a very young person. He grew up watching giants of the industry. He learned how they worked and how they thought. He got to work with his creative heroes on a peer-to-peer basis over a period of years, with important innovations to his credit. "It wasn't because Bell Labs sent me to a class on innovation," says Ditzel.

"Creativity has a gigantic dynamic range," says Nathan Myhrvold. "There are productivity studies for programming, which show that the best programmers versus the average programmers are better by a giant factor. It's not like someone's twice as good. The difference between the best and the average can easily be a factor of a thousand or more." The more radical the results you want to get, the more radical things you are going to have to try.

"The biggest challenge is always the status quo," says Glenn Renwick, CEO of Progressive. "Those who embrace the status quo are unlikely to have even the intellectual curiosity to challenge it. Our culture attracts people that display a curiosity for advancing business models—and they enjoy doing it," Renwick explains.

When traditional managers commission separate creative development groups or a corporate venture task force and they don't otherwise promote creativity, everyone else in the company gets the message that it is not their job to have or implement new ideas. But H3s consider everyone in their organization to be a creative resource. Everyone can be a part of the creative community and make creative contributions on one level or another, regardless of his or her specific job, talents, or position in the organization.

That is not to say that all people have the same creative skills. "Just because somebody is good in traditional marketing doesn't mean they are going to be good in new product development," Dan Dillon says. At Welch's, there is a dedicated new product development team, although they mainly work on line extensions, and an assortment of skunk-works in which team members break the rules on purpose.

Well-intentioned rulebreaking is part of everyone's job description at H3 organizations. Lend Lease, for example, describes its own culture as "disobedient"—people are encouraged to challenge the system as long as they can produce positive results. Capital One has a "Speak Up!" program whereby all associates can make creative contributions, voice their ideas, and expect feedback from the appropriate manager. "This interactive suggestion box gets results," says Dennis Liberson, vice president of human resources. "Through the company's intranet, associates can send their ideas to a special team, who route the ideas to the right department or person and then follow up within twenty-one days on the status and outcome of the idea."

MAGNETS

It's not an everyday occurrence when an executive moves an entire company to another location just to attract new talent, but when David Cole met Linda Dozier, a technology specialist at Systems Research and Applications (SRA), that's ultimately what he did as he was building Navisoft, a navigation software company, which he eventually sold to AOL. "The more we got to know her, the more excited we became about having her work at Navisoft. We were less concerned about the technology designs and more concerned with finding a way to bring her in." After some negotiations, Cole executed a license agreement, which included bringing some of SRA's people on board. Dozier came over to be chief technology officer.

"We weren't sure exactly what our company would be," admits Cole, "but we were sure we wanted to build it around Linda. We moved the company to Santa Barbara, which met some of her personal needs. It allowed her to hunker down and do what she really does best—designing system architecture along with recruiting and motivating the technical team to get from technology to product. That's how Navisoft was created. We mobilized the company around a specific talent."

The idea of talent as the sun around which the rest of your organization revolves is new for traditional organizations. Many businesses start as talent-centric, with a talented entrepreneur as the center driver, but as they grow into larger organizations, management tends to become more important than talent. Many H^3s attract talent and shape their organizations around it. For example, Capital

One and Macromedia hold talent at a premium. Corning is built around 2,000 of the world's best scientists; Palm attracts people who want to create breakthroughs; Macromedia gets the crème de la crème of engineers and designers; the world's top cancer researchers are drawn to Genzyme.

Building around talent sometimes means going to where the talent is, as Navisoft did. But what if your talent is scattered around the world, as is the case with Lend Lease's boards and executive teams?

Lend Lease has figured out a way to be wherever the top talents are. The chairman and CIO work in Boston; the CEO and CFO, in London; headquarters and a few directors are in Sydney; other directors reside in Singapore, Switzerland, London, Boston, and so forth. The concept works well for Lend Lease. If someone in Atlanta or Dubai has knowledge or a good idea about a product that can be transferred to Australia, it's just a matter of a telephone call. "If it's a good idea, it will be done," says chairman Jill Ker Conway. "There isn't a large bureaucratic structure that gets in the way."

Far-flung talent has, in many ways, worked well for Lend Lease in terms of innovation. The company was the first to launch a global real estate investment fund, which has since been copied. It was the first to offer soup-to-nuts real estate services with financing, design, construction, securitization, and management businesses, each of which could be based in different countries. A Lend Lease customer could have its buildings designed in one country, developed in another, and financed in third. "I think our best service to a client comes when we can put all these things together," says Conway.

CLUSTERS

For all of his companies, David Cole has had to bring in a lot of new minds quickly. The biggest push was at AOL. "We would go out and buy groups of talented people who were already working together in a business," says Cole. The leadership issues had already been established. The culture was readily discernible. "It was part of our strategy," explains Cole. "We said, 'This is the smartest way to grow.' With these clumps, we were able to get a lot more done. In hiring innovative, pre-existing groups, not only did we move faster, but we knew more." Often, AOL acquired whole companies with the expressed goal of getting their talent groups. Cole calls it "capitalized recruiting."

TALENT MARKET

Early in his career at Bell Labs, Ditzel set out to stack the deck. He went outside his own division to the VP of the computer division and said, "I've got this new idea that I'm calling RISC microprocessors and it's really important. We need to be doing it here, but it's not going to happen in this structure. I want you to give me some money, and let me pick people out of your division and my division and other divisions and let us work together on this project." And he did it. Ditzel became a market maker for talent.

It's part of a lesson he learned from watching Steve Jobs in action. "When Jobs was working on the Mac, he didn't ask or negotiate for talent," recalls Ditzel. "He just approached the talent he wanted and said, 'Hi, I'm Steve. I'm starting this new project and you're going to join it.' He didn't care if that person was in the middle of another project. He just walked over to this guy's computer, pulled the plug out of the wall, and said, 'Follow me to your new office.' That's one of the reasons I have a lot of respect for Steve Jobs. He wins in the talent market."

Ditzel built his new company, Transmeta, the same way. Once he developed confidence in his general idea for the Crusoe Chip, once he realized it could happen, he was able to convince some of the best talent in the industry, such as Linus Torvalds—developer of Linux, the most widely used open source operating system—to join his cause.

At Enron, talented people who suggested ideas for a new business were charged with building and growing that business—a variation on building a business around talent. When John Sherriff first thought of the online commodities trading model months before the idea was presented to CEO Jeff Skilling, he assembled his choice of talent around him and grew the business, sparking other new businesses designed around the same model. Three hundred and fifty people in the company thought the idea had enough merit to warrant spending their personal time and allocated their budgets to bring this new business concept to life. Anyone in the company could try to win over other employees with new ideas. If they were able to convince enough of the right people to contribute their creative talents and resources, they could build the business together. Ideas are for sale in the talent marketplace.

When I asked Jeff Skilling what he would do if I, an outsider, came to him with an idea for a new business, he said, "OK, tell me how you are going to come on board and run it for me. We are only constrained by the availability of talent."

The market for talent was very liquid at Enron. When Sherriff's group came up with the concept of a credit derivative business, he figured he should see how Skilling felt about it, since it was fairly different from other Enron businesses. "I didn't want to surprise him. I wanted his support," says Sherriff.

Skilling didn't skip a beat. He said, "Go!"

"It was really a pretty short conversation," Sherriff recalls.

Lend Lease also innovates by redefining talent markets. "When we tackle a new question or problem, we mix up a group of talented executives from all the different businesses," explains Jill Ker Conway. "No matter whether it was a financial services problem or an engineering one, we expect them to work together and work it out. It is, in essence, an idea swap meet. Normally, there's an agenda worked out and there are consultants brought in. But, sometimes, they throw it all out, change the agenda, and do it another way. It's very organic."

At Capital One, anybody who has a new idea can test it. No one needs permission. The company offers its support, providing access to a modest stipend. Employees can test their creative abilities in the real marketplace, with real customers.

DREAM TEAMS AND SOLO FLIGHTS

Some creative people contribute better in teams; some work better solo. Teams have become a fairly standard way of working and now, there is little opportunity for people to spend time creating alone.

"One of the most important lessons for me in my career," recalls David Cole, "was when I had a whole group of great programming guys. They had the right procedures; they had the right meetings, and they had the right Coke, coffee, and doughnuts and all that stuff. And they were tasked with doing a 16-bit version of a product for the IBM PC. Then I had another guy who was a loner. He didn't want to be with any other guys, but he was very gifted. So, I just took him, gave him two junior programmers of his choice and a red Mustang, and simply said, 'Beat this team of guys!' and they did—and not just by a little bit, but absolutely by a mile! Everybody agreed it was a great product, and it was done long before those other guys could have done it. It was dBaseIII, Ashton-Take's most successful product."

While new technologies have enabled sharing and collaboration, others have made innovation increasingly possible by single individuals. The scale on which individuals can contribute to innovations continues to change dramatically.

Ditzel, for example, needs solo time up front. He went off on his own for a few months before he emerged with the plan for Transmeta. "I'm a person who doesn't really like to talk about things until I have them worked out," Ditzel says. He supplied the vision and he brought in seven others to help work out the details and make improvements. Tod Machover, the renowned contemporary composer, known for his creative collaborations with top artists such as Peter

Gabriel, Bono and U2, David Byrne, and Joshua Bell, also works with large creative squads as in his highly acclaimed Brain Opera project. But, Machover prefers to form and develop compositions in private time and space before jumping into the team stream.

ATTRACTIONS

Creative talent tends to be most attracted by situations that let or even help them do what they want to do, the way they want to do it. It's about freedom and pursuing dreams.

"I find the biggest help here is that people trust that they can do exciting things. They can talk about and be proud of their ideas," says Henri Termeer. "It's possible to do something that doesn't necessarily have anybody's buy-in. We have both an introspective and a searching environment. People have a lot of fun here despite the fact that their work has such high stakes."

The playful creative culture of Macromedia makes that company an exciting place to work. "It's a magnet for West Coast creative types," says Betsey Nelson, "and they attract people who aspire to join their ranks." But an even stronger draw is the stimulation and encouragement aiding the development of new ideas. "If you have good ideas," Nelson says, "you're going to get a chance to present them. You're welcome at the discussion table or planning session so long as you make a contribution. Even if you're a senior vice president but not really contributing, you'll be asked to find something else to do."

Dreams can also serve to pull people together. The constant questions at Macromedia are "What can you not do today that you want to do? What dreams are you able to realize?" Those questions led to the revolutionary development of Dreamweaver.

"People come here because they want to work here," says Nelson. "I don't have to be the top offer necessarily—people like to work here because they can pursue their dreams, and I want to cultivate that. It ultimately helps our customers, and it breeds loyalty as well, because customers want to work with a company like us. That's why we still have a 70 percent market share. I think it's a kind of virtuous circle."

If your people identify with others outside of the organization more than they identify with you inside, their ideas will leak out and, often, their bodies will follow. Young talent is especially hard to hold. Ditzel was the youngest full-time staff member Bell Labs had ever hired. "What you'll find interesting about Bill Gates, Bill Joy, me, and others who started very, very young in this is that once we got our education technically, learned how the culture works, and learned how to run with it, we were still young enough to leave and go do something about it." If an organization is attractive enough, talent stays.

SYSTEM CHECKS

You still have to determine how much an employee is worth relative to your innovative mission. The typical vertical evaluation systems don't work well when organizations and environments are changing quickly.

Jeff Skilling explains the problem by using the analogy of the child's game of "telephone" in which a message is conveyed along a line of gossipers. "The message is never the same at the end. Someone at the top says, 'The world is changing, and we have to change direction.' I guarantee you that if you have ten people reporting to you, maybe four of them get it, four say they get it but they really don't, and two are actually hostile to it. Even with the four who get it, by the time it gets down to the bottom, a very different message is received."

"At Enron, we moved to a horizontal performance evaluations system," explains Skilling. "We put everybody in four organizational levels and evaluated each by a committee of twenty-five people chosen by me for their excellent understanding of our mission." It is a forced ranking system. "Instead of the lines of somebody's boss and boss and boss, I know there's an absolute direct line, through this committee, between our employees and our goals," Skilling says.

Controversy over forced ranking abounds. Some people are horrified by it, believing it is an invitation to discriminate. But Skilling, who believes strongly in the economics of free markets, strongly disagrees: "People who think that there is not a forced ranking at their company are out of their minds!" he exclaims. "Ultimately," he explains, "you have to pay people a salary—and there are only a certain number of dollars to go around. Compensation and reward have to be tied to specific evaluations. People have to figure out who gets the dollars and who doesn't. That's forced ranking!" he says emphatically. "You can either be explicit or implicit about it. We prefer to be explicit because we think it gives better feedback. In the old days, before we made the change, 95 percent of the employees had received outstanding or above performance evaluations. *Ninety-five percent!* What kind of feedback is *that?*"

The Number One objective at Enron was to build value for the company rather than to just please the boss. If your boss doesn't like your idea, but you can convince the committee that it has merit, you can move out to a more hospitable place. This option allows you to transfer flexibly across the organization, with the assurance that wherever you go in the organization the same committee will evaluate you later.

DYNAMO HUM

In traditional organizations, people interested in advancement usually want to be associated with the core business because that's where most of the revenue is. The more revenue that is managed, the higher the compensation is for the managers, and the better their chances are for promotion and greater reward. They are, in essence, incentivized to stick with core business initiatives. The problem is: that's not where innovation comes from.

If, instead, you want people to aspire to be innovators and develop new businesses, you need to get a fresh bunch of carrots. One of the first things to figure out is what kind of creativity you want to have. What problems do you need to solve? What are your innovation goals? Do you have a small number of big problems or a large number of small problems? Are they better tackled inside or outside your organization?

An important aspect of innovation management is figuring out a process by which you can get certain kinds of creativity to happen. "You have to be careful," Nathan Myhrvold warns. "Some companies will say, 'We'll give you a bonus for every new patent.' And they get lots of bogus patents they don't do anything with."

If you withhold rewards from people when their ideas don't work, that is not good. If you compensate people based on how long they've been at the company, that is not good either. So, what *is* good?

Some H³s such as Corning and MIT's Media Lab reward people for crossing organizational and functional boundaries. At Corning, Ackerman and Loose set goals that span across units and divisions. Enron rewarded people for starting businesses. Capital One rewards them for developing new products.

Lend Lease takes into account how much they improve culture and enhance relationships both inside and outside of the organization. As the company has grown through acquisition and global expansion, managers needed to build a common culture. Cash-poor because they were integrating many new businesses, Lend Lease couldn't create financial incentives. So the company created a system, similar to airline mileage programs, which it calls "culture credits." Anybody who is a real innovator in finding ways to bring different parts of the organization together in action, spirit, or values builds up a credit account. The innovator can use the credit in spending a day with a senior executive team or in working on a particular business problem, or even having lunch with the chairman.

The opportunity to work side by side with the top executive team is a great incentive for everyone at Lend Lease, including the most junior. "The idea is to find the people who are building their collective culture and to put them in touch with senior executives," explains Jill Ker Conway. "They get their shot at solving new kinds of business problems. They also gain incredible experience and visibility."

H³s also have enlightened compensation structures in line with the risk that executives take. At Corning, for example, in addition to more traditional stock options, if profit and sales goals are met in a very embryonic business, those business builders get a special bonus. It is almost like creating an inside stock deal: Instead of just being tied to the company stock, employees are tied to their own numbers. When Corning wants to sell a business, added incentives are available if the sale price is high.

Corning also has unique incentive programs that reach down to the workforce in each manufacturing unit, although not all unions are happy about relinquishing such power over compensation. In effect, everybody in the company can have up to a 10 percent bonus, and even possibly more, based on "local sets of objectives." Corning practices risk-sharing and gain-sharing at every level. Although each plant has its own set of circumstances, Ackerman claims to have a principle of continuous proof, as illustrated by a steadily climbing gross margin, at times approaching 42 percent, and sometimes as much as doubled productivity gains. As many as seventy operations evaluate themselves and each other, setting a higher bar for local objectives each year. "Gain-sharing is unique," says Ackerman. "It gets everybody very interested in what they're doing in each location. It's one thing that unites us all together." A fourth of a unit's rating is based on the company's earnings performance, whereas three quarters of it is measured by the local unit performance.

Gain-sharing need not be profit-oriented. It can be a business goal—for example, to get a certain market share, win back a customer, or reach a safety goal. "That's unique," Loose believes. "I don't know of any other company that does this."

While everyone at Enron had stock options, Jeff Skilling was vehemently opposed to equity participation in specific initiatives. "One of the keys in our organization is that we are trying to create a meritocracy," Skilling explained, trying to take "luck" out of the mix. Take the case of broadband business. If people who worked in broadband had equity participation, they would have been multimillionaires overnight. But that all crashed. At the same time other people were building a steel business, a much more mundane business, but then that industry began to do exceptionally well. Enron's meritocracy insured that people in both groups got compensated equally. He believed this unification helped long-term development in the organization. "If they are smart," he said, "people should be paid regardless of what business unit they are in or what luck comes their way."

David Cole arranges for senior executives to be owners out of the block. He wants them motivated right away. If anyone leaves to take another job, the company buys back the stock. "The critical thing to grab," says Cole, "is the opportunity to really have a stake in the business and have a unity of interest with the shareholders." Cole uses different systems and changes his approach depending on the characteristics of the leadership that he is attracting into the organization. Cole believes shareholders should adapt to a new way of thinking, allowing for more flexibility and creativity in their hiring and evaluation criteria to better match the needs of a unique talent.

Cash and creature comforts are not all that attract people. In fact, some H^{3}s have found that a generous supply of resources for a creative individual or team can be even more rewarding. For example, Corning recently spent over $3 million to build specialized facilities for one senior researcher so he could conduct the experiments he wanted to pursue in melting glass. Giving an individual or a team the staff, equipment, space, time, and budget to pursue dreams can have the biggest impact of all.

There are a number of ways to tool things up so you can meet the unique needs of your executives. It starts by asking your most talented people, "What's important to you?"

MACRO STRUCTURE

Imagine telling your employees, "You can organize any way you want. I don't care." You might expect utter chaos and complete dysfunction. But Corning, one of the most innovative and successful companies in the world, is managed just that way. "There is no one right way to organize things," says Roger Ackerman. "We offer unique incentives so that people look at businesses as if they were their own. There is no cookie-cutter structure. There have been a lot of permutations and combinations."

H^3s tend to take an "Erector set" approach to organizational structure, and the model is never done, the bolts are never fully tightened. Sometimes the structure is adjusted to accommodate or incentivize talent, or to take advantage of market opportunity, or to stimulate innovation. "We reorganize all the time," says Peter Lewis as he scans his thirty-five-year history as chairman and CEO of Progressive. "That's good! We get a new focus. This keeps people on edge—and that's good for innovation. We have a fluid organization because we change it every year. I give people the authority to organize the way they want to—so long as they're motivated and they get the job done, and they keep innovating."

Beyond autonomous organization, H^3s have developed some interesting new structures. Taking some positives from the re-engineering movement, such as flattening structures, while avoiding the weaknesses, such as lack of attention to top-line growth, the new organizational designs are largely geared to foster innovation. While re-engineering flattened to increase efficiency by cutting cost and streamlining operations, H^3s tend to like flat structures because they produce better interaction and better ideas.

"I thought the whole re-engineering fad was pretty bogus," says Dave Ditzel. "I like a shallower structure, in part because of better communication. When you get too many levels deep, it's hard to know what's really going on. My second most important issue is about empire building and avoiding it. If you have lots of titles, then people play the game according to whatever you make the game to be." In traditional organizations, people realize that title promotions and salaries are largely based on how many people report to them. So, they'll work to hire more and more people. "We try to avoid titles wherever possible," says Ditzel. "I have a number of people that have been VPs in other organizations and here they're just 'engineer' or 'member of staff.' That's OK, because we don't make title a big peer-respect thing. You get respect out of the work that you do."

BUDDY SYSTEMS

Innovative organizations tend to play well with others. As discussed in earlier chapters, they tend to form new kinds of relationships that can help in all aspects of the innovation process, from ideation to commercialization. Partnership, in general, is not a new concept. What is new about H^3 partnering is that it has become de rigueur. In contrast to traditional companies, which may form one or two partnerships, H^3s such as Genzyme form many.

Many are moving beyond traditional partnerships to form new models, such as new spins on the Japanese keiretsu, a cluster or clan-based organizational structure. Venture-capital firm Kleiner Perkins Caufield & Byers developed a new keiretsu model, with Netscape at its core, that encourages member companies to feed each other business, share information, services, and synergies, temporarily exchange key executives and board members, and still remain independent and unfettered. Keiretsu members enjoy new economies of scale and thrive on such collaborations and cross-pollination of talent, skills, shared resources, and ideas.

The way John Seely Brown sees it, innovators need to "marinate" in a lot of diverse information and nuance. "When you marinate, serendipity happens," says Brown, "and the keiretsu is like ten different marinades all seeping together and interacting." Brown is developing an innovation keiretsu that will help form and support a network of corporate keiretsus. "I want to create a symphony of peripheral innovations," he says.

MIT's Media Lab has developed many new concepts in partnerships, one of which is an innovation consortium. Currently, the Lab is the only place on earth where competitors such as Agfa, Fuji, and Kodak sit around the same table and talk openly about the future of photography. Of course, conferences and symposia bring rivals together, but those venues are more guarded and much less collaborative.

According to Rudy Burger, in order to do meaningful world-class research, a company has to spend a minimum of $50 million a year to set up its own lab. But consider, if that same company put $1 million a year into a consortium, pooling its contribution with that of 200 other non-competitive members, each would have access to a $200 million research project. The choice is having access to an annual contribution of $200 million for research, sharing the intellectual property (IP) with those companies—as opposed to securing an exclusive license to the intellectual property generated by one's own $100 million investment in research. "I think companies will eventually recognize that the shared IP model is the better one," says Burger.

This model is already starting to play out in genomics, where individual companies are discovering new genes, properties, and molecules. Instead of trying to patent, they're putting their discoveries out for anyone's potential use in any potential development of new applications.

If a company such as ImClone, for instance, discovers a gene, it has two choices: It can patent the gene, or it can leave it open so that others have access to the gene. In patenting, there are the standard protections and licensing issues. In the open model, any company, university, or individual can take the new gene and develop new applications for it or create new products from it. The new products are then patented by the product developer, but the gene developer receives no royalty in this case and has no jurisdiction in the use of the new product. The gene developer can also develop a new product based on the gene, itself. In this case, it would patent-protect the product but not the gene.

PRODIGIOUS PROGENY

Business incubators have gone in and out of vogue. In the last decade, over 800 new incubators cropped up in the heat of to tackle the New Economy. Some, such as idealab!, CMGI, e-Hatchery, and Internet Capital Group (ICG), reached stratospheric market caps. They crashed, along with their progeny, when the bubble burst. Now, for many, "incubator" is a dirty word. If you examine the ruins, you'll find more evidence that the particular eggs these incubators were hatching were duds, with deeply flawed business models. However, the concept of an incubator—a mother-group that supports infant companies, speeding and strengthening their development until they are strong enough to fend for themselves—still has merits.

Therics, Incorporated, a Princeton-based biotechnology firm, was incubated at the Trenton Business and Technology Center and was sold to publicly traded Tredergar Corporation in 1999 for $13.9 million. Tredergar committed to invest $60 million into expanding Therics's tissue engineering business over a three-year period.[8] For some, the line between incubators and venture capital firms is very blurry. In some cases the terms are even used interchangeably. For example, Kleiner Perkins Caufield & Byers has worked as an incubator would in having its hatchlings share a nest of resources. AOL, Intuit, Sun, and Netscape were stellar examples of a brood fostered by KPCB.[9]

Incubators can facilitate and encourage the flow of ideas between different hatchling companies and can provide nourishment, resources, facilities, and expertise that would be otherwise inaccessi-

ble. Critics may charge that entrepreneurship cannot be system-
atized, but this is not about "systemization." It's about leveraging
innovation assets.

Many new incubators are seeded with venture capital. Some are
beginning to coordinate their hatchlings to build one macro set of
core competencies. Some companies set up internal incubators to
keep the best budding ideas from walking out the door. The more
talent you have inside the company, the more likely they are to leave
to start or join new businesses that can better capitalize on their
ideas. There is no better example of that than Xerox, a company that
spawned numerous other companies, such as Adobe and 3Com.

Rudy Burger proposes setting up an internal incubator as a fundamental component of the research environment, with a permeable membrane between the incubator and R&D activity, to facilitate more successful commercial application. A company can build
its own internal incubator to generate ideas and grow new businesses in-house.

Although Enron's idea marketplace worked fantastically well, the
company began a controversial new initiative called the Accelerator.
One floor in the Houston headquarters was set aside and divided
into six areas to serve as a kind of internal incubator for new ideas.
The Accelerator team's mission: Canvas the company in search of
rough new concepts, pick their six favorites, set them up with space
and other centrally funded resources, and develop them into new
businesses. The big questions became: Would the ideas be as good,
and would the businesses be as strong as those that came from Enron's culture of personal passion and sacrifice?

TRACKERS

Henri Termeer wanted to buy a company that could grow human
skin. There were a large number of orthopedic and cardiovascular

surgical procedures that could have benefited greatly, if they had biological materials, such as skin and bone, to work with instead of plastics, metals and fabrics. The market opportunity was big. Termeer and his executive teams had an epiphany: Genzyme already had a number of product development programs, which could dovetail nicely with some emerging technologies, solve the materials problem, and capture the market. By combining programs, they could actually grow skin, cartilage, and other biological materials for use in grafts, replacements, plastic surgeries, and the like. Termeer saw a perfect fit and a great acquisition opportunity in Biosurface Technologies. The question was: How to do the deal and how to structure the business?

Termeer wanted to develop this new business with as little constraint as possible—to be free to experiment, to bob, weave, and commercialize fast. None of the typical models of ownership appealed to Termeer, who is an economist by training—not total absorption, business units, subsidiaries, spin-offs, split-ups, carveouts, special purpose research corporations (SPARCs), or research and development limited partnerships (RDLPs). To Termeer, they all had too many drawbacks. Genzyme has a reputation of being very creative with financial models. The innovative answer here was to combine Biosurface Technologies with Genzyme's internal tissue engineering business and create the Tissue Repair division, which Termeer then structured as a new kind of tracking stock. Termeer used a similar tracking stock strategy in forming Genzyme Molecular Oncology and Genzyme Biosurgery.

Tracking stocks are like internal spin-offs. Typically the parent retains ownership of all the underlying assets of the business, while it sells some of its economic interests to investors who want a "pure play" in their portfolios. Investors don't own any part of the tracking stock company itself and have no voting rights. Tracking stocks offer unique benefits to companies, such as certain tax and risk-management advantages, providing both consolidated and separate financial statements. They are a way for a parent company to operate a completely different kind of business without stepping too far out on the ledge. Each tracker has its own CEO, management team, employees, and shareholders.

The concept of a tracking stock is a relatively recent creation. In vented by General Motors in 1984, it was, at least in theory, a way of "unlocking" value for shareholders. It was developed as a structure for optimizing GM's acquisition of Electronic Data Systems (EDS)[10] and used again in 1985 when GM acquired Hughes Electronics. The company believed these two businesses, if separately valued, would achieve higher overall valuations than those that GM had determined at the time of acquisition. By the mid-1990s, a few other companies followed with similar offerings, such as USX/Marathon, US Steel/Delhi, and Continental Baking/Ralston Purina. Genzyme was the seventh company ever to try tracking stocks. In 1998, Sprint issued the Sprint PCS tracker, whose success triggered seven more companies to give tracking stocks a try that year. More were contemplated as established companies attempted forays into Internet businesses, although most of those never made it out before the dotcoms crashed. Some argue that the problem was in the dotcoms' flimsy business models, not in the tracking stock structure.

Today Genzyme Corporation trades as four entities: three tracking stocks—Genzyme General (GENZ), Genzyme Biosurgery (GZBX), Genzyme Molecular Oncology (GZMO)—and one publicly traded subsidiary, Genzyme Transgenics Corporation (GZTC). There is no stock for the parent corporation itself. "While the largest division, GENZ, is very profitable, the newer divisions, such as GZMO, are still unprofitable," says Gail Maderis, president of Genzyme Molecular Oncology. "We can't apply all of Genzyme General's profits back into its own R&D, because Genzyme shareholders are looking for a regular increase in earnings per share (EPS)." Genzyme Molecular Oncology trades as more of a discovery engine and can take much bigger longer-term risks. Its losses don't tarnish Genzyme's stock value.

Most management, operations, and finance functions are kept

separate for each tracker. But Genzyme developed a new spin: the science and technology is shared. GM and EDS couldn't do that, nor could any other parent/tracker ensemble.

"Our Genzyme affiliation gives us far more leverage than most companies have," says Maderis. "At Genzyme, in addition to the infrastructure synergies, we get enormous leverage from sharing the technology base. I'm not aware of others where the leverage is so fundamental to the core competency and strategy of the entity." Each tracker can access the Genzyme's clout, leverage its brand, and share its resources, including R&D staff, technology, manufacturing facilities, intellectual property, and clinical personnel. The cost of these resources is allocated and charged to each division based on how much it uses.

Termeer's tracking stock structure promotes innovation by building in diversity. It allows the company to explore opportunities in a variety of markets such as oncology, genetics, and biomaterials. This facilitates one of the key dynamics of innovation: two or more different knowledge bases intersecting. In addition, the financial and strategic objectives of Genzyme's three businesses differ according to their stages of development. Genzyme's corporate structure allows its emerging businesses to invest in more research and development, while preserving the capacity of its more established business to generate earnings growth.

Not everyone is sold on the benefits of tracking stocks.[11] Of the thirty-one tracking stocks issued since 1984, only nine have outpaced the S&P 500, including AT&T Wireless and three from Genzyme.[12] Some investors fear that Genzyme might set the tracking stocks up to turbocharge pricey new product development, then snatch rewards away in a buy-back when the products are close to market but before the public has an understanding of their value. Maderis argues, "We can't trade on inside information. If we were an independent company, Merck or Bristol-Meyers could buy us at any time. And gosh knows what the premium would be! It could be higher or lower than the 30 percent to which we have committed. So it's not necessarily any different than any other situation."

Through these structures, Genzyme is able to devote significant amounts of money to nurture new ideas along. And that's one of the main points. For example, when GZMO got great data on one of its clinical trials, the company pushed the button mid-year to go from one trial to five trials. "If I'd been under a budget constraint, worrying about quarterly earnings in the general division, I couldn't have just immediately turned the faucet and quadrupled the trials," Maderis explains. "We've got a billion in cash to work with. Most start-ups and spin-offs can't say that."

MODULES

Over 56 percent of inductees into the National Inventors Hall of Fame made their discoveries as individuals or at small firms they founded. Only 27 percent came from large organizations. If you believe, as many H^{3}s do, that ownership is a key driver of performance, strategic size becomes more of an issue. If a group is too big, each stake is small, and the drive is weaker. If it is too small, it doesn't have the ability to scale.

Beyond public ownership dominated by institutional investors, the ownership of most traditional companies is concentrated at the very top of the organizations, with little or none trickling down to employees. They tend to favor economies of scale and clout. They want developments to happen under their own roofs and are reluctant to cut a budding prospect loose, even if it can fly higher and faster as a smaller bird.

The founder of idealab!, Bill Gross believes that a group of ten to one hundred people is the right size for an innovation-focused organization. He sees them as "tribes" in which everyone knows each other well and has emotional connections. There is greater intimacy, better communications, and more camaraderie. "Within a tribe, people still feel like one clan fighting a common enemy," says Gross.[13]

Large sizes can be limiting. They can be paralyzing. It's not surprising that many large companies have to struggle hard to gain lift through innovation. For the most part, the pharmaceutical industry can't figure it out. Companies merge because they don't know quite how to develop the science by themselves. Henri Termeer, like Gross, advocates strategic sizing. "If large companies endeavor for great scientific success, and if they allow themselves to be broken up at times, then they could reseed, reconfigure, and re-challenge their people," he suggests.

Obviously, you have to be careful about that strategy. Thermo Electron Corporation is a scientific instruments manufacturer that created twenty-three companies out of its activities, only sixteen of which were left standing. That the other seven companies went out of business may or may not be a good thing, but the point is that such division into smaller parts is a decision that has to be thoroughly considered before rushing to the chopping block. "We created many smaller companies too," explains Termeer, "but we will change the size and structure of our companies freely, as opportunity dictates." For example, with little exception, if you or anyone you know has ever undergone amniocentesis testing, Genzyme's genetic testing division was behind it. "We made it a public company where we needed to finance it as a subsidiary. Then we liked it so much, we brought it back into the general division," explains Termeer. "Things never need to stay the same for very long. You build a company, you don't build a division. And just because a division is the way to structure today doesn't mean it needs to be structured tomorrow in that fashion."

This smaller-piece structure, favored by many H³s, is analogous to the structure of information available on the Internet, and it is curious that the two structures have developed side by side. In contrast to traditional media such as books, magazines, and television, where content is presented whole and integrated, the Internet often gives us small and discrete pieces of information, all of them available at any time. True, we can read an article from the *New York Times* online, consult a job description on monster.com, or find an item for sale on eBay, but in the Internet's world of piecemeal information retrieval the data can come from any number of sites and users. Thanks to better technology, as well as lower prices and lower barriers to entry, the number of sources of information available in the online structure is practically infinite.

Some argue, however, that if you structure the organization right, you're never going to be too big. "My job is to listen," says Dave Ditzel. "I can't listen to 200 VPs. When there's an important issue, I go another level below that and listen in more detail. I don't think that's unworkable. I watched it work at Sun, where there were 15,000 people. CEO Scott McNealy could get down to another layer of VPs, and there weren't too many people. Someone on the staff level talks to the same people that the general manager of the division talks to. Quite often, people are too operationally focused. They will get so busy in meetings that they don't have time to go and talk to people. That's why we've split up that role in Transmeta."

Lend Lease splits things into modules called project control groups or PCGs. This is an engineering concept. PCGs are central to the company's organizational strategy. It is all about designing a critical path to an endpoint, figuring out what has to happen at every stage along the way to success. "We have a very project-driven company," says Conway. A PCG forms for each big project, with directors who typically include an assortment of outside experts and stakeholders. Similar to SPWI's Leading Edge Expert Network, a PCG could include top-notch architects, anthropologists, entertainers, CEOs of other companies, artists, and so forth, together with Lend Lease directors. Like a board of directors, a PCG governs a project, checking in periodically, being available for consultation, and holding feet to the fire.

PCGs are similar to Enron's project groups. They both are primarily autonomous and self-organizing, and they are both directly responsible for building businesses. They share structural ideals with other H³s, incorporating a big-picture focus, emphasis on creative talent, and no-holds-barred communications.

> "We're open to new corporate capital structures that allow us to be involved in lots of innovation—and not just what's in-house. This also helps us in attracting and retaining great employees over the long term."
>
> —Betsey Nelson

If all this structural autonomy and change sounds as though it can result only in organizational chaos, if the possible design options seem too overwhelming or even contradictory, consider the notion that our lives and the world around us are designed just this way. If we are successful, we hold it together with our vision, our mission, and our macro-approach. The way Robert Wilson sees it, "Paris is a beautiful city, with many different styles that hold together. I can design something—Frank Gehry has a different personality and will design something altogether different. Then there are different designs throughout history. But, the city has an architectural cohesion. Take, for example, the apartment building in which you live: You like it minimal, and I like it baroque, and we live next door to each other, but the building has a cohesion, an organization that fits each personality."

PHYSICAL ENVIRONMENTS

A large two-story corkscrew slide gives the corporate offices of Macromedia the air of an amusement park. Ping-Pong tables occupy a lot of space in the employees' cafeteria. Physical environments can either support or frustrate innovation activities. People have different preferences and needs—at times wanting lots of stimulation, open communal spaces, and face-to-face contact, at other times desiring peace and quiet, privacy, and virtual technologies.

One of the most important issues to raise debate is over communal versus private space. The trend over the past twenty years—particularly evidenced by the cubicle, the open bullpen, and the disappearance of the personal office—has been toward openness and togetherness.

John Sherriff, CEO of Enron Europe, casts a strong vote for the collective experience. "We just jam people together, really close," he says. He tries to maximize IQ per square foot. He wants interactions at the coffee pot, elevator banks, and the bathrooms. On one floor, the company had 500 people from thirty-five different nationalities and all different kinds of backgrounds. The noise level was far higher than at most places. When I asked, "What about private space? Might hyper-interaction all the time actually hurt creative ambitions?" Sherriff responded, "Yeah, but, that's what the weekends and holidays are for, right?" Sherriff's offices collected a half a billion pieces of information a day. He believes that Enron's innovation advantage started with an information advantage, and that it's best to have open, unobstructed access to that information.

Although one can applaud Sherriff's statement of this ideal, we note with irony, however, that investors have complained about receiving confusing information from the company in its "opaque" financial statements.

John Loose would agree with Sherriff about the value of communal space. He tells of one scientist who, while walking around, happened upon another group of scientists who were having repeated problems trying to cut through a special kind of glass. The glass would shatter and spray shards everywhere. This scientist, through other meanderings, knew of a special fluid that binds only to glass and suggested that it be used to keep this glass intact while it was being cut. As Loose points out, big breakthroughs in Corning's fiber optics business happened just the same way—through a casual conversation in passing.

Communal space works for Corning, but not for everyone. "I tried that when I was CEO at Ashton-Tate," says David Cole. "I was twenty-eight years old, and I believed in the concept of the 'open office.' I even put my office out in the middle of a big open-floor plan. It was very strange. People knew what I was doing all the time. It didn't work. It didn't last long." Cole and his employees found open space to be a real distraction. In certain circumstances—for instance, tech support and telesales—people can share lessons learned and pump each other up to deal with inevitable rejection. But for settings where high levels of concentration are needed, it helps to have access to both communal and private space. Acirca's headquarters have some cubicles but everybody doesn't sit out in an open-floor plan.

For many, creative thinking requires some degree of physical separation at some points along the way. "People have so little time these days to actually sit by themselves to solve a problem and see something through," laments composer Tod Machover. "We spend so much time brainstorming or solving problems, often poorly. At the Media Lab, people spend hours and hours just thinking by themselves, trying to solve a problem without having to explain it to somebody until they are far enough along. Obviously, it is great to have places that are open, informal, and invite encounters that you didn't expect," says Machover. "But I think it is also important to be able to have a quiet place where you go away by yourself or with a small group, where you are not going to be interrupted or inhibited."

Genzyme has no campus. Instead, people work in various locations, some in Kendall Square in Cambridge, Massachusetts, some in Genzyme's state-of-the-art manufacturing facility near the Harvard Business School, some in Framingham, some in Fall River, and many others on the road. "We don't want a campus," says Termeer. "We will never have a research center surrounded with ponds and geese, where everyone can tightly meet in a corner, have coffee together, and exchange thoughts. It doesn't work in this company.

Size, bulk, and pushing people together in circumstances, where the surroundings become more important than the person—all that is troubling. It blinds the mind. There is an assumption of power—all of these monuments and beautiful campuses that large companies can so easily develop are shown off throughout their annual reports, with the best intentions—but it does not create productivity. It creates the expression of power, but it doesn't create a heart, and it doesn't create a way to make things happen."

Macromedia aims to create an environment where people want to work, day in and day out, even late into the night. "We try to create sort of a bond, not just to the other people in the company, but to the space itself," says Betsey Nelson. The building becomes a very real second home for many of the founders and employees. They need to personalize it. "If you're in a sort of cookie-cutter environment, it feels too much like a production line, and it's harder to create that emotional bond," Nelson says.

Whether environments are high-tech, high-touch, or some combination, they can be stimulating and inspiring. Some H^3s design spaces to connect with nature; others have peaceful Zen rooms; still others have game rooms. Several create inspiring environments with art.

Although corporate art collections are not new, some H^3s are using art to inspire and lift people's spirits. It's not just for decorating blank walls. Widely considered one of the top companies in supporting the arts, Corning, for example, owns Steuben Glass, and the Corning Museum houses one of the finest collections in the world of art glass. Glass sculptures are everywhere throughout the Corning complex, and a different major work of art graces each of four atria; the center houses a huge Dale Chihuly sculpture. "People can be sitting around having coffee and looking up at beautiful sculptures," says Roger Ackerman. "It helps in many ways, like a ripple effect in their creativity. Art and science, creativity and research, they're all connected here."

Peter Lewis considers art to be an integral part of how his company innovates and operates. He believes artists are the seers of our society and that visual provocation has great value. "The company is, in a sense, as idiosyncratic as I am," says Lewis. "We have what is possibly the finest collection of 1980s and 1990s paintings, better than anyone else's in the world." Over 5,000 pieces hang in 350 Progressive offices around the country and the collection is featured on their company website so that customers and potential customers see art as a part of the business. Some were valued as little as $1,000, but none originally cost more than $10,000. Of course, they are worth much more today. Lewis adds the "undiscovered" to his vast collection of Rauschenbergs, Lichtensteins, Warhols, Stellas, and the like. "Some of it is even screwier than the stuff that's hanging around here," he says as he gestures toward the walls of his Manhattan penthouse. "At one of our last board meetings, I made a crack that when I retired, I feared the art would go also. I think that would be a serious mistake. The board

> We live in a country that sees the arts as an extra—a "we-can-live-without-it" thing. The arts are the first to be axed when school boards need to tighten their belts. All the arts—the fine arts, music, theater, writing, and so on—teach self-discipline, problem-solving, and independent thinking. Those things aren't extras.
>
> —Annette Lemieux

might see it as an unnecessary cost. But, the feedback I got from our senior people was '*Au contraire,* we understand its power.' I was very gratified by that."

For others, music is key to their environment. "Music actually stimulates as many, if not more, parts of the mind at once than almost anything else," says Tod Machover. "It obviously has the ability to get you in the gut and stimulate all kinds of very visceral primitive powerful responses. But it also has some strong connection with our general reasoning. In many ways music does tell stories."

If someone comes up with an idea for something beautiful, some way to build a stronger, healthier, more productive environment, or something wonderful for children or elderly people in a community, Lend Lease tries to develop it. The company has long been known for its enlisting the world's most influential architects, urban designers, and anthropologists, bringing them in early as part of the project executive team, as the company did with Fox Studios Australia. As Jill Ker Conway says, "In the long run this community will flourish, and we won't be driven totally by the numbers."

Whether it's with contemporary art, classical music, or fantastic architecture, many H^{3}s are designed to inspire and support the creative efforts of their people, partners, and customers. As we've seen in this chapter, this applies to the cultures they create, the quality of their creative leadership, and their views of art in the workplace— both physical or environmental art and the art of working. As we will see in Chapter 7, their philosophy about environments extends far outside their physical office spaces into the local and global communities.

. 7 .

MAKING AN APPLE PIE

Beyond the Organization

Experience is not what happens to you; it's what you do with what happens to you.

—Aldous Huxley

Over the past decade, work has become practically all-consuming. We have less time to do more things. We have more opportunity to keep working, even outside of the office, at any hour of any day. Thanks to our laptops, cell phones, beepers, Palm VIIs, and Blackberries, more and more of our personal time has been encroached upon. While a certain amount of stress and tension is good for creativity, many of us have too much for our own good. We can develop a collection of health problems, neglect our families and friends, and virtually starve ourselves to the point where our creative potential is greatly compromised.

New ideas at work, and the creativity it takes to conceive of them, come from people who are creative beings as a whole. As the emphasis on creativity and innovation for organizations can transform a company, it can also transform the way we live our lives. You must create something new in yourself into order to create something else. As Carl Sagan said, "If you wish to make an apple pie from scratch, you must first create the universe."

How will we integrate these new approaches to creativity and innovation with the whole-life experience? Creativity extends into home life, community, philanthropy, and other pursuits. Holistic creativity enhances all aspects of living.

This chapter looks beyond the organization, beyond the world of work. We see how a sampling of H³ companies and individuals create new sweetness for their communities, families, friendships, and themselves. We examine how creative philanthropy fosters future creative generations, how H³ people live with ambiguity, yet purposefully, with infinite passion—how they live the lives they imagine. They put something in the universe that wasn't there before, nurturing seeds and souls.

CREATIVE PHILANTHROPY

Strolling down a long lacy-petalled row of dwarf heirloom apple trees on a spring afternoon is a heavenly experience that delights the eye with fresh, soft colors, the nose with sun-warmed apple blossoms, the ear with chickadees and phoebes. The experience can transport us to a plane that is movingly different from the rest of our lives, and we think of things we don't normally think of, often in ways we have never tried before.

David Cole has taken many of these walks, especially after one such walk a few years ago triggered a new set of desires. He wanted to leverage his formidable corporate leadership talent by applying it to his interest in conservation. He began by plunking down a few million dollars[1] to buy a worn-out 500-acre farm named Sunnyside about seventy miles west of Washington, D.C., bordering a pocket-

sized town called Washington, Virginia. To support his other passion—good food—Cole set out to build an organic farm unlike any
the world has seen.

Organic food was already on its way to becoming one of the
hottest trends around, growing at a clip of about 24 percent a year,
on average, throughout the 1990s. There were a lot of reasons why
more people began to prefer organic foods. For one thing, organics
are perceived as being healthier than food genetically modified or
exposed to herbicides, pesticides, and chemical fertilizers. But beyond their own health, many people found organic foods more appealing because they began to care more and more about the
planet's health and its ecosystems. Demographics pushed the trend
along, since many Baby Boomers developed a high level of health,
social, and environmental consciousness. Cole was among them.

One of the top leaders in the high-tech industry, Cole began to
wonder if he could take a "new technologies" approach to organic
farming—using information to replace chemicals and increasing
both productivity and profitability, just as info-tech did with many
other industries. He pulled together some of the brightest minds in
both environmental and computer sciences to look at the intersection of those two disciplines. "At Sunnyside we are taking systems
and remote sensors, and integrating information technology into
organic production," he says. "No one else is doing this."

One of the great fortune-makers in the PC and Internet booms,
Cole could have easily just written a giant check to environmental
conservation organizations. But as a serial entrepreneur, he saw the
farm as a way to make a big, positive difference in the world *and* a
big, profitable business. He figured that the networking concepts
that exponentially expanded Silicon Valley could be applied to the
sunny fields of Rappahannock County.

Farming, always a tough way to make a living, has been getting
even tougher, especially for independent farmers. The tougher it
has become, the more they have needed to rely upon chemical technology to boost yields and cut costs. As a consequence, however, the

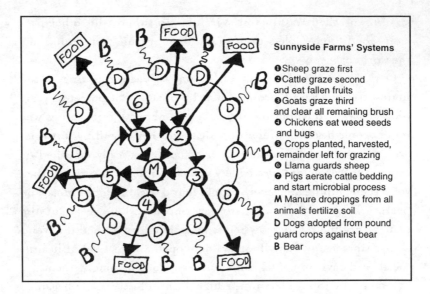

Sunnyside Farms' Systems

❶ Sheep graze first
❷ Cattle graze second
and eat fallen fruits
❸ Goats graze third
and clear all remaining brush
❹ Chickens eat weed seeds
and bugs
❺ Crops planted, harvested,
remainder left for grazing
❻ Llama guards sheep
❼ Pigs aerate cattle bedding
and start microbial process
M Manure droppings from all
animals fertilize soil
D Dogs adopted from pound
guard crops against bear
B Bear

more they have wrecked their own soil. Commercial growing techniques have depleted the land. Cole envisioned Sunnyside as a hub,
feeding and reviving a set of smaller farm spokes, to form a network
of strong, profitable organic farms. He designed a model that he
believes can be replicated in any agricultural area to help that area's
local farmers not only survive, but flourish. In addition, the project
helps heal the planet and strengthen our bodies.

It took almost $12 million and two years to get Sunnyside's soil
healthy and wriggling with fat earthworms again, to bring in cutting-
edge technologies that dramatically improve farm management, and
to fill the fields with organic crops and herds. Applying systems
thinking to the concept of crop and grazing rotation, Cole used a
succession of cows, then sheep, then goats, and then chickens to
keep the fields maintained, reducing the need for human and
chemical labor.

Sunnyside is a foodie's dream. Hundreds of Kobe beef cows,
called Wagyus, happily and freely roam the pastures. Dozens of toma-
toes, exceptional in their taste, color, and variety, as well as bright-
tasting berries, luscious orchard fruits, flowers, herbs, and vegeta-

bles, many of heirloom or gourmet variety, grow abundantly. Chickens freely range over the farm. Their eggs—with intense school-bus yellow yolks—are sold by a local Sunnyside market, or by Fresh Fields, a national chain of natural food markets, as well as by natural food stores up and down the East Coast. Sunnyside also supplies some of the most prestigious restaurants in Washington, D.C., as well as the Inn at Little Washington, where dinner is a sumptuous three-and-a-half-hour event. And that's not because the service is slow.

The farm is a conservationist's dream. "We're re-conceptualizing the farm as a living lab for our nonprofit institute," Cole says. Sunnyside Institute experiments with hundreds of new crop varieties and organic growing methods, and shares the results with farmers, food manufacturers and processors, as well as government agriculture czars from around the world. The institute also serves as an interpretive center to show how different living systems—hydraulic, ergonomic, and biologic—work and are related to each other and to profitable food production. "As far as we know, that's a new collision of forces," says Cole, "and we've got world-class thinkers working on that."

Beyond organic farming, Cole thinks the institute will increase understanding of sustainable systems by studying the biological and technical nutrient cycles and their relationships. Fungi, for example, play a role in metabolizing organic material, preparing it for microbial activity. The institute experiments with using fungi to produce nutrients to improve soil productivity. "There's a stupendous level of ignorance in terms of how these systems interrelate," Cole says. He believes it is a function of what he calls "Betty Crocker" farming, which encourages farmers to use predetermined formulae of chemical cocktails based on a pre-fab decision tree of factors such as temperature, cycle time, and so forth. "It's like thermonuclear war: They spray and kill everything in the soil," he laments. As much as we now know about the many systems that affect our lives, the interrelationships of these living systems are not all that well understood. Thousands of species live in the soil, but our agricultural schools and research labs have hardly begun to investigate them fully. What, for instance, is the interrelationship between mycelia and bacteria and plant roots in the system?

If you don't understand how the fungi operate, you're definitely not in the loop: You don't have a holistic view of what's happening—if you did, you could use fungi in your agricultural programs. By examining ways in which information systems can be smarter about biological systems, Cole seeks to move from biology as a "descriptive" science to biology as "predictive" one—that is, he wants to do more than just analyze the list of physical and behavioral characteristics of various species. He wants to understand the evolutionary paths species are likely to take in response to changes introduced to them and to their environment. The change is going to reshape strategies for innovating agriculture.

As vast as the genome project has been over the past few years, it is not big enough for Cole. So far, it has focused mainly on the human genome. He wants to look at earthworm and mushroom genomics to see how they interrelate, particularly with larger systems. "We want to use it, not only to change our farming methodologies, but also to influence others," he explains. For example, the institute is experimenting with mycofilters, which are actually mushroom filters with billions of mycelia, to turn wastewater into clean water, putting the clean water back into the system. "It is a $20 million effort, which is really big in the world of permaculture," he says, referring to the principles of perennial agriculture that employs renewable resources and rejuvenates local ecosystems.

Cole has turned his passion for saving the world into a carefully designed, innovative cluster of for-profit and not-for-profit enterprises, including Acirca, Sunnyside Farms, the Sunnyside Institute, and Cole Gilburne Bioinformatics and Life Sciences. Each member of this cluster feeds the others, and the group grows together, striving to reach at least as high as the most successful high-tech businesses have grown. "Conservation," Cole explains, "is really the game that's important to me as a philanthropist. There's no higher calling in life, as far as I'm concerned, given the environmental conditions that we are faced with here in the world."

Naysayers may think we've gone too far down the road for people, businesses, and governments to change. Cole counters this pessimism, saying, "I know for a fact that the history of extraordinarily high-performing companies is really a history of people who manage change and embrace consumers' changing needs and desires."

Cole, the former president of AOL Internet Services, aims to use his exceptional business talents, financial resources, and top-shelf connections to change the food and agriculture business in the United States and around the world. He believes corporate America and Europe have already begun to embrace the possibility of operating in an earth-friendly way. It is happening piece by piece. For some, it's coming up with a non-toxic green dye; for others, it's developing better-tasting meat substitutes; for others, it might be not cooking the French fries in animal fat. Cole, who is also a director of the American Farmland Trust and of the World Wildlife Fund, and former director and current adviser to the Nature Conservancy, has helped in developing a successful program for sustainable harvesting of fish and timber. In conservation, this is incredible progress, a world of change from where we were twenty-five years ago to where we are today.

It's easy to be cynical when you're in a transaction-oriented environment. So many of us serve on a project team, trying to sell something as soon as possible. But there are larger forces. "There are these tectonic forces that are moving beneath your feet that you really can't sense because you're in a narrower, problem-solving frame," says Cole, "but they are happening in our lifetimes."

Some of these things take a while to turn. Cole believes that even if it takes twenty, thirty, or forty years, somebody's got to have that horizon and start planting seeds now. "It's planting sequoias versus parsley," he says.

It is no surprise: it is all about economics. "I found out a long time ago, when you go to southern China, Indonesia, or Papua, New Guinea, and talk to politicians there, and you say you want to talk about conservation, their eyes glaze over. If you say you want to talk about economic development, they're all excited." Accordingly, Cole built an economic platform into the conservation initiative. He figured out a way for economic plans to have a strong, conservation component and vice versa; for example, if you plant crops in certain configurations and rotations, using organic methods, you not only prevent soil erosion, chemical seepage into the groundwater supply, chemical residues in food crops, and super-bugs, but you can also reap higher profits. Cole believes the best economic investments are those that do not scar the environment. "We found that the conservation dog is wagged by the economic development tail," he quips. "You can't just promote a good cause, you have to learn to speak economics."

If Cole is right, all corporations—not just those in the agriculture industry—will see the tremendous value of conservation as a component of their entire operations, from waste disposal to production to shipping and distribution. And if that is true, the items an accountant measures are likely to change. Look for "natural capital"— that is, money earmarked for conservation and other environmental concerns—to appear as a new item on the balance sheet.

STRATEGIC PHILANTHROPY

Corporate giving and social activism are not new, but they are taking on creative new forms and new purposes. Ben & Jerry's was one of the first companies to say publicly on its packaging that 5 percent of profits would go to protect the rainforests, a policy now adopted by Stonyfield and Bath and Bodyworks, among others. Corporate responsibility is being built into the business model. New global alliances are being formed for the express purpose of benefiting people in need. The H³ business world is teaming up with the nonprofit world in ventures of social innovation, which is now viewed as a boon to both the companies and the communities of people in need.

What's also new is the gargantuan scale of the new philanthropy. Many successful H³ leaders have built their for-profit mega-companies from scratch in well under ten years. Many have made more money than anyone could ever dream of and have significantly transformed the way we work and live. Now they believe they can do tremendous things, in the same fast, mammoth way, to improve society. They are becoming "social entrepreneurs."

They want to work with a new, results-oriented approach to corporate giving that links business interests with specific programs that are important to their stakeholders. Some focus on specific community problems, an approach called "strategic philanthropy," which differs from the ad hoc approach corporations have traditionally taken to giving.

H³s such as Capital One, Acirca, and Lend Lease have discovered that this new form of corporate giving can be a powerful tool. With a smart strategy, it can result in positive benefits such as stronger customer loyalty, higher employee satisfaction, and better relationships with the community. It's more than writing a check, however. It requires that businesses find out what is important to their stakeholders and become more directly involved in their communities. In essence, strategic philanthropy uses good business sense. It begins with a vision based on a company's values and a set of objectives. It supports the overall corporate strategy. It makes "social investments." And investors expect a significant return on both sides of the fence. Some call it a return on social investment (ROSI).

Strategic philanthropy quickly yields a win-win. Supported by companies such as Dreamworks SKG, Universal Studios, Motown Records, and Arthur Andersen, the Los Angeles-based Fulfillment Fund, for example, mentors troubled kids and grooms them so well that they are in heavy demand for internships and jobs with those sponsors. Incorporated as a nonprofit organization in 1977, the Fulfillment Fund has become the largest private donor of scholarships to students in the L.A. Unified School District.

Share Our Strength

Food has become a sophisticated art form over the past decade in the United States, as evidenced by the virtually ubiquitous splashes of balsamic vinegars, rounds of molten goat cheese, salty sun-dried tomato pillows, sushi-grade tuna, and champagne truffles. Restaurants have become exalted meccas. The Food Network, a widely popular cable channel devoted entirely to the preparation and enjoyment of food, has cast chefs as celebrated artistes, way beyond the likes of Julia Child and James Beard.

While a select few in prosperous circles indulge their taste buds, millions of people throughout the world are malnourished or starving. To help fight hunger, Bill Shore, the former chief of staff for Senator Robert Kerry and legislative director for Senator Gary Hart, organized a group called Share Our Strength (SOS), which leverages the knowledge, talents, and connections of star chefs and food professionals, among them Charlie Trotter, Daniel Boulud, Jean-Georges Vongerichten, Danny Meyer, and Tom Colicchio.

One of the leading anti-hunger organizations, SOS mobilizes thousands of individuals and organizations to develop such programs as Taste the Nation, a series of food- and wine-tasting events held annually across North America. Leading local chefs and vineyards prepare samples of their best dishes and libations for attendees. In 2000, at one event alone, 65,000 people paid $75 each to attend. What's more, *all* the proceeds went directly to hunger relief—an unheard-of feat in the not-for-profit world, but standard for SOS events. Since September 11, 2001, a number of restaurants around the world followed suit by donating proceeds to victims of the World Trade Center disaster.

At SOS, the operative phrase is "community wealth," a term referring to tangible assets and resources that are used to benefit the community of stakeholders, business partners, and needy recipients who come together in the fight against hunger and poverty. SOS wants to promote social change through financially profitable relationships—corporate partnerships and ventures—within the community. Community Wealth Ventures, the consulting arm of SOS, "was launched on the premise that every organization can increase its social impact by building on its own internal assets, rather than relying on support from external sources."[2]

Mark Rodriguez has actively participated in SOS since he was CEO of Danone International Brands, makers of Evian, and Dannon Natural Spring Water. When Rodriguez joined Acirca as its new CEO, he wanted to develop a winning business strategy for its ambitious growth. Immediately he thought of partnering with SOS in a symbiotic relationship never before achieved between a for-profit and not-for-profit organization: They give to each other.

Corporations have long been donors to CEOs' pet causes, but the Acirca case is different. In addition to prominently displaying the SOS logo and call to action on its packaging and marketing communications, Acirca executives offer their management and marketing expertise to SOS. In an even more unusual twist, SOS superstar chefs will act as a dream team of product development consultants to Acirca, helping the company to understand food and beverage trends and issues, and assisting with R&D, formulations, and manufacturing processes. Each organization is helping the other to grow.

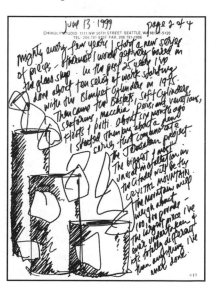

RECIPES FOR GIVING

Getting strategic about philanthropy involves the same kind of vision and planning skills as any other kind of strategic development: You have to get the ingredi-

ents right. Corning, Inc., for example, supports the work of glass sculptor Dale Chihuly and other artists because they push the medium of glass beyond currently known limits. They discover new forms and properties, pointing to new applications that Corning hopes to incorporate into its next product innovations. So first, it's important to decide what your mission is within the context of your existing organization. Consider your competencies, capacities, culture, and market opportunities. Then, decide which causes or areas of need are most important to you and others in your organization—and why. Creativity comes in determining where corporate mission and societal needs intersect.

Venture Philanthropy

The high-tech and Internet booms created a new generation of millionaires and billionaires, who feel the power of their money and know its potential to make the world a better place for people in need. A number of family foundations—for example, the Cole Family Foundation—have been created around Seattle, Silicon Valley, and other pockets of high-tech activity worldwide. This burst of philanthropic activity has brought investments in programs for long-term change in education, job creation, and the environment. They are merging social innovation with leading-edge business management practices.

Social Venture Partners (SVP), for example, is a pioneer in a hot new concept in giving called "venture philanthropy." Started in

1997 by Paul Brainerd, founder of the prodigious Pagemaker desktop publishing software company, Aldus Corporation,[3] SVP sets up charitable foundations and helps existing ones grow. It uses the same tools that venture capitalists and incubators use: experts in strategy, technology, media, HR, finance, fund-raising, and other areas who help create highly successful nonprofit organizations. SVP specifically targets mid-level managers at high-tech companies, who have a lot of disposable income, to suggest appropriate philanthropic endeavors.

Donors are considered partners at SVP. Not only do they contribute money to a fund that invests in a portfolio of local charities, concentrating on children's and educational programs, but they also take lead roles in guiding the charities' strategy. For example, they may help develop brands, build infrastructure, and network with alliance partners.

Based in San Francisco, the Roberts Foundation, with over $100 million in assets, runs a $3 million program called the Roberts Development Fund, which links nonprofits with for-profit executives. The objective is to build for-profit businesses in the San Francisco area. In addition to philanthropic work in support of low-income families, formerly homeless and disabled individuals in the Bay area, the RDF also sponsors fellowships for MBAs who work at the charities, helping them to manage and grow more productive.

Gary Hirshberg, president and CEO of Stonyfield Farm, founded the Social Venture Institute (SVI), a venture philanthropy incubator, in 1996. SVI provides an interactive and affordable way for socially conscious business ventures to explore new paths to succeed. It established the Social Venture Network, which offers leaders of socially responsible businesses and innovative not-for-profit organizations expert advice, mentoring, and a forum where both problems and best practices can be shared.

Three young Wall Street traders who struck it rich started a charity called the Robin Hood Foundation, which has become one of most innovative philanthropic organizations in the United States. The founders had the idea of applying business skills and the stock picker's mentality to building and managing a venture philanthropy foundation. With a staff of business-savvy attorneys, Ivy League grads, and newly minted MBAs, the foundation takes a hands-on, activist approach, providing $18 million to over 100 eclectic programs in 2000 alone. The Robin Hood staff helps creative philanthropic entrepreneurs build successful organizations, and, like managers of any well-run business, they demand results. The recipient programs make commitments to achieve predetermined goals. Robin Hood audits each program to make sure it's using sound business practices. If programs fail to meet those goals, Robin Hood helps them learn how to do things better. If they still don't cut the mustard, Robin Hood cuts off their funding.

Robin Hood's board has included the late John F. Kennedy, Jr.; Kenneth Langone, founder of Home Depot; Bob Pittman, president of AOL; news anchor Diane Sawyer; and Jann Wenner, founder of *Rolling Stone* and chairman of Wenner Media. At a recent benefit, The Who performed gratis, and Robin Williams and Gwyneth Paltrow emceed. George Soros has been among those who have contributed several million dollars.

VENTURE PHILANTHROPY BROKERING

H[3] leaders who have made their fortunes in their twenties and thirties still have a very long, productive life, perhaps fifty years or more, ahead of them. Some choose to start new business ventures. Many turn to philanthropy as a "second career." But many don't know whom to support, or how.

An organization called Seachange runs a program called the Social Venture Network. The Network members include over 400 leaders of "socially responsible businesses." SVN links donors with the nonprofits that best match their personal and corporate philanthropic profile and preferences. Beyond donating funds, Seachange matches donors who want more hands-on experience with start-ups that can benefit from their advice, guidance, and connections. Guy Kawasaki, founder of garage.com, is helping Seachange develop a website modeled after his popular garage.com site, which links venture capitalists with start-ups looking for funding. The new site will be a "nonprofit version to attract engaged philanthropists."[4]

Funds raised by a few hundred venture philanthropies now account for about 5 percent of the $22 billion in total charitable contributions raised each year—a clear indication of a major change in philanthropic giving. H^3 leaders are coming together to raise lots of money with the same lightning-quick speed that they use in running their businesses. One venture philanthropic organization, for instance, raised over $13 million in a few weeks to save a pristine portion of the Cascade wilderness. Think about how long most environmental groups take just to make a tiny dent.

NEWFANGLED MEDICIS

The Medicis, one of the wealthiest families in Europe during a significant part of the fifteenth and sixteenth centuries, were known for their patronage of the arts and artists. Lorenzo de' Medici (1449–1492) was patron to Michelangelo and Botticelli, among many other artists. While Medici interests were largely motivated by complex political, economic, and religious concerns, the family members also loved art for its own sake. Likewise, some of today's patrons love not only the art, but also the idea that art can bring new innovation success to their own organizations.

Paul Allen and Laurie Anderson

When Laurie Anderson, the world-renowned multimedia artist, particularly interested in the intersections of art, music, and technology, returned from a concert tour in 1995, she was ready for a change. "We had lots of trucks and sets and people sitting around," recalls Anderson, "and we said, 'Now what'll we do?' I put the stuff in storage and began to look around for another commission. I wondered what would it be like if I could work anywhere and any way I wanted. I put all my work in a distressingly small box—books, tapes, records, photos, CD-ROMs, and laser disks—and sent it to Paul Allen, with a note: 'Will you be my Medici?'"

Co-founder of Microsoft and, by some accounts, the second richest man in the world after Bill Gates, Allen was interested in finding new technologies and new ways to help people communicate.[5] In 1992, he had founded Interval, a pioneering research lab devoted to this kind of exploration. Allen recognized an opportunity for Anderson to help his researchers to develop new music and audio technologies, which could ultimately be commercialized. For almost three years, Interval acted as Anderson's patron, sponsoring a series of her experiments, as well as small productions and staffing.

As Anderson recalls, "In exchange for this support—which turned out to be the fun part for me—I went out to Interval a few times a year and looked over their shoulders." There she helped researchers develop the Talking Stick, a wireless sound sampler, as well as a digital turntable and other creative tools for generating and transmitting audio-visual messages.

Dale Chihuly and Hilltop Artists in Residence

In the Seattle-Tacoma area, a number of at-risk teenagers are becoming "glass kids." They are learning the art of glassblowing from one of the master craftsmen in the business: Dale Chihuly. Sponsored in part by the National Endowment for the Arts (NEA), the

Hilltop Artists in Residence program identifies young people, often from disadvantaged backgrounds, who can profit from the discipline and inspiration of working with an artist like Chihuly. Since 1994, Chihuly has taught hundreds of these teenagers how to blow and shape spirals of colored glass.

Hilltop is the brainchild of Kathleen Kaperick, who co-founded the venture with Joseph Carston. Because glassblowing is an art that requires the delicate handling of hot materials and full attention to details, it is perfect for giving these teens the kind of discipline that can translate into successful lives or careers. Chihuly provides the technical know-how and specialization in glass art, not to mention the inspired mentoring that often comes in working with a great artist one-on-one.[6] In this case, the glass artistry is repairing what possibly otherwise would become society's shards.

Watermill Center

In a golden stretch of Long Island, New York, known as the Hamptons, where celebrities such as Steven Spielberg, Billy Joel, Meg Ryan, and Rob Reiner have their beach retreats, the Watermill Center brims over with artists, scientists, students, interns, and business leaders. They come together each summer to this international facility to learn from each other and create new works of visual and performance art. Watermill Center is truly a creative laboratory environment.

Founded by the artist Robert Wilson, Watermill Center provides a sanctuary where participants can "see many ways of bringing together many different fields of study, through art, to create new ideas for us all. At the Center, it's possible to start with a blank book and write your own text," says Wilson, who believes we are all becoming so specialized, compartmentalized, and isolated that it's increasingly more difficult for us to speak each other's language and know each other. He wants his center to mix and mingle an array of thinking, to ask questions and develop concepts that otherwise might never come to be. "Our communities need a crystal cube that can reflect both the universe and the core of the village," he says.

"As an artist, I was always interested to see art, but I would have to go to a museum to see it," explains Wilson. "The Center is a place where art can just happen, where it can begin its journey out into the world. It's a place where anything can happen." In the past decade, Watermill Center workshops have spawned over fifty major works for theaters and museums around the world.

The Watermill Center is sponsored by a number of for-profit and not-for-profit organizations and private individuals, including Giorgio Armani, Bacardi USA, Inc., and Donna Karan. Its board includes a spectrum of influential artists and business leaders, including Armani, Karan, Isabella Rosselini, Jessye Norman, Lou Reed, Susan Sontag, Richard Serra, Philip Glass, Tom Krens, and Tom Waits.

Watermill Center is not only a hatchery for Wilson, his collaborators, and his students, it also helps to fire up other organizations such as Aventis, the pharmaceutical giant. The Aventis Foundation contributed €1.7 million to finance the Web of Life Project, a combination of art, technology, and cultural development. Watermill Center hosts the Aventis Triangle Forum—a collaborative venture of the Aventis Foundation and the Center for Applied Policy Research—which brings together business leaders, scientists, artists, and government leaders to study the future of sustainable development on a global level. Representatives from countries around the world, as well as from international institutions such as the United Nations, investigate how networking is affecting our lives and what it may mean for our future. Beyond the expected discussion about the role of biotechnology in agriculture with respect to feeding the burgeoning global population, the forum has taken on such questions as "How can our lives become more and more linked with everybody else's?" and "How might we create added value through our interplay?"

TECH-PHILANTHROPY

New technologies are opening up opportunities to do good on a scale never before seen. The Internet can connect donors and recipients in new ways. Genomics can help find new cures for disease, aid in conservation initiatives, as well as help improve and increase food production to fight world hunger.

Web of Life

The Web of Life Project is an interactive arts and sciences initiative that presents the aesthetic power of global networks. One element is a dramatic large-scale interactive installation of a giant screen, over three meters high and ten meters long, in a darkened room at the Center for Art and Technology, in Karlsruhe, Germany. A continual metamorphosis of patterns suggests a living network. Four remote terminals, communicating via the Internet, periodically present images from sites such as the Guggenheim Museum in New York, the InterCommunication Center in Tokyo, the Australian Center for the Moving Image in Melbourne, and the Ars Electronica in Linz, Austria.

Visitors can place their palms on an interactive screen, which displays their unique palm lines as they activate visual and musical changes in the network and evoke theoretical correlations. Each visitor is said to breathe new life into the immersive web of life experience. Another aspect of the work is a book that explores the hows and whys of social, organizational, and ecological networks, asking questions such as "Can the interlinkage of hundreds of millions of people through technologies such as the Internet initiate a new era of human evolution?" The project includes an on-going dialog among viewers via a linked website.

e-philanthropy

Leveraging the power of the Internet, some H³s have come up with creative giving programs that increase the reach, efficiency, and effectiveness of contribution flows. Beyond powerful new culture-building networks, the Web links philanthropic donors and recipients in innovative ways. The concept of "e-philanthropy" involves finding ways to make charitable giving easier, just as e-commerce makes it easier to buy and sell. These companies attract people to their sites or a partner's site by promising to donate a portion of food, money, or some other form of aid every time someone visits via the Internet. The potential is great: A study conducted by Walker Research in 1997 found that when price and quality are equal, two-thirds of customer populations said they would switch brands to those of the more socially responsible companies.

Greatergood.com and 4charity.com, for example, link with major retailers such as amazon.com and llBean.com. When customers make online purchases through charity sites, the companies donate anywhere from 2 percent to 20 percent of the purchase price to one of hundreds of allied nonprofit causes. Those contributions are tax deductible, of course, although customers receive no tax benefit from their purchases.

Thehungersite.com donates a cup and a half of rice or grain a day to the United Nations World Food Program every time somebody clicks the button that says "donate free food."[6] The website 4charity.com hosts an online charity mall. Here you can buy a virtual storefront, which will donate a percentage of every purchase to charity. The service promises to deliver "eyeballs," a measure of how many Internet users actually see the site you have constructed. Advertisers get a low-cost medium for their messages, while building customer loyalty. By any measure the practice of e-philanthropy is a win-win for all participants.

HELPING EMPLOYEES TO GIVE

At the heart of all of Capital One's philanthropic programs are its associates, who generously give their time as volunteers each year. In 2000, more than 5,000 Capital One associates worked together to help the communities in which they live and work, donating over 50,000 hours of service. Associates are given the opportunity to volunteer both during and outside of regular work hours, combining their business skills and their altruistic spirit. The VolunteerOne program further rewards those who do volunteer work by making contributions to organizations where associates volunteer at least 100 hours a year.

Associates mentor young children and teens, build and repair homes, as well as collect food, clothing, school supplies, and holiday gifts for families in need. During the 2000 holiday season, for example, associates donated more than 5,500 substantial gifts, including computers and bikes, as well as 40,000 pounds of food. Other associates participate in the Kids' Café program, which feeds 6,000 children a day in ninety-three Kids' Cafés across the United States.

In another example, the Australian Council of Trade Unions (ACTU), which represents nearly 2 million Australian workers, first teamed up in 1981 with Lend Lease Corporation to form the ACTU-Lend Lease Foundation. This foundation continues to help disadvantaged people to gain skills for work while it improves the lives of employees outside of their conventional workday and enhances employees' relationships to their own communities. Lend Lease employees, for instance, help train people and apprentice them to some 140 businesses or nonprofit companies in the community. Over 30,000 apprentices in various trades and services are working and gaining valuable experience required for career advancement. They represent 16 percent of the total number of apprenticeships in Australia.[7]

Many traditional companies have workplace giving programs that match the gifts its employees make. Almost $5 billion in charitable donations pass through these programs annually. But many H[3] organizations are also encouraging employees to go beyond checkwriting and take a more active role in improving their communities. Philanthropic programs inspire employees. Beyond doing good for the recipients of these funds, they do good for the companies. Among other things, they dramatically increase employee loyalty: According to a recent study, almost 90 percent of employees reported that they feel a stronger sense of loyalty in companies with workplace giving programs.[8]

VIEWS ON GIVING

Not everyone agrees on the appropriateness of company philanthropy. Some H[3]s don't have the time to devote to it. Some leaders choose to concentrate on building wealth now and letting the giving come later, although this decision can spark a lot of public criticism, as it did with Bill Gates for most of his career at Microsoft. Eventually, he created the Bill and Melinda Gates Foundation, one of the wealthiest in the world, which focuses on promoting global health and addressing issues in education.

Peter Lewis thinks differently about philanthropy. He has an unusual point of view: "I don't want my company to give away five cents," he says in all seriousness. "I'm a very generous person. I give away millions and millions of dollars. But I don't think the company should do that. It is our job to make money for our shareholders. Then they can choose to give it to whomever they wish." Lewis asserts, "I'm not against giving. I just don't think that companies should be doing it."

In contrast, David Cole has made creative giving part of his personal creative strategy. He has found that he has gone through three phases of giving: "The first is what I'll playfully call the 'Ritchie Rich' phase, where you now have resources and can begin to impact things by your ability to write checks. Often, that's more about you than it is about what you're writing checks for. And so, it's responding to other people coming to see you with another narrow set of opportunities or problems, whether it's safeguarding the arts or building a building for a university."

"In Phase Two you go beyond that and think thematically about what you're doing," says Cole, "so that you begin to connect the dots over a multi-year timeframe and you shift to think more about the philanthropic action itself."

The third phase is a multigenerational look, "extending the themes to go way beyond the work you can achieve in your own lifetime. That contextual shift moves you into building institutional capacity." Through the Cole Family Foundation, Cole is investing in the creation and development of socially conscious corporations. He works just as hard at his philanthropic endeavors as he did in building his own for-profit empire.

REFILLING THE WELL

Philanthropy adds to an already jammed agenda. We pay a price for our workaholism, both on an individual and societal level. Although philanthropic pursuits have a restorative effect on a personal level, creative people also need to replenish their creative energies and

keep their juices fresh. Creative leaders have a better balance between time-crunch and time-off.

Balance

The traditional work model is one of hard work. Work-life balance
is a newly emerging concern.

If you want to get ahead, you work hard and long hours, and you
push yourself. As the New Economy geared up, it was fairly typical to
see people working practically nonstop, seemingly around-the-
clock, to beat the clock. The lure of big, fast money and the pressure
to produce at lightning speed drove people relentlessly. As their
companies grew older and bigger, people at the dotcoms and the
software companies, as well as "establishment" employees, began to
rebel against the 24/7 work-style. Many people wanted their lives
back. They wanted time to be with families and friends. They
wanted a more balanced pace.

At some of the more evolved H^3 companies, leaders lead by example. Vinod Khosla, managing partner of Kleiner Perkins Caufield
& Byers, makes sure he gets home to have dinner with his family at
least a few nights during the week. Khosla tracks family time like any
other system indicator. He promotes putting metrics around life
priorities in addition to those around work priorities. David Cole
builds in major vacation time to spend time with his family and on
his own—for example, taking six weeks off to hang out on a beach in
the south of France, while many of his peers insist on keeping their
workaholic schedules.

Michael McGrath, head of PRTM, instituted a program, called
Sunny Days, in which employees are expected to take one day off (usually Fridays) in their grueling workweek to spend on themselves.
Having worked intensely, for long hours Monday through Thursday, when Friday comes, they are expected *not* to come into the of-

fice, attend meetings, or work at home. Rather, they are expected to take care of personal business, invest in personal growth, regroup, and relax. The intention is to help people restore mental and physical energy so they are free to work better and smarter the rest of the time. *Sunny Days* are documented on time sheets. If an employee is found repeatedly to be reporting for work, that behavior gets immediate attention and reprimand.

The giant accounting firm Cap Gemini Ernst & Young has been making major efforts to become more H^3. One initiative focuses on life balance issues for employees, in an attempt to reduce the burnout rate for overstressed employees. An Office of Retention was established to create work-life programs and policies governing flextime, casual attire, telecommuting, and day care. Some of the programs go further to offer concierge services or to equip employees' home offices to enable telecommuting. Others address burnout prevention by monitoring time sheets and intervening if an employee is working beyond a reasonable number of hours. The balance between life and work is now tied to compensation, as the company seeks to reduce travel requirements for consultants and adds a life-balance component to each project at its outset to assure people won't get burned out on the project. An HR representative serves on all major project teams, and the company provides the Life Balance Matrix, a database that describes best practices for life-work balance.[9] Similarly motivated programs include sabbaticals, satellite offices to reduce commuting, paid time-off intervals, and paid time for volunteer work.

Personal Creative Strategy

One summer, when my son was six years old, he needed to practice his creative writing. He had trouble deciding what his writing should be about: What story should he tell and how should he tell it? I suggested that he write about what he thought he wanted to be when he grew up.

"When I grow up," he wrote, "I want to be me." Here was the foundation for a personal creative strategy—a plan and a commitment to lead a creative life. I was, of course, delighted to see such a response.

People who enrich their personal lives by seriously playing music, painting, dancing, writing, engaging in extreme sports, traveling, teaching, learning, meditating, volunteering, and intensely pursuing a host of other interests have a personal creative strategy. The effects of those pursuits spill over into their professional lives, cascading into fountains of creativity whose reach seems to have no limit. Peter Lewis, chairman of Progressive Insurance, builds several layers into his creative strategy. In addition to serving as chairman of the Guggenheim Museum and contributing enormous amounts to the arts, he frequently travels around the world, exploring new places on his high-tech luxury tugboat. He works from the boat and is fully connected to the office—when he wants to be.

David Cole has a particularly unique creative strategy that guides his whole life. "I made a commitment to myself and to my wife that I would never do anything for more than three years. I would never do the same thing. I owed it to our relationship, and I owed it to myself to push for new experience. I knew that by staying anywhere for more than three years, and doing the same thing, I was virtually assured of falling into the familiar, into the comfort, and indeed the tyranny of the routine."

John Seely Brown's personal creative strategy includes eclectic travel to out-of-the-way places on a regular basis. He spends lots of time on his orange BMW motorcycle on back roads. Sometimes he travels to remote areas in the United States, to get in touch with the world outside of Silicon Valley. Or he may take his motorcycle to an underdeveloped country, where he comes down to earth and finds simplicity as he sees raw, rudimentary innovations that transform whole villages. For example, Brown recounts seeing how a forty-five-horsepower pump allowed a whole village to change its economy by doubling rice harvests through increased irrigation.

When I asked Timothy Greenfield-Sanders, "How do you stay excited about what you are doing?" he replied, "I grow raspberries at my country house in upstate New York. I have a family." Whether he grows the fruit for its colorful aesthetics or just because he likes raspberries, it helps to rejuvenate and inspire his creativity; likewise, his family is a constant source of inspiration in simple day-to-day living. As he puts it, "People who are smart try to make whatever they are interested in even more creative."

Leading-edge creative people are notorious for indulging their passionate natures outside of the office, matching their passions for their work. From insatiably collecting art, memorabilia, cars, and guitars, to voraciously reading and traveling, to pursuing their own artistic muses, many H^3s are driven by personal callings.

PERSONAL CALLINGS

It's more than a job, more than the next paycheck. For creative leaders, there is a higher purpose in life, something that beckons them, asking them to continually reach for a higher place of service or a more intense personal experience

Walking down the street one day in a small town in New Jersey, Robert Wilson saw a thirteen-year-old boy being arrested for throwing a rock through a church window. Observing that the boy was acting strangely and was not very intelligible, Wilson assessed that he was a deaf-mute, a fact that had escaped the policemen, who were roughly handling the child. Wilson intervened and got the boy released. To most, the boy was a nameless individual, a trouble-maker, a child with a police record. His name was Raymond. When he was taken home, Wilson discovered that Raymond was living,

without parents, under troubling circumstances. He was about to be institutionalized by "guardians" who did not understand his condition. Wilson again
intervened, this time before a court where
he convinced the judge to let him adopt
Raymond. His argument: "It will cost you a
lot of money to take care of him. If I adopt
him, you won't have to spend that."

Raymond lived and traveled around the
world with Wilson, who was then trying to
establish himself as an avant-garde artist
and theater director. In helping Raymond
overcome his disabilities, Wilson encour-
aged him to tell stories through pictures and movement. Raymond's
creativity blossomed with his newfound joy of expression, which inspired Wilson even more. Together, they created *Deafman Glance*, a
silent opera, which became a major hit in Europe, where Wilson
and Raymond got rave reviews from the intelligentsia. They received
invitations to the top European arts festivals, including Spoleto and
Avignon. The opera was a lightning rod for Wilson's career and
electrified his fame and fortune. He is now widely celebrated in the
world of avant-garde visual and performing arts.

o   o   o

When things begin to get boring, depleted, or stuck, anywhere in
our world, it is a signal, not only for the need for new ideas, but for
new ideas about developing new ideas.

Classic approaches to innovation development can still have
merit, but they all have significant limitations. They are mostly relegated, compartmentalized activities, quite separate from daily life;
they are mainly routinized programs. But we don't need to be cor-
ralled by them.

We can, instead, *become* innovations—we can become new ideas.

Each H³ we saw was a new idea in and of itself, with a new business model, a new internal structure, a new culture, or a new perspective. And when we look ahead to the next crop of H³s, we will, no doubt, find a fresh cache of next ideas about new ideas to explore.

New challenges are certain to keep appearing before us. But if we face them, and grow because of them, we will always develop new ways to get past them. If we develop and maintain a high creative priority, if we always search for ways to innovate in everything we do, we can potentially innovate every process and spike every outcome. Skill is not enough. Intelligence is not enough. Without imagination and talent, we are merely running in place—and possibly even slipping behind. The H³s we see are not only compelled by creative priority and centered on talent, they are driven by a creative passion.

> You must be the change you wish to see in the world.
> —Mahatma Gandhi

Like them, we can elevate the level of every initiative to a new creative platform—from making breakfast to making a living to making a difference. We can keep a creative agenda and be guided by an innovation strategy. We can look at everything through more aesthetic lenses. We can bring more art into our lives and continually push for more art in our solutions.

As Mahatma Gandhi said, "You must be the change you wish to see in the world." Creative leaders first have to have creative ideas, which in turn make them more creative leaders who may then have even more creative success, and on and up they go, with more new ideas at each level, creating more and more of the future—making it up as they go. For many, creativity outside of work both drives and is driven by creativity at work, in a limitless upward spiral. As many H³s can attest, we have to continually *be* new if we want to see new.

Featured Organizations and Individual Profiles

Acirca, Inc.

A leader in the organic foods industry, Acirca uses new manufacturing, distribution, and management strategies and technologies—including several from the biotech, telecommunications, and software industries. The company was founded by **David Cole.** Cole was the president of America Online's Internet Services during that company's extraordinary rise to prominence as the largest U.S. Internet provider. He now serves as chairman, while **Mark Rodriguez** is CEO of Acirca, whose name is derived from the phrase "a circle of life." It was founded in 2000 and is based in New Rochelle, New York. Recognizing that the organic food category is the fastest growing specialty of the U.S. food industry, Acirca markets organic foods and products under the Walnut Acres brand. It acquired Millina's Finest and Frutti Di Bosco, which have brought Acirca an approximately 22 percent share of the U.S. market for gourmet organic pasta sauces. It also acquired Mountain Sun (the Number One brand of organic juice) and ShariAnn's Organics (the second largest ready-to-eat certified organic soup company in the United States, and it continues with an aggressive acquisitions plan.

Laurie Anderson

Musician and performance artist Laurie Anderson has recorded several major albums, beginning with her 1986 debut *Big Science*. She is perhaps best known for multimedia performances, including an adaptation of Herman Melville's novel entitled *Song and Stories from Moby-Dick*. Her latest album (as of August 2001) is entitled *Life on a String* (Nonesuch). Anderson teamed up with Paul Allen, the co-founder and former president of Microsoft, to develop new digital communications tools. She has also collaborated with David Bowie, Lou Reed, Peter Gabriel, Brian Eno, Robert Wilson, and others. Anderson is based in Manhattan.

Joshua Bell

Recognized at age thirty-two as one of the world's greatest living violin virtuosos, Joshua Bell began as a prodigy, making his debut in 1981 at age fourteen with the Philadelphia Orchestra. He has performed with the world's major orchestras and records on the Sony Record label. In addition, he teaches master classes at the Royal Academy of Music in London. He was featured as the violinist for the movie *The Red Violin*.

Capital One Financial Corporation

Named by *Fortune* as one of the best places to work in the United States for three consecutive years (1999–2001), Capital One Financial Corporation began as an independent company. Originally a division of Signet Bank, Capital One was founded in 1995 by Richard D. Fairbank, now CEO, and Nigel Morris, the current president and COO. Headquartered in Falls Church, Virginia, it now has over 19,000 associates, who have helped the company build a reputation for excellent customer services and its information-based strategy (IBS). With over 38 million customers and managed loans of over $35 billion, Capital One ranks as one of the top ten financial institutions in the United States. **Marge Connelly** is executive vice president for operations, and **Dennis Liberson** is executive vice president for human resources and corporate real estate.

Dale Chihuly

Shattering conventional tastes and expectations, glass sculptor Dale Chihuly is well known for his flamboyant, colorful, and distinctive designs, which appear in installations the world over. In 1995, he mounted a large-scale exhibition of glass works over the canals of Venice, and in 1999 he showed fifteen enormous pieces within the walls of an ancient fortress, now the Tower of David Museum in Jerusalem. He has exhibited in over 200 museums around the world, including the Metropolitan Museum and the Louvre in Paris. Over forty galleries worldwide feature his creations. Chihuly's studio is housed in his 30,000-square-foot boathouse in Seattle, Washington.

David Cole

Former president of America Online's Internet Services, AOL New Enterprises, and AOL International, David Cole founded and now serves as chairman of Acirca, and oversees Sunnyside Farms, an organic farm network he also founded. Cole also serves a chairman of the Cole Gilburne Fund, which among others, served as lead investor for Macromedia, Inc., Tops, Inc. (acquired by Sun Microsystems) and Shiva Corporation (acquired by Intel). Cole also founded Navisoft, Inc., which he sold to AOL in 1994. Prior history includes his serving as president of Ziff Communications and chairman, president, and CEO of Ashton-Tate.

Active in international conservation efforts and early childhood education, Cole serves on the boards of the World Wildlife Fund, American Farmland Trust, Island Press, and the Sesame Workshop (formerly known as Children's Television Workshop).

Corning, Inc.

Corning, Inc. began in 1851 as a Massachusetts-based glass company. A century and a half later, it employs over 40,000 people, has an entire city named for it (Corning, New York), and has moved far beyond the manufacturing of the glass used in light bulbs. After successful products such as its Pyrex line of cookware have been spun off or sold, Corning is now focused on fiber optics (it holds a 70 percent share of the market, twice as much as its nearest competitor), LCD glass for use in laptop computers and other products, high-powered mirrors used in space exploration, and microarrays, which are used in biotechnology, especially genomics research. **Roger Ackerman** served as chairman and CEO during Corning's stellar rise in the 1990s. Today, **John W. Loose** is president and CEO, having served as a sales and marketing manager at Corning since 1964. Corning's 2000 sales topped $7.13 billion.

EMC² Corporation

Specializing in data storage systems for businesses, the Hopkinton, Massachusetts-based EMC² has been one of the fastest growing companies in the high-tech industry. The information age is growing at such a rapid rate that companies are reeling in reams of data. They need some way of managing, storing, accessing, and retrieving this vast body of information, and EMC² has for several years been practically the sole player in the data storage and retrieval industry. The former CEO and currently executive chairman of EMC², **Michael Ruettgers,** oversaw a period of stupendous revenue growth, a seventy-four-fold increase to $8.9 billion in 2000. That growth represents an 80,000 percent increase in one decade. During the bull market of the 1990s, EMC²'s stock was the single highest performing one among publicly traded companies.

Enron

Despite the difficulties which have brought down the business energy producer and the top seller of natural gas in the United States, Houston-based Enron has been a leader in innovation, whether in the development of products and services, in marketing, or in commodities trading. Former CEO **Jeff Skilling** is credited with turning an "Old Economy" company into one geared for the New Economy. The company became the leading buyer and seller of natural gas in the United States. It operated a highly successful online commodities market for such products as coal, paper, electricity, and bandwidth. Enron has ranked among the top companies in *Fortune's* list of fastest-growing companies, the best places to work, and size (its 2000 sales topped $100.7 million). Citing personal reasons, Skilling resigned as CEO in August 2001. Chairman **Ken Lay,** who has led the company since 1985, assumed the role of interim CEO. In December 2001, because of repercussions from alleged financial reporting irregularities, Enron filed for Chapter 11 protection.

Frank Gehry

Frank Gehry is said to be the world's greatest living architect. His design for the Guggenheim Museum in Bilbao, Spain, brought him world attention and fame. Now a startling design for a new Guggenheim Museum, to be built in lower Manhattan on the East River, will be added to an impressive list of his other buildings, including the Walt Disney Concert Hall (Los Angeles), DG Bank Building (Berlin), Vitra Design Museum (Weimam-Rhein, Germany), Case Western's Weatherhead School of Management (Cleveland, Ohio), Paul Allen's EMP (Experience Music Project) rock and roll museum (Seattle), the Frederick R. Weisman Art Museum (Minneapolis), and the Nationale-Nederlanden Building (Prague). Frank O. Gehry and Associates is based in Santa Monica, California.

Genzyme Corporation

Cambridge, Massachusetts-based Genzyme is making innovation happen, in part, by appealing to a new breed of investors and finding new ways to increase the flow of resources to its new business ventures. **Henri Termeer** serves as CEO, chairman, and president. **Gail Maderis** is CEO of Genzyme Molecular Oncology (GZMO), one of four tracking stocks that trades on the New York Stock Exchange. That division is concerned primarily with gene research for the diagnosis and treatment of cancer. Other divisions focus on orthopedic products and cardiothoracic surgical supplies, experimental drugs for rare diseases such as Gaucher's disease, and transgenic proteins used in treating certain illnesses. Genzyme's 2000 sales were over $903 million. The company employs about 4,400 people.

Philip Glass

Chicago-born, Manhattan-based, composer Philip Glass studied at the Julliard School and in Paris with Nadia Boulanger in the 1960s. A minimalist, he has described his compositions as "pure sound events." Works include a collaboration with Robert Wilson entitled *Einstein on the Beach*, operas (*Satyagraha* and *Akhnaten*), and several film scores, including *The Thin Blue Line*, *Hamburger Hill*, *Koyaanisqatsi*, and *Kundun*, for which he received an Oscar nomination. Considered one of the greatest living composers, Glass is always in demand. A prolific creator, Glass continues to collaborate with numerous artists including Wilson, Doris Lessing, Brian Eno, and David Bowie.

Brian Greene

Professor of physics at Columbia University, Brian Greene is a leading physicist and proponent of String Theory, one explanation of the building blocks of the universe. He has delivered many public lectures and published user-friendly articles and books on String Theory, the most significant of which is *The Elegant Universe,* a best-selling book in 1999–2000. He has also been featured on the award-winning Nova series (PBS).

Timothy Greenfield-Sanders

Photographer, filmmaker, and award-winning artist, Timothy Greenfield-Sanders has photographed some of the best-known personalities of the twentieth and twenty-first centuries, including Hillary Clinton, George Bush, Monica Lewinsky, John Malkovich, Robert Mapplethorpe, Andy Warhol, and Orson Welles. Based in Manhattan, he has exhibited his work at the Museum of Modern Art, the Metropolitan Museum, the Whitney Museum, and the National Portrait Gallery in London. Greenfield-Sanders won a Grammy for his documentary on Lou Reed.

Guggenheim Museums

Beyond the famed white circular Guggenheim Museum building designed by Frank Lloyd Wright on New York's Upper East Side, the Guggenheim now extends to Venice, Bilbao, Berlin, and Las Vegas. Under the direction of **Tom Krens**, the museums are among the world's most frequently attended sites for exhibitions of great art. As director since 1988, Krens himself is an extraordinary innovator, having reached to the Internet in his effort to create a brand around the Guggenheim name. He now oversees a complex network of art, artists, patrons, civic leaders and politicians, movie stars and designers. Architect **Frank Gehry** is currently at work on a new Guggenheim museum for New York near the World Trade Centers site.

IBM–Life Science Solutions Division

The IBM Life Sciences Solutions Business Unit, headed by vice president **Caroline A. Kovac,** provides the IT infrastructure that researchers in biotechnology, pharmaceutical research, genomics, proteomics, and healthcare need to turn data into scientific discovery and new treatments for disease.

On December 6, 1999, IBM announced a $100 million research initiative to build the world's fastest supercomputer, "Blue Gene", to tackle fundamental problems in computational biology. The Blue Gene system will be capable of performing more than one petaop/sec. (1,000,000,000,000,000 operations per second). It will achieve this performance through a combination of massive parallelism (1 million processors), and new computer architecture approaches: The system will be built through the replication of a large number of identical chips, each containing multiple processors, memory, and communication logic. The Blue Gene project will use this computer for large-scale biomolecular simulation to advance our understanding of biologically important processes—in particular our understanding of the mechanisms behind protein folding.

ImClone Systems

New York City-based ImClone focuses on pharmaceutical therapies to cure cancer. Having recently gained "fast-track" approval from the FDA, ImClone's drug therapy C225 promises to be a major contribution in the war against cancer, as well as a major revenue producer (some market watchers predict $500 million in sales by 2005). Other areas of research and product development include angiogenesis inhibitors, vaccines for various diseases, and stem cell research. The $3 billion company had sales of $1.4 million in 2000, and employed approximately 270 people.

Founder **Sam Waksal,** president and CEO of ImClone Systems, is both a scientist and a prolific patron of the arts. His brother Harlan Waksal is executive vice president and COO.

Intellectual Ventures

Nathan Myhrvold sold his first software company to Microsoft when he was thirty years old and became its chief technology officer. In 2000, after ten years at the helm with Bill Gates, Myhrvold left Microsoft to form his own investment partnership, the Seattle-based Intellectual Ventures. Focusing largely on high-tech and biotech industries, as well as philanthropic goals, IV is developing a portfolio of companies to rival the number of life-altering changes introduced by the Internet. Myhrvold holds postgraduate degrees in theoretical and mathematical physics, mathematical economics, geophysics, and space physics. He is also a certified mountain climber, scuba diver, and formula racer as well as an avid hunter of dinosaur bones in the Northwest.

Annette Lemieux

Mixed-media artist Annette Lemieux studied at the Hartford Art School (University of Hartford) and teaches art classes at Harvard University. Her solo exhibitions have appeared in various museums and galleries, including the Museum of Modern Art, New York; the Whitney Museum of American Art; the Solomon R. Guggenheim Museum; the Wadsworth Athenaeum; the Museum of Fine Arts, Boston; the Fogg Art Museum, Cambridge; the Davis Museum and Cultural Center; and the Rose Art Museum at Brandeis University. Her sculptures playing on human feet were featured at the Whitney Museum's exhibition of American artists for the 2000 Biennial.

Lend Lease Corporation

Sydney, Australia-based Lend Lease Corporation is truly global in its operations and projects. It began as the combination of two Dutch companies in the early 1950s in Sydney, Australia, and grew to have over 100 subsidiaries, with offices in North and South America, Asia, and Europe. The company specializes in real estate, project design and development, insurance, and many other services. Early projects in Sydney included the Harbour Heights Estates, the city's first skyscraper, Caltex House, and the Sydney Opera House. Later projects included buildings such as Newington Olympic Village (built for the 2000 summer games), Darling Park, Fox Studios Australia, and Grand Central Terminal in New York. In 2000, the company had sales of over $7.7 billion and employed nearly 10,000 people worldwide. Lend Lease's chairperson is **Jill Ker Conway,** the former president of Smith College and well-known author of two memoirs.

Macromedia

With Shockwave and Dreamweaver, two of its best-known software products for web designers, San Francisco-based Macromedia has passed all challengers, both in terms of its 70 percent market share and in its ability to attract the creative new talent and innovative managers it needs to stay ahead. Executive vice president and CFO **Betsey Nelson** offers some unconventional advice for financial officers who have been schooled to go strictly by the numbers when it comes to evaluating innovation assets (see Chapter 3). The company's 2001 sales were approximately $390 million, representing a one-year's sales growth of almost 48 percent. The company employs just over 1,000 people.

MIT Media Lab

The famed MIT Media Lab is a hot spot for geniuses, young and old. From robotics to artificial intelligence to genomics to product design, the researchers and scientists at the Lab are the bright stars of today and the future. **Rudolph (Rudy) Burger** is CEO of Media Lab Europe; **Tod Machover**, considered to be one of the most important and influential composers of his generation, is Professor of Music & Media, Head of the Opera of the Future/Hyperinstruments Group, Co-Director of the Things That Think (TTT) and Toys of Tomorrow (TOT) consortia at M.I.T.'s Media Laboratory. In addition, Machover is a highly acclaimed designer of new technology for music. He is the inventor of hyperinstruments, which use smart computers to extend the range of possibilities in musical instruments. Performers such as Yo-Yo Ma, Joshua Bell, the Los Angeles Philharmonic, Prince, and Peter Gabriel have used these hyperinstruments. **Steve Eppinger** is co-director of the Center for Innovation in Product Design. **Joe Paradiso** is technology director of the "Things That Think" consortium, a group of some fifty companies and ten research groups that focus on the use of computer technology in everyday objects—for example, electronic ink and paper, toys with minds of their own, and "smart" highways.

Philip D. Noguchi

Philip D. Noguchi is director of the division of cellular and gene therapies at the Office of Therapeutics Research and Review Center for Biologies Evaluation and Research at the U.S. Food and Drug Administration.

Palm, Inc.

Based in Santa Clara, California, Palm is currently the leading maker of hand-held devices, or personal digital assistants (PDAs). Beginning with the Palm Pilot, these devices have been improved to the extent that today's VII model offers wireless Internet access, as well as regular features such as an address book, games, and memo functions. Palm was acquired in 1995 by U.S. Robotics, which sold it to 3Com in 1997. Three years later, the company was spun off from 3Com. Palm's 2001 sales topped $1.56 billion. **Satjiv Chahil**, Palm's chief marketing officer, marshals a variety of marketing experiences at IBM, Apple, Xerox PARC, and Sony. He is credited with making the Apple the computer of choice in Japan, having built its dominance in multimedia creative performance. At Palm, he has been responsible for establishing the brand and building the marketing emphasis on customer relations.

Progressive Insurance Corporation

The fourth largest auto insurance company in the United States, the Progressive Insurance Corporation has led the industry in many innovations, including being the first to sell insurance on the Web and the first to actively market itself to high-risk individuals. It recently launched its "immediate response" program, which offers claim resolution at the accident site on a twenty-four-hour basis. Some 30,000 independent agents in the United States sell Progressive's products. Sales in 2000 were approximately $6.8 billion. Chairman **Peter Lewis** has created something of a museum of contemporary art at the company headquarters in Mayfield Village, Ohio. **Glenn Renwick** serves as president and CEO.

PRTM

The management consulting firm of Pittiglio Rabin Todd & McGrath (PRTM) was founded in 1976 by **Michael McGrath** and Robert Rabin. Headquartered in Waltham, Massachusetts (with other offices worldwide), the company provides high-tech, information- and web-based solutions to help companies improve cycle time, product development, supply chain operations, and time-to-market. McGrath innovated PRTM's product-development consulting practice, or PACE® (Product And Cycle-time Excellence®), which has been successful in improving the performance of clients in a variety of industries, including automotive and industrial products, medical devices, chemicals, telecommunications, and software. McGrath is founder and chairman of IDe.

Richard Serra

Born in San Francisco and educated at Yale, Richard Serra started out working in steel mills. That experience had a lasting impact in that as a major sculptor Serra has been fascinated with the uses of enormous plates of steel, some weighing many tons and extending hundreds of feet. His installations can be seen at the Dia Center for the Arts in New York City ("Torqued Ellipses"), the Federal Plaza in New York City ("Tilted Arc"), Bochum, Germany ("Terminal"), Videy Island near Reykjavik, Iceland ("Afangar"), and other locations worldwide. Serra's studio is located in Manhattan.

Sunnyside Farms

David Cole initially invested $11.5 million in Sunnyside Farms, a 500-acre organic farming venture located in Washington, Virginia, near Washington, D.C. The farm had been in existence since the middle of the eighteenth century, growing apples and other fruit, cattle, and timber, but over the years had not fared well. Part of its original 1,000 acres had been incorporated by the federal government into the Shenandoah National Park. Since the mid-1990s, under Cole's leadership and ongoing investments, the farm has been transformed through the addition of many species of herbs and vegetables, a very high-quality line of cattle (producing Kobe beef), an "open" pasture and poultry system, and collaborative ventures with other organic farming groups. Sunnyside is creating a nonprofit center for teaching organic farming techniques and benefits.

Transmeta, Inc.

Transmeta, Inc. developed a hybrid software-hardware solution to the problem of microprocessors that generate high levels of heat and thus demand a lot of battery power. Transmeta, led by company founder **David Ditzel,** markets the Crusoe family of chips that run at much cooler temperatures than Intel chips, thereby saving energy and providing longer battery life. Major computer manufacturers using Transmeta's technology include Sony (for its Vaio laptops), Fujitsu, Hitachi, Toshiba, and Sharp. Ditzel's career has spanned years at Bell Labs, where he helped develop the first RISC processors, and at Sun Microsystems, where he was CTO of the microelectronics division. He left a prestigious research position in 1995 to found his own company, where he serves as CTO and vice chairman. A relatively new IPO (in 1999), Transmeta is the only major software/hardware company that is challenging Intel's dominance in this market. Its 2000 sales were $16.2 million, and the company employs about 400 people.

Welch Foods, Inc.

Welch's is the food processing and marketing arm of the National Grape Association Cooperative. Organized in 1945, National Grape is a grower-owned, agricultural cooperative with 1,461 members. Headquartered in Concord, Massachusetts, Welch's is the best-known producer of grape products from jellies and jams to juices and juice bars. It operates processing plants in Washington, New York, Pennsylvania, and Michigan, and it exports products to over thirty countries. **Daniel P. Dillon** is CEO. Sales for the most recent accounting period (2000) amounted to $679 million, with net proceeds of $78.1 million. The company harvested over 311,000 tons of grapes and sold 309,000 tons—part of which went into the 17.5 million cases of bottled red, white, and purple grape juices it sold in 2000. New products (including new kinds of packaging) accounted for 29 percent of 2000 sales. Welch's employs about 1,300 people.

Robert Wilson

Multi-media artist, director, Robert Wilson is one of the leading experimental artists in the world. In 1971, he composed a "silent" opera, *Deafman Glance*. For over three decades he has produced a distinguished body of works, many done in collaboration with artists such as Philip Glass (*White Raven* and *Einstein on the Beach*), Laurie Anderson (*Meltdown on the South Bank*, as well as an adaptation of Euripides' *Alcestis*), Allen Ginsberg, David Byrne, William S. Burroughs, Tom Waits, Susan Sontag (an adaptation of Henrik Ibsen's *Lady from the Sea*), Lou Reed (*POEtry*, a work based on the poems and stories of Edgar Allan Poe), and opera star Jessye Norman (*Jessye Norman Sings for the Healing of AIDS*). Wilson also runs the Watermill Center, an international center for new work in the arts, which he founded in 1992. Overseen by a stellar board of directors, including Giorgio Armani and Donna Karan, the center, based on Long Island, New York, provides space and funds for workshops, internships, independent study, and collaborations. To date, it has provided support to several hundred aspiring artists and students.

Xerox PARC

Since 1970, when it was founded, Xerox's Palo Alto Research Center (PARC) has been a hotbed of innovation—it's the birthplace of the first computer mouse, the Ethernet, and Graphical User Interface, or GUI.

Although most of its creative efforts have not been effectively developed and leveraged, PARC has become almost a synonym for innovation. Its PAIR program (PARC Artists In Residence) represents one of the first attempts by a major corporation to bring artists and researchers together in an institutionalized setting.[1] Chief Xerox scientist and the former director of PARC, **John Seely Brown** is a world-renowned innovator. Co-founder of the Institute for Research on Learning, he is particularly interested in artificial intelligence, the digital culture, organizational learning and innovation of all sorts. He now serves as a member of the board of directors of Corning. In 1997, he published *Seeing Differently: Insights on Innovation* (Boston: Harvard Business School Press). In 2000, he published *The Social Life of Information* (Boston: Harvard Business School Press).

Notes

Introduction

1. Geoffrey A. Moore, *Crossing the Chasm: Marketing and Selling High-Tech Products to Mainstream Customers* (New York: HarperBusiness, 1999).

2. In its 1998 annual survey of leading technological firms in the United States, the Industrial Research Institute (IRI) in Washington, D.C., found that making innovation happen had jumped from fifth place in earlier years to become the industry's biggest single problem.

3. Corning researchers created Pyroceram glass ceramics in 1957, which were found to be ideal for cookware. The company entered the consumer products market with its Pyrex brand, selling that business in 1998.

4. World Biochip Markets, Frost & Sullivan, available at www.biotech.frost.com.

5. On Sept. 16, 1998, the SEC sent a 23-page letter to Enron "raising questions related to accounting and disclosure." The SEC sent a separate letter to Enron on Jan. 26, 1999. Lisa Sanders, *Enron's shares decline—again*, CBS.MarketWatch.com, Oct. 30, 2001.

Chapter 1

1. The comparison is made to the Crusoe processor model TM5400. See Alexander Klaiber, "The Technology behind Crusoe™ Processors," Transmeta Corporation, January 2000, available at http://www.transmeta.com.

2. Brian Greene, *The Elegant Universe: Superstrings, Hidden Dimensions, and the Quest for the Ultimate Theory* (New York: Vintage, 2000), p. 4.

3. *Columbia Encyclopedia,* sixth edition, Paul Lagassé, ed. (New York: Columbia University Press, 2000), p. 692.

4. Selected highlights, adapted from www.bio.org/timeline/timeline .html.

5. The phrase is borrowed from Michael Lewis, *The New New Thing: A Silicon Valley Story* (New York: Penguin, 2001).

6. This timeline is adapted from Corning's 2000 Annual Report and its website available at www.corning.com/discovery_center.

7. ClirCode was acquired by Isotag in 1999.

8. See, for example, Catherine Arnst, "The Birth of a Cancer Drug," *BusinessWeek,* July 9, 2001, p. 96.

9. Hoover's Online.

10. Arnst, p. 96.

11. Deepak Chopra, "What Is the True Nature of Reality?" Lecture presented at the Seattle Center, May 18, 1991, available at www.wisdombase. org/chopreality.html.

Chapter 2

1. Austin K. Pryor and Michael E. Shays, "Growing the Business with Intrapreneurs," *Business Quarterly*, March 22, 1993, p. 42.

2. Cited in Anna Mudio, ed., "The Art of Smart," *Fast Company,* July–August 1999, pp. 85-86.

3. Michael Schrage, *Serious Play: How the World's Best Companies Simulate to Innovate* (Boston: Harvard Business School Press, 2000).

4. The genome is the total hereditary material of a cell, comprising the entire chromosomal set found in each nucleus of a given species. See The Biotechnology Industry Organization, *Guide to Biotechnology* (Washington, D.C.: Biotechnology Industry Organization, 2001), p. 107.

5. See Kevin Maney, "Myhrvold Explains Why New Economy Isn't Dead," August 31, 2001, available at usatoday.com/money/columns/ maney/2001-08-08-maney.htm.

6. Christopher Helman, "Charlotte's Goat," *Forbes Global*, February 19, 2001, available at www.forbes.com.

7. "The Fire This Time," *Time*, October 25, 1999, p. 1.

8. "The Edison of the Internet," *Fortune*, February 15, 1999, p. 84.

9. Clayton M. Christensen, pp. 171-175.

Chapter 3

1. Industry Canada, "Measuring and Reporting Intellectual Capital," paper published by the Strategic Policy Branch, September 1999.

2. Baruch Lev, the Philip Bardes professor of accounting and finance at New York University's Stern School of Business, as cited in Alan M. Webber, "New Math for a New Economy," *Fast Company,* January-February, 2000, p. 214.

3. Deepak Chopra; see chapter 1, note 11.

4. As of September 2001, based on approximate market capitalization, the No. 1 biotech company was Amgen, followed in order by Genentech, Serona (a private company), and Genzyme.

5. Malcolm Gladwell, *The Tipping Point: How Little Things Can Make a Big Difference* (Boston: Little, Brown and Company, 2000).

6. Chart from www.skandia.com.

7. Bill Birchard, "Intangible Assets Plus Hard Numbers Equals Soft Finance," *Fast Company* (October 1999), p. 316.

8. www.skandia.com.

Chapter 4

1. The Gehry exhibition at the New York Guggenheim closed on August 26, 2001, and moved to other Guggenheim museums, beginning in Bilbao. The exhibit catalogue is available. See *Frank Gehry: Architect,* ed. J. Fiona Regheb (New York: Guggenheim, 2001).

2. Michael Schrage, *Serious Play: How the World's Best Companies Simulate to Innovate* (Boston: Harvard Business School Press, 2000), pp. 155–176.

3. Ibid., p. xvi.

4. Barnaby J. Feder, "I.B.M. Meets with 52,600, Virtually," *New York Times* online, May 28, 2001.

5. I. Peterson, "Simplicity Makes for Superfast Computing," *Science News Online,* December 11, 1999.

6. Marty Bates, Syed H. Rizvi, Prashant Tewari, and Dev Vardhan, "How Fast Is Too 'Fast'?" *McKinsey Quarterly*, no. 3 (2001).

7. Information about Symyx's parallel processing is available at http://www.symyx.com.

8. Enron press release, available at www.enrononline.com/docs/marketing/PressRoom/05_23_01/.

9. Ibid.

10. Interview with Satjiv Chahil.

11. See, for example, the website for the Association for Business Simulation and Experiential Learning, ABSEL, www.towson.edu/~abset/Simpack/package.html.

12. John Tagliabue, "How Ducati Roared onto the Internet," *New York Times*, April 18, 2001.

13. Susan Gregory Thomas, "Getting to Know You.com," *Personal Tech*, 127.19 (November 15, 1999), p. 102.

Chapter 5

1. One rare exception in recent history is Baron von Thyssen-Bornemisza, who gave over 800 paintings from his collection to Madrid's Prado Museum in 1992.

2. Information from the British Museum website.

3. While sales dropped off considerably in 2001, the decline has been attributed to a problem with inaccurate forecasting.

4. Larry Hand, "Computing for Cancer Research," *BioSino*, n.d., available at www.biosino.org/bioinformatics/01508-5.htm; see also Kevin McKean, "Tap the Power of Your PC to Fight Cancer," *PCWorld.com*, April 3, 2001, available at www.pcworld.com/news/article/0,aid,46143.00.asp.

5. Malcolm Gladwell, *The Tipping Point: How Little Things Can Make a Big Difference* (New York: Little, Brown, 2000), pp. 19, 21. See also Geoffrey A. Moore, *Crossing the Chasm: Marketing and Selling High-Tech Products to Mainstream Customers* (New York: HarperBusiness, 1999) for a discussion of the so-called adoption cycle.

6. See Steve Jurvetson, "What Is Viral Marketing?" CNetNews.com, June 22, 2000, available at www.news.cnet.com/news/0-1274-210-3287297-2.html.

7. Richard Dawkins, *The Selfish Gene* (New York: Oxford University Press, 1976).

8. Seth Godin, *Unleashing the Ideavirus* (Dobbs Ferry, N.Y.: Do You Zoom, Inc., 2000); Emanuel Rosen, *The Anatomy of Buzz: How to Create Word-of-Mouth Marketing* (New York: Doubleday, 2000).

9. Michael Pollan, "Naturally," *New York Times Magazine*, May 13, 2001, p. 32.

10. "Organic Futures," *Vegetarian Times*, March 2001.

11. Estimates are provided by Acirca, Inc.

12. Leticia Williams, "Wal-Mart to Stop Sharing Sales Data," CBS.MarketWatch.com, May 12, 2001.

13. Cited in Saul Hansell, "Credit Card Chips with Little to Do," *New York Times*, August 12, 2001, p. 24.

Chapter 6

1. Skilling stepped down as CEO in August 2001, citing personal reasons.

2. Randall Lane, "The 50 Best CEOs," *Worth Magazine*, May 14, 2001.

3. Thane Peterson, "Climbing on the Organic Gravy Train," *BusinessWeek Online*, August 21, 2001.

4. Brian Greene, *The Elegant Universe: Superstrings, Hidden Dimensions, and the Quest for the Ultimate Theory* (New York: Vintage Books, 2000), p. 15.

5. Scott Woolley, "Giving Wall Street the Cold Shoulder," *Forbes*, May 14, 2001, pp. 222–224.

6. "Clockspeed" has numerous meanings in the business context, but Charles H. Fine makes a useful distinction in describing the various rates of evolution that products, processes, companies, even entire industries undergo. A product such as a microprocessor, for example, may have a useful life of no more than a few years, whereas an automotive model may remain unchanged for several years. See *Clockspeed: Winning Industry Control in the Age of Temporary Advantage* (Reading, Mass.: Perseus Books, 1998), pp. 6-7.

7. For more details, see Agis Salpukas, "Firing Up an Idea Machine: Enron Is Encouraging the Entrepreneurs Within," *New York Times*, June 27, 1999.

8. Peg Brickley, "Synergy in St. Louis: Business Incubators Aim to Breed Biotech Startups," www.the-scientist.com, July 24, 2001.

9. Melanie Warner, "Inside the Silicon Valley Money Machine," *Fortune*, October 26, 1998, pp. 128-140.

10. EDS was spun off into a separate company in 1996.

11. Cory Johnson, "The Tracking-Stock Conundrum," CBS.Market Watch.com, July 26, 1999.

12. Spin-Off Advisors report, www.spinoffadvisors.com.

13. Bill Gross, "The New Math of Ownership," *Harvard Business Review*, November-December, 1998, p. 68.

Chapter 7

1. Reports range from $10 million to $30 million.

2. Acirca, Inc. press release.

3. Aldus was sold in 1994 for $450 million.

4. Colin Crawford, "Networks Link Entrepreneurs and Nonprofits," *Wall Street Journal*, March 29, 2000.

5. Allen's wealth ranking fluctuates within the top five richest people in the world, depending on economic and market conditions.

6. "Charity Begins with a Click," *Newsweek*, June 5, 2000.

7. Lend Lease corporate website available at www.lendlease.com.au/IIweb struct.nsf/webcommunity/L3?open document.

8. Tony Schwartz, "Tell the Truth," *Fast Company*, August, 2000, pp. 228–230.

9. Pamela Kruger, "Jobs for Life," *Fast Company*, May, 2000, pp. 236–252.

Featured Organizations and Individual Profiles

1. Craig Harris, ed., *Art and Innovation: The Xerox PARC Artist-in-Residence Program* (Cambridge: MIT Press, 1999).

Credits

Chapter head art for all chapters: Shira P. White. All interior sketches not attributed to others are by Shira P. White.

Chapter 1: Spark Soup

Page 25: Dale Chihuly sketch—*In the Light of Jerusalem*
Page 26: Dale Chihuly sculpture—*Jerusalem White Tower*
Page 46: Timothy Greenfield-Sanders photo—*Laurie Anderson*

Chapter 3: Bargaining with the Future

Page 98: Dale Chihuly photo—*Red Saguaros*

Chapter 4: Going Live

Page 132: Frank Gehry sketch—*Lewis residence*
Page 133: Frank Gehry design process model—*Lewis residence*
Page 135: Frank Gehry CATIA model—Experience Music Project
   Final design model—Experience Music Project
   Sketch—Experience Music Project (1)
   Sketch—Experience Music Project (2)
Page 136: Frank Gehry sketch — Guggenheim Museum Bilbao
   CATIA model—Guggenheim Museum Bilbao (1)
   CATIA model #2—Guggenheim Museum Bilbao (2)
   Design Process model—Guggenheim Museum Bilbao
   Final Design model—Guggenheim Museum Bilbao;
Page 137: Frank Gehry final design model—Walt Disney Concert Hall
Page 137: Timothy Greenfield-Sanders photo—Richard Serra

Page 139: Richard Serra sketches
Torqued Ellispses
Torqued Ellispses Partial Roll Out
Torqued Ellispses Roll Out Flat
Photo—*Torqued Ellispses*; DIA exhibit.

Chapter 5: Integrated Circuits

Page 192: Timothy Greenfield-Sanders photo—*Lou Reed*
Page 193: Timothy Greenfield-Sanders photo—*self portrait*
Page 200: Timothy Greenfield-Sanders photo—*Philip Glass*
Page 202: Tod Machover music score—*Texture Blob 1*

Chapter 6: Rocket Science

Page 216: Timothy Greenfield-Sanders photo—*Elaine de Kooning*
Page 218: Joshua Bell handwritten score—*Bell's Cadenza for Mendelsohnn's Violin Concerto in E Minor, Opus 64*
Page 263: Dale Chihuly sketch—*Floats in the Ancient Village*

Chapter 7: Making an Apple Pie

Page 277: Dale Chihuly sketch—*June 13, 1999 Jerusalem Cylinders*
Page 278: Dale Chihuly photos—*Jerusalem Cylinder #1* and *Jerusalem Cylinder #2*
Page 294: Timothy Greenfield-Sanders photo—*Robert Wilson*

Notes

All artwork and photos courtesy of the artists listed:

1) Frank Gehry art and photos © Frank O. Gehry
2) Richard Serra art and photos © Richard Serra
3) Dale Chihuly sketches and photos © Dale Chihuly
4) Timothy Greenfield-Sanders photos © Timothy Greenfield-Sanders
5) Tod Machover score © Tod Machover
6) Joshua Bell score © Joshua Bell
7) Shira P. White art © Shira P. White

Index

Acirca, 54, 116–117, 142, 198,
 224–225, 229, 262, 272,
 275, 277, 297
Ackerman, Roger, 29–31, 59, 61,
 88, 98–99, 221, 230, 233,
 246, 247, 249, 264, 300
ACTU-Lend Lease, 288
Adversity, 217–220
Aldus Corporation, 279
Allen, Paul, 26, 282, 298, 316n5
Altered states, 84–87
amazon.com, 199
Anderson, Laurie, 16, 26, 114,
 210, 282, 297–298
AOL, 74, 102, 118, 151, 159, 170,
 193, 218, 238, 239–240,
 252, 273
Apple, 124, 141, 164, 210, 240
Ariba, 105
Art
 aesthetic factor for, 115–116,
  209–213, 223, 263, 313n1
 collections in, 174, 223, 264,
  314n1
 computer-aided design (CAD)
  in, 135–136
 in storage, 177
 live with, 91, 98
 philanthropy for, 281–286

physical environment and,
 263–265
science and, 209–210
seeing simplicity in complexity
 in, 99–100
visual *vs.* language for, 56–57
Artist, 75, 216
 characteristics of, 68–69, 192,
  233, 294
 discipline of, 69
 naïveté of, 46
 perpetual innovation, 25–27
 portfolio of, 126
 R&D for, 136–139
 vision of, 8, 132–14
Assets
 hard, 119–120
 soft, 97–98, 105, 110–111,
  119–120
Australian Council of Trade
 Unions (ACTU), 288
Automation, 154–155
Aventis Foundation, 284–285

Ba, Dr. Sujuan, 183
Bell Labs, 105–106, 232, 235,
 236, 240, 244
Bell, Joshua, 15, 86, 217, 218,
 298, 306

"Big Pharma" *See* Pharmaceutical
  industry
Bilbao, Spain, Guggenheim
  Museum, 57, 115, 132–134,
  137, 175–179, 209, 313n1
Bilbao effect, 175–176
Biochips, 6
Bioinformatics, 179
Biotechnology, 5–6, 221. *See also*
  Gene; Genetic engineering;
  ImClone; Human Genome
  Project
  approach to diseases by, 35–36,
    49, 60, 107–108, 121–124,
    225–226
  Blue Gene Initiative and, 147
  variation of company structure
    in, 125–126, 254–257
  competition for, 64–65, 313n3
  demand for, 63–64
  drug discovery of, 6, 35–36, 39,
    44–45, 48, 90, 151, 179
  endless genesis
    (problems/solution
    continuum) in, 32
  enzyme development in, 71
  financing of, 226
  genes and, 57–58, 147–148, 179,
    251–252
  growth for, 62, 63–65
  maintaining rights of, 9, 36
  pharmaceutical companies *vs.*,
    168–170, 168f
  physical laws, limitations and,
    65, 66–67
  standards for, 64
  THINK, information sharing
    and, 183–184
  timeline of, 27–28, 312n4
  virtuous cycling for, 64

BMW (Bayerische Motoren Werke
  AG), 176
Bowie, David, 26, 55, 126
Brainerd, Paul, 279
Brainstorming
  beyond, 52–55
  developing parameters for, 53
  limitations of, 52–53
Brand name, 115, 177, 198–199,
  211
Brown, John Seely, 47, 80, 85,
  180, 182, 185, 188–189, 213,
  215, 250–251, 292–293, 310
Burger, Rudolph (Rudy),
  234–235, 251, 305–306
Buyout, private, 228

C225 See ImClone
California Public Employees'
  Retirement System
  (CALPERS), 112
Cancer
  experimental approaches to, 60,
    122
  problem in finding one cure
    for, 33–37
  research, 183–184
  War on, 33–34
  See also ImClone, GenzymeCap
  Gemini Ernst & Young, 291
Capital One Financial
  Corporation, 108–110, 112,
    148, 167, 185–187, 194–195,
    203–204, 237, 238–239,
    242, 246, 275, 287–288,
    298
Carroll, Lewis, 59
Carston, Joseph, 283
Chahil, Satjiv, 124–125, 141, 164,
  180, 210

Chihuly, Dale, 25–26, 73, 283, 298–299

Chip industry, 62–63. *See also* Crusoe Chip

Christensen, Clayton M., 4, 90

ClirCode, 33

Cole, David, 54, 116–117, 142–143, 151–152, 161, 196–198, 217–218, 221–222, 224–226, 228–229, 238, 239–240, 242, 248, 262, 268–274, 289, 290–291, 292, 297, 299, 307–308

Collaborations, 146–147

Commitment, unconscious, 42–43

Commodities, 156–158, 162–163

Communication, 184, 185, 188
buzz in, 191–193

Compensation, 244–246

Competition, 74, 201
advantage through creativity for, 19
giving ideas to, 80
growth and, 64–65
urgency about, 229

Concept Development Group, 165

Connelly, Marge, 148, 186, 204, 298

Conservation, 218, 268–269, 271–274

Conservatism, 29
retreat to, 17–18

Continuous innovations, 4

Conversation pieces, 146–147

Conway, Jill Ker, 78, 218–219, 239, 241, 247, 259, 265, 305

Corning, 16, 91, 210, 263–264, 299–300
biotechnology of, 5, 6, 221
continuous leaps of, 4–5

cookware and, 311n2
development with customers of, 165
inspiration, different ideas and, 88, 101, 127
loose-tight management of, 230–232, 247, 249
mixing voices (perspectives) in, 73
R&D investment by, 98–99, 212
successes from mistakes at, 59, 61
talent of, 239, 246–247, 248, 261
transformations of, 29–31, 49, 98–99, 137, 196, 227, 228, 261, 312n6

Corporations
ideas more important than, x
innovation as biggest problem for, 311n2
leap innovation for, 12–14
small evolutionary change by, 24–25
social responsibility by, 116–117, 274–277, 286–287, 289
See also Organizations

Cosmology, 27, 37–38, 216, 225, 230

Creative philanthropy, 268–274

Creative pressure, 78
altered states of thinking with, 84–85
inspiration, different ideas and, 87–88, 127, 153, 183
release *vs.* understanding of, 81
separation and, 84–87
status quo, new idea and, 79–80, 237
tensile strength of, 82–84

tension for, 79–82
troublemakers in, 80
Creative process
constitution of, 21
operation of, 54
prototypes in, 145, 147
sticking point in, 143–144
Creativity
accomplishment with, 233–234
as way of life, 51, 54
breaks for, 77
for competitive advantage, 19
holistic, 268
MBA and, 3–4
mirror, 16
New Economy's influence on,
17–19, 151, 187
priority of, 7–15, 99
range of, 237–238
sensitivity with, 100–101
strategy for, 77–78
talent and, 232–234
top echelon of, 12, 235–238
unorderliness of, 28–2
value of, 111–112
See also Innovation
Credit cards, 109–110, 186
Crick, Francis, 34, 211–212
Crusoe Chip, 24, 196, 240, 311n1
Customers, 74, 141, 194, 313n7
beyond, 75
changing attitudes of, 273, 286
development of more, 102, 103,
144, 165, 187
friendly to needs of, 81, 117,
188–189
listening to, 194–196
measurement of transaction
behavior of, 109–110
rare creative leaps by, 72

real time feedback for, 166–167,
186, 194–195
relationship to, 198–199
social attitudes of, 286
Customizing live, 166–167

Danone Group, 224, 277
DCF (Discounted Cash Flow)
103–106
Development, 137
customer, 102–103, 144, 165,
187
cycle time and costs of, 124, 150
scared by new, 71–72
time and process of, 153–157
Development chain management,
207
DigitalESP, 105
Dillon, Daniel (Dan), 13–14,
38–39, 198, 237, 309
Discontinuous innovations, 4
Discount factor See DCF
Ditzel, David (Dave), 12, 15–16,
23–25, 41, 49, 85–86,
87–88, 105, 234, 235–236,
240, 242, 244, 249–250,
259, 308
DNA technology, 28
Dotcom. See New Economy
Dozier, Linda, 238
Dreamweaver, 8, 243, 305
Drug discovery, 6, 39, 45, 48, 151,
179, 312n7
Fast Track for, 45
leap innovation in, 35–36,
75–76, 90
limitations/difficulty imposed
on, 39, 44
Dyson, Esther, 74
Ducati, 165–166

Eastman Chemical Company, 33
eBay, 100, 115, 118
Ecology, 271–274
Economic slowdown, ix, 226–228
Economy, creative, 179
    cancer research and, 183–184
    ecology of services and, 180–183
    networking and, 180, 182–183
Edison, Thomas, 20, 30
Einstein, Albert, 34
EMC² Corporation, 62–63,
    188–189, 300
Employees, 4, 245
    empowerment index of, 119
    personal time for, 291
    philanthropy and, 287–288, 291
    turnover, 120, 245, 291
    See also Talent
Eno, Brian, 26
Enron, 16, 20, 145, 155, 159, 217,
    226, 300
    loose-tight management of,
        230–234, 244–245, 253,
        260, 261
    Online, 154, 156–158, 166, 170,
        220
    problems for, 20, 227, 311n5
    talent at, 239, 241, 246, 248, 261
Entrepreneur, 46. See also Leaders,
    creative
Environmentalism, 116–117,
    271–274, 279, 281, 285
Eppinger, Steve, 306
Erté, 55
Ethernet, 80
Experience
    factor, 112–113
    paradox, 160
Experimentation
    neophyte and, 160

on the Internet, 166, 220–221
    rough-start strategy for,
        141–143, 163
    See also Models, live

Failure, 20
Fairbank, Richard D., 109, 298
Family, 290–291
Fast Company, 150
FDA, 39, 43–45, 49, 60, 225
    Fast Track of, 45
    protocols of, 39, 43–44, 49,
        225
Fear, 43
    naiveté and, 46–47
    passion over, 49
    safety vs. opportunity and, 44
Fiber optics, 30, 31, 88, 101, 196,
    261
Financial organizations, 15–187,
    108–110, 112, 119–120, 148,
    167, 194–195, 203–204, 237,
    238–239, 241–242, 275,
    287–288, 298. See also
    Commodities
Flexibility factor, 116
Focus groups, 127–128
Ford, Henry, 65
Food, 13–14, 71–72, 91, 93–95
4charity.com, 286
    alternative (enzyme) in, 71–72
    fighting hunger and, 276–277
    organic, 54, 116–117, 142–143,
        161, 197–198, 224–225, 229,
        269–271, 289
    slow, 229
Food and Drug Administration,
    U.S. See FDA
Fruit of the Loom, 115
Fulfillment, 118

Fulfillment Fund, 275

Gabriel, Peter, 26
Gates, Bill, 42, 282, 289
Gehry, Frank, 56–57, 115–116,
    131–137, 161, 175–176, 209,
    233, 260, 301, 313n1
Gene
    research, 57–58, 147–148, 179
    standards for, 57–58
    See also Genetic engineering;
        Human Genome Project
Genesis, endless, 29–33
Genentech, 90
General Electric, 20, 52, 68
Genetic engineering
    pasting genes among species in,
        66
    sharing new gene in, 251–252
Genzyme, 66, 107–108, 111,
    122–123, 125–127, 143–144,
    145, 225–226, 227, 228,
    232, 239, 254–257,
    262–263, 301
Gladwell, Malcolm, 111, 191
Glass, Philip, 26, 56, 69, 114,
    200, 284, 301–302
Gnutella, 201
Godin, Seth, 193
Going live. See Live; Time
Grants, 234
greatergood.com, 286
Greene, Brian, 11, 16, 27, 37–38,
    86, 101, 216, 225, 230, 302
Greenfield-Sanders, Timothy, 16,
    55, 69, 92, 216, 293, 302
Greenspan, Alan, 29
Gross, Bill, 153, 257–258
Growth
    competition for, 64–65
    demand for, 63–64

of biotechnology and high tech,
    62, 63–65
of business, 230
physical laws and, 65
rate of, 109
standards for, 64
through innovation, 227
virtuous cycling for, 64
Guggenheim, Peggy, 173–174
Guggenheim Museums, 57,
    115–116, 132–134, 136–137,
    173–175, 176, 286, 292,
    302–303, 313n1. See also
    Bilbao, Spain
Internet and, 178, 199

H3 (hot, hip, and happening)
    organizations, x-xi, 7, 8, 49,
    55, 128–129. See also Leaders,
    creative
age of, 17
as loose-tight creative machines,
    215–216
conditions changing in, 25, 54,
    101–102, 137, 226
creative leadership of, 216–238
creative strategy for, 77–78,
    80–81, 98, 147, 159, 237
customer and sharing of
    development by, 165
employees, philanthropic
    programs and, 288
expected problems in, 45
flexibility in, 116
innovation core of, 11–12, 101,
    129, 171, 210
innovation project portfolio for,
    91
integration for, 213
internal incubators for,
    252–253

intuition for, 123–124
loose-tight management in,
    230–234, 244–245,
    249 250, 253, 260
partnerships for, 250–252
physical environments of, 17,
    260–265
restlessness of, 29, 89–90
risk and, 107–108, 134
size variation with, 16, 257–260
social and environmental
    concerns of, 116–117,
    274–277, 286–287, 289
surrendering to uncertainty in,
    11, 102, 125
talent of, 106, 238, 248
time utilization by, 150–157, 159
tracking stocks for, 253–257
employee movement within, 245
troublemakers, creative tension,
    and, 80
Hamel, Gary, 166
Hawkins, Jeffrey, 161
Healthcare, 182–184
Heart, trusting of, 77
Heisenberg's Uncertainty
    Principle, 103
Hilltop Artists, 283
Hirshberg, Gary, 279
Hodgkin's lymphoma, 68
Hotmail, 192–193
Human Genome Project, 4, 28,
    64, 147–148, 272, 312n4

IBM, 52, 146–147, 205–206, 230,
    303
IDe, 154–155, 157, 206–208
idealab!, 153–154, 252, 257
Ideas, x, 148
    as currency, 101, 241
    blockbuster, 221

competition and, 79–80,
    201–203
creative pressure and different,
    87–88, 127, 153, 196
execution of, 142, 144–145, 178
flow, 187–188, 253
meme, 192–193
rapid ideation and, 155
searching for, 196
shared, 221
status quo and new, 79–80
thought-virus and, 193
Identification marking systems,
    32–33, 312n7
ImClone, 9, 16, 35–37, 45, 49,
    57–58, 90, 169, 226, 251,
    303–304. See also Waskal, Sam
Incubators, 151, 153–154, 182,
    252–253, 257
Information
    strategy based on, 109–110
    diminishing returns of too
        much, 44
    integration of, 206–208, 213
    privacy of, 201–204
Information Age, 30
Information storage systems,
    62–63, 188–189
Information technology (IT), 161,
    163, 178–179, 201–204
    aesthetic aspects of, 209–213
    complexity and, 205–206
    context for, 208–209
    information sharing and,
        183–186, 206–208, 212, 213
    social dynamics influence on,
        185
    success, failure, communication
        and, 213
    visibility, integration and,
        206–208

Innovation. *See also* Creative
    process; Creativity; Leap
    innovation
as core, 11–12, 101, 129, 161, 178
awards for, 68
beginning point of, 23–29
biggest problem of various
    industries, 311*n*2
competencies, 129
continuous/discontinuous, 4
creative talent for, 8
definition of, 183
endless genesis of, 29–33
freedom for, 230–232, 243
in the fringe (outsiders), 88–91
playing with, 145
product/process as, 136
project portfolio for, 91
R&D and, 9–10, 98–99, 213,
    227
radical, 24
restrictions on, 190–191
return of assets on, 120
strategy development for,
    157–160, 170–171
success through, 21, 145, 165
transformations in, 29–31
Innovation action, 173–175
    Bilbao Guggenheim Museum
        and, 175–179
    communal lines, boundary
        objects and, 188–191
    competition and, 200–201
    confluent flows, customers, and,
        185–187
    creative economies and, 179–184
    idea flows of, 187–188, 253
    inflows for, 194–196
    information technology,
        convolution evolution, and,
        201–213

    lead users, viral marketing, and,
        191–194
    new touchpoints in, 196–200
    openness and privacy in,
        201–204
    power (networking) grids, social
        dynamics, and, 184–185
    visibility, dashboards, and,
        206–208
Innovation assets, 110–111
    Return on (ROIA), 120
Innovation strategies, 170–171
Insurance, 57, 79, 81–82, 88–89,
    96, 119, 170, 219, 221, 223,
    237, 249, 306–307
Intel Corporation, 24, 184
Intellectual capital, 118–120, 119*f*
Intellectual property, 120–121, 251
Intellectual Ventures, 9, 54, 62,
    304
Internal benchmarking, 127
Internet, 4, 106, 148
    brand names and, 198–199
    business models of, 117–118,
        258–259
    Enron Online, 154, 156–158,
        166, 170, 220
    inflow of customer information
        with, 194–195
    instant messaging on, 156, 193
    museums and, 178, 199
    ratings on, 113
    security, 204
    shopping, 109, 114, 115, 118,
        166–167, 179, 198–199
    small *vs.* large structures for,
        258–259
    thought-virus and, 193
    Web of Life Project and,
        285–286
    webcast on, 164

Interval, 282
Interviews, x–xi
Intuition, 76–77, 121–125
Inventory, 32
Italian government, 173–174

JAVA, 15–16
Jobs, Steve, 240
Johnson, Philip, 55
Joy, Bill, 87
Jurvetson, Steve, 192

K-mart, 199
Kaperick, Kathleen, 283
Keiretsu, 179, 250–251
Kleiner Perkins Caufield & Byers,
    250, 252, 290
Knowledge, 73–74
Knowledge management. *See*
    Information technology
Khosla, Vinod, 290
Kodak, 10, 251
Koolhaus, Rem, 211
Krens, Tom, 115, 174, 177–178,
    284, 302

Land, Edwin, 40
Language, 56, 96
Lay, Ken, 227, 230, 300
LCD, 30, 31, 59, 61, 88
Leaders, creative
    adversity for, 217–220
    as magnets, 238–239
    balance in, 290–292
    changing vision of, 229, 292,
        295–296
    creativity desired by, 15,
        232–234
    difference between everyone
        and, x
    dream teams *vs.* solo, 242–243

economic downturn and,
    226–228
encouragement from,
    220–222
high-speed decision making of,
    228–229, 315n6
holistic perspective of,
    223–226
loose-tight, 230–232
macro structures for, 249–250
partnerships for, 250–252
passion of, 221, 222–223,
    232–234, 235, 293
performance checks by,
    244–245
personal callings of, 293–296
personal creative strategy for,
    292–293
physical environments for,
    260–265
prodigy, 217
selection of talent by, 232–235,
    239–242
talent, attractions, and keeping
    of, 243–244
talent-centric, 232–234,
    238–239
top creative echelon utilized by,
    235–238
See also Philanthropy
Leap innovation
    growth of family of questions
        and, 47–48
    in traditional companies, 12–14
    incremental change, questions
        and, 39, 45
    into unknown, 4
    new company, 25
    passion, vision *vs.* fear in, 49
    unlikely from current staff, 4
Lemieux, Annette, 16, 264, 304

Lend Lease Corporation, 78, 219,
        226, 237–238, 239, 241,
        246–247, 259, 265, 275,
        288, 304–305
Levi Strauss & Company, 43
Lewis, Peter, 81–83, 88–89, 106,
        131–133, 137, 219, 221, 223,
        231, 249, 264, 289, 292
Liberson, Dennis, 238, 298
Licensing, rights vs., 9, 36,
        169–170
Life, transformations, 142–143
Limitations
    biotechnology, physical laws and,
        65, 66–67
    of brainstorming, 52–53
    on drug discovery, 39, 44
    psychological, 42–43
Live, 171
    customizing, 166–167
    inventing help, 167–170
    models, 160–166
    See also Time
Location, 17
Loose, John, 6, 61, 73, 230–231,
        233, 246, 247, 261, 300
Luczo, Stephen, 228

Machover, Tod, 10, 15, 149,
        159–160, 199–200, 202,
        242–243, 262, 265
Macromedia, 8, 17, 103–104, 106,
        160, 228, 233, 239,
        243–244, 260, 263, 305
Maderis, Gail, 143–144, 255,
        256–257, 301
Malcolm Baldrige National Quality
        Award, 68
Management, gestalt vs. list, 226
Manufacturing, 190

Marketing
    "rent-a-rep," 169
    first in positioning, speed, and,
        151–152
    free and, 193–194
    individualizing of, 167, 168, 179
    MBA and, 3
    old vs. new, 168–169, 168f
    positioning of new benefits in,
        71–72, 91, 112, 124, 150
    scared by new developments and,
        71–72
    telemarketing vs. inflow for,
        194–195
    viral, 192–193
MBA, 1–3
McGrath, Michael, 154, 161–162,
        206–207, 291, 307
Media Lab (MIT), 10, 15, 149,
        159–160, 196, 199–200, 201,
        202, 234–235, 246, 251,
        262, 305–306
Mendelsohn, Dr. John, 34–37,
        75–76
Messer, Tom, 173
Millennium Pharmaceutical
        Corporation, 170
Microarrays, 6, 30
Microsoft, 9, 42, 54, 62, 141, 150,
        193
Mistakes, success from, 59, 61
Models, 133–134, 137, 145, 147.
    life as working, 147–149
    live, 164–166
    massing, 160–163
    old vs. new, 169, 169f
    simplifying of, 162
    virtual reality with, 149, 163
    See also Prototyping
Moore, Geoffrey, 4

Moore's Law, 62

Morris, Nigel, 109

Motorola Corporation, 68

Museums
  collections in, 174, 177
  constellations of, 174, 176–178
  Internet and virtual, 178, 199
  See also Guggenheim Museums

Music, 24, 26, 46, 72–73, 86,
    149, 265

Myhrvold, Nathan, 9, 54, 62–64,
    65, 70, 147–148, 237, 246,
    304

Naïveté
  as an asset, 45–47, 149
  fear and, 46–47

Napster, 201

National Endowment for the Arts
    (NEA), 283

Navisoft, 238

Nelson, Betsey, 8, 17, 233, 243,
    260, 263, 305

Networking, 114, 180, 182–184,
    186, 200

New Economy (dotcom), 18, 62,
    117, 187, 228, 290
  belief in, 62
  collapse of, viii, 17–18, 151, 159,
    187, 198–199, 252

New Idea Development Groups,
    73

Nexia Biotechnologies, 66

Nixon, Richard M., 33

Noguchi, Philip D., 306

Opportunities
  beginning of, 67–70, 187, 196
  between services of companies,
    182

fear of, 44
looking for, 41, 222
lost of, 105
unclear in finding of, 58

Organic food, 54, 142–143, 161,
    229, 274, 289
  growth of, 197–198, 224–225,
    269
  high-tech approach to, 116–117,
    269–271
  See also Conservation; Ecology;
    Sunnyside Farm

Organizations , innovating
  size of, 16, 257–260
  traditional, 8, 12–14, 167–168,
    168*f*, 203, 249–250, 257
  See H3 (hot, hip, and happening)
    organizations

Palm, 124, 141, 161, 179, 193, 203,
    210, 239, 306

Paradiso, Joe, 199, 306

Parkinson's disease 107–108, 121.
    See also Genzyme

Partnerships, 250–252

Passion, 49, 216, 220, 221,
    222–223, 235, 293

Perfection, 37–42, 140, 171
  optimally done *vs.*, 141–143, 151

Performance, old and future, 110

Pharmaceutical industry, 48,
    168–170

Philanthropy
  art, 281–285
  creative, 268–274
  e, 286–287
  employees and, 287–288
  giving at different times for,
    288–289
  strategic, 274–277

tech, 285–286
venture, 274–281
Photography, 55, 69–70
Physical environments, 17,
    260–265
Picasso, Pablo, 126
Planning, no major product from
    formal, 52
Play, learning through, 145, 148
Polaroid, 40–41, 52, 115
Privacy, 201–202, 201–204
Problems
    continuum of solutions and,
        31–33
    perfect, 33–37, 48
    safe, 45
    See also Questions
Process
    as product, 134–149
    development, time, and,
        153–157
    parallel, 155–156
    See also Creative process
Prodigy, 217
Product
    formal planning effectiveness,
        52
    life of, 315n6
    process as, 134–149
Profits, social and environmental,
    116–117, 274
Progressive Insurance
    Corporation, 57, 79, 82, 91,
    96, 106, 170, 219, 221, 223,
    237, 249, 264, 292,
    306–307
Project control groups (PCG),
    259–260
Prototyping
    as boundary objects (for
        manufacturing), 190–191

in creative process, 145, 147, 171
    rapid, 144
PRTM, 307. *See also* McGrath,
    Michael
Psychology
    of creative person, 54–55
    self-limitations of, 42–43

Quality control, 68
Questions
    blurring the edges of, 39, 48, 59
    changing nature of, 41–42
    discovering the perfect, 40–41
    first definition of, 42, 48
    growth of family of, 42–43
    perfect basic, 37–42
    right place for right, 39
    timing important in, 39
Quinn, James Brian, 52

R&D
    cooperative, 251, 253
    for innovation, 98–99, 213, 227
    funded by customers, 141
    in art, 136–137, 212
    innovation not necessarily
        correlated with, 9–10
    manufacturing and, 190–191
    scaled back, 18, 29, 212
Rauschenberg, Robert, 55, 100,
    114
Real estate, 78, 219, 237–238,
    239, 241. *See also Museums;*
    Physical environments
Reed, Lou, 26, 70, 192
Reflect.com, 167
Relationships, 113–114; 290–291
Renwick, Glenn, 12, 81, 82, 216,
    307
Research and development. *See*
    R&D

Research Triangle Park, 17
Rewards, 246–247
Richards, Dr. Graham, 183
Rights
    licensing vs., 9, 36
    privacy vs., 202–204
Risk, 134, 168
    appropriate, 233
    execution, 142
    valuation and, 102–103,
        104–105, 107–108, 120–121,
        125
Roberts Foundation, 279
Robin Hood Foundation, 280
Rodriquez, Mark, 223–225, 277,
    297
Rosen, Emanuel, 193
Rosenquist, James, 57
Rough-start strategy, 141–143, 163
Ruettgers, Michael, 188–189, 300

Sagan, Carl, 268
Santana, Carlos, 72–73, 79
Schrage, Michael, 60, 145
Sculptures, 25–26, 69, 137–139,
    263–264
Seachange, 281
Seagate, 227–228
Security, 204
Self, imaging with, 10
Self-limitations, 42–43
Senses, 10–101
Serra, Richard, 69, 137–139, 307
Share Our Strength (SOS),
    276–277
Shareholders, 125–126, 226. See
    also Stocks
Sheriff, John, 158, 162, 166, 220,
    241, 261
Signal interruption, 36–37
Simulators, 163

Six Sigma, 68
Size, small vs. large, 15–16,
    257–260
Skandia, 119, 119f
Skilling, Jeff, 217, 220–221, 223,
    229, 231, 233, 234, 240,
    244–245, 248, 300
Silicon Valley, 17, 80, 269, 278,
    293
Smart, Geoff, 232
Social dynamics, information
    technology (IT) influenced
    by, 185
Social responsibility, 116–117,
    274–277, 286–287, 289
Social Venture Institute (SVI), 279
Social Venture Network (SVN),
    281
Social Venture Partners (SVP),
    279, 281
Solutions
    continuum of problems and,
        31–33
    lacking in one, 2–3
Sony Corporation, 24
Spaces
    art and, 139
    communal, 261–262
    physical, 260–265
    separation of, 262–26
    sizzling, 5
    small, 67–70
    spark, 61–62
Specialization, as interrupting
    innovation, 11
Speed. See Time
SPWI Group, 33, 71, 73, 127, 165,
    180, 259
Stakeholder, 196–198
Status quo, 79–80, 95, 237
Stocks, tracking, 254–257

Stonyfield Farm, 279
Strategic philanthropy, 274–275
String Theory, 225, 230
Success
    in the fringe (outsiders), 89–90
    information technology, failure,
        and, 213
    innovation critical to, 21
    of youth, 46–47
Sun Microsystems, 15–16, 23–24,
    86, 87, 259
Sunnyside Farms, 142, 229,
    268–271, 307–308
Sunnyside Institute, 271–272
Symbols, word *vs.* images in, 56–57
Symyx Technologies, 155–156

Talent, 227
    attraction and keeping of,
        243–244
    clusters of, 239–240
    compensation/rewards/incentive
        s for, 244–248
    creativity and, 232–234
    dream teams *vs.* solo, 242–243
    experience paradox with, 160
    hires and promotion of,
        232–234, 239–240
    macro structures for, 249–250
    news potentiality important for,
        29
    organization revolving around,
        232, 238–239
    performance checks of, 244–245
    physical environments for,
        260–265
    selection of, 232–235, 239–242
    spotters *vs.* trainers of, 235–236
    top echelon of, 12, 235–238
    value of, 8, 105–106
Target Corporation, 211

Technology, 29, 205–206, 256,
    269
Telemarketers, 194–195
Tension, 79–82
Termeer, Henri, 107–108, 111,
    121–124, 125–127, 145, 160,
    222, 243, 253–254, 258,
    262–263, 301
Terrorism, 29
Testing, 148
Tharp, Twyla, 114
Thermo Electron Corporation, 258
THINK, 183–184
Time, 39
    as human construct, 37–38
    customizing live, 166–167
    in live models, 164–166
    management of, 77
    marination and solo, 153
    real, 156–158, 165, 166
    slowness, decisions, and,
        150–152, 229
    speed, decisions, and, 150–152,
        153–154, 187–188, 226,
        228–229, 290, 315n6
    timetables and, 159–1160
    unreal, 157
    variation of procedures for,
        153–156
    virtual reality and, 149, 163
    See also Live appropriate
Torvalds, Linus, 24, 240
Tracking stocks, 253–257
Transmeta, 12, 17, 41, 49, 88, 196,
    240, 242, 308
Trans World Airlines, 115
12 Entrepreneuring, 182

Uncertainty, 29, 103, 106–107,
    125, 127
    surrender to, 11

Valuation
   context important in., 101
   discounted cash flow (DCF)
      factor in, 104–106
   diverse perspectives in, 126–127
   holistic, 128–129
   ideas as currency in, 101
   in talent, 8, 105–106
   innovative portfolios for,
      125–126
   intuition and., 121–125
   market-set *vs.* traditional, 97
   new metrics for new, 110–118
   of core operations, 102
   of intellectual capital, 118–120,
      119*f*
   risk and, 102–103, 104–105,
      107–108, 120–121, 125
   seeing simplicity in complex in,
      99–100
   soft assets in, 97–98, 105,
      110–111, 119–120
   struggle in, 94–96
   vision *vs.*, 95–99
Values, new, 110
   "world citizen" factor for,
      116–117, 197–198
   aesthetic factor for, 115–116
   brand factor for, 115
   creative factor for, 111–112
   experience factor for, 112–113
   flexibility factor for, 116
   model factor for, 117–118
   relationship factor for, 113–114
Venture capitalists, 151, 250, 252,
      281, 290
Virtual reality, 149, 163
Vision, 70–76
   changing, 229

   for new markets, 74
   reality *vs.*, 133–134, 226
   value *vs.*, 95–99
Visuals
   of photography, 69–70
   words *vs.*, 56–57
Volatility 106
VolunteerOne, 287–288

Wal-Mart, 199, 201–202
Warhol, Andy, 55, 114
Waskal, Sam, 9, 35–36, 45–47,
      49, 57–58, 60, 75–76, 90,
      169, 211–212, 216, 226–227,
      303–304
Waksal, Harlan, 35, 304
Watermill Center, 283–285
Watson, James, 34, 211
Web of Life Project, 285–286
Welch Foods, Inc., 13–14, 38–39,
      198, 237, 308–309
Wilson, Robert, 114, 155, 196,
      200, 228, 260, 284,
      293–294, 309
Witte, Larry, 57
World citizen, 116–117, 197–197
WorldJam, 146–147
Wright, Orville and Wilbur, 65

xeno-transplantation 107–108,
      225
Xerox Corporation, 52, 115, 253
Xerox PARC, 47, 80, 196, 210,
      232, 309–310

Yahoo, 199
Youth, success of, 46–47

About the Author

Shira P. White is president of the SPWI Group, a leading innovation management and new product development consulting firm, based in New York City. Clients include a diversity of companies such as Viacom, Eastman, Thomson, Clairol, Kraft, Hearst, Avery Dennison, Procter & Gamble, Pfizer, and Citibank. Shira has deep and varied experience in creative direction, strategic planning, business development, qualitative research, trend analysis, and future studies.

Prior to founding the SPWI Group, Shira held creative and development positions at top international agencies such as Ogilvy & Mather Partners, Saatchi and Grey Advertising in New York City. In addition, she served as new products consultant for BrainReserve.

Shira received an MBA from NYU Stern Graduate School of Business, a Fine Arts degree from the School of Visual Arts, and completed undergraduate studies at Temple University. She served as an instructor at the Pratt Institute and as a guest lecturer at NYU Stern Graduate School of Business and the School of Visual Arts. Shira is a noted speaker and writer on the subjects of innovation, product, service, and business development as well as creativity in business. She has been invited to speak at major conferences for organizations such as the Product Development & Management Association, the Commercial Development Association, the Society for Cosmetic Chemists, the International Institute for Research, the American Marketing Association, and the World Future Society, as well as internal seminars for corporations. Shira is featured in The Hidden Intelligence: Innovation through Intuition (Butterworth–Heinemann) and is currently working on a book manuscript under contract with Marcel Dekker, Inc. Her articles on innovation and new product development have appeared in numerous trade publications. Shira received the Edward J. Davies award for best paper and presentation for her work entitled "New Ideas about Old Ideas," presented to the Commercial Development Association. Shira is an accomplished painter, with a large body of work in both corporate and private collections throughout the United States. She is the founder of Hope Harvest, a not-for-profit organization distributing food surplus to those in need.

To find out more about New Ideas About New Ideas and the SPWI Group or to contact Shira White please visit our website: www.newideasaboutnewideas.com.

G. Patton Wright, who contributed invaluable guidance and advice for this book, has worked on various books and articles dealing with business management, retailing, supply chain management, the New Economy, and innovation, including *The Horizontal Organization* (Oxford University Press), *The Innovation Premium* (Perseus Books), *The Circle of Innovation* (Knopf), *Reengineering Management* (HarperBusiness), *Clockspeed* (Addison-Wesley), *Corporate Kinetics* (Simon & Schuster), and *The Clickable Corporation* (Free Press). Pat has worked with authors such as Tom Peters, James Champy, and Rosabeth Moss Kanter. In addition, Pat has worked on major business publications for A.T. Kearney, Arthur Andersen, Andersen Consulting, Price Waterhouse, Deloitte & Touche, and Ernst & Young. He has edited books for the University of California Press, Humanities Press, Simon and Schuster, John Wiley and Sons, Addison-Wesley/Perseus Books, and many others.

A graduate of Duke University, he received his M.A. and Ph.D. degrees from the University of North Carolina at Chapel Hill and taught literature and writing courses at the university level for 25 years. In 1989, he received a Fulbright lectureship and taught at the University of Warsaw.

Pat is currently based in Cambridge, Massachusetts.